EUGENIC FEMINISM

EUGENIC FEMINISM

Reproductive Nationalism in the
United States and India

ASHA NADKARNI

 University of Minnesota Press
Minneapolis
London

Portions of chapters 1, 2, and 3 were previously published as "Eugenic Feminism: Asian Reproduction in the U.S. National Imaginary," *NOVEL: A Forum on Fiction* 39, no. 2 (2006): 221–44. Copyright 2006 Novel, Inc. All rights reserved. Reprinted by permission of Duke University Press. www.dukeupress.edu.

Portions of chapter 3 were previously published as "'World Menace': National Reproduction and Public Health in Katherine Mayo's *Mother India*," *Nation and Migration: Past and Future,* special issue of *American Quarterly* (2009): 303–25. Reprinted with permission of The Johns Hopkins University Press. Copyright 2008 by the American Studies Association.

Published by the University of Minnesota Press
111 Third Avenue South, Suite 290
Minneapolis, MN 55401-2520
http://www.upress.umn.edu

Library of Congress Cataloging-in-Publication Data
Nadkarni, Asha.
    Eugenic feminism : reproductive nationalism in the United States and India / Asha Nadkarni. Includes bibliographical references and index.
    ISBN 978-0-8166-8990-3 (hc : alk. paper)
    ISBN 978-0-8166-8993-4 (pb : alk. paper)
    1. Feminism—India. 2. Feminism—United States. 3. Eugenics—India.
    4. Eugenics—United States. 5. Birth control—India. 6. Birth control—United States. I. Title.
    HQ1742.N32 2014
    305.420954—dc23

                                                                    2013028375

Printed in the United States of America on acid-free paper

The University of Minnesota is an equal-opportunity educator and employer.

20 19 18 17 16 15 14   10 9 8 7 6 5 4 3 2 1

To my parents,
Ravi Nadkarni and Sara Nadkarni

and my sisters,
Maya Nadkarni and Neela Grace Nadkarni

CONTENTS

INTRODUCTION

Eugenic Feminism and the Problem
of National Development

SPEAKING IN A 1935 RADIO BROADCAST in Bombay titled "What Birth Control Can Do for India," American birth control pioneer Margaret Sanger outlined the importance of reproductive control to the incipient Indian nation. Long sympathetic to the cause of Indian independence (at this point still twelve years away), Sanger trotted out the usual arguments about the necessity of birth control for maternal and familial health. Eugenic concerns, however, were at the forefront of her address. Saying she is "[bringing] this message at a critical time in [India's] history," Sanger proposed that "[India's] first consideration must be the primary one of what kind of people you are going to have in the future. You need as never before, the finest men and women possible, the strongest, spiritually, intellectually and physically. This means you must give consideration to what kind of children you are now bringing into the world to take up the responsibilities of your nation in the future."[1] Linking birth control to the project of Indian nation building, Sanger deliberately aligned her message with Indian feminists who used precisely such eugenic arguments to create a space for feminism within nationalism. Middle-class Indian nationalist feminists such as Rani Laxmibai Rajwade, Lakshmi Menon, and Sarojini Naidu similarly mobilized a language of eugenic reproductive futurity as the motor of nationalist feminist politics, arguing for right reproduction as the way to assure a more perfect national and feminist future. Taking literally the nationalist symbol "Mother India," such feminists posited the reproductive agency of India's women as the key to a reinvigorated Indian nationalism. As Sarojini Naidu memorably put it in her 1904 poem "To India" (first recited at the Eighteenth Session of the

Indian National Congress), Mother India must shake off her "gloom" and "beget new glories from [her] ageless womb."[2]

Sanger may have focused on a positive eugenic message of making "the finest men and women possible" in her 1935 radio broadcast, but her interest in India was also motivated by a negative eugenic concern with improper reproduction on a world scale. Her explicit aims in visiting India (as described in a letter to eugenicist C. P. Blacker) were "first, to bring the poorer and biologically worse endowed stocks the knowledge of birth control that is already prevalent among those who are both genetically and economically better favored, and secondly, to bring the birth rates of the East more in line with those of . . . the civilizations of the West."[3] Her choice of India was not incidental, as colonial censuses and famine control policies from the 1870s onward had painted a dire picture of India's high birth and death rates, creating the global perception that India was desperately diseased and overpopulated.[4] For Indian nationalists, colonial mismanagement was at fault (even as there was a national injunction toward right reproduction), while for imperialist feminists like Sanger the problem was irresponsible reproduction by the "poorer and biologically worse endowed stocks."

Despite her overtly racial interest in birth control in India, Sanger was positively received by Indian eugenic and women's organizations (indeed, the All-India Women's Conference passed a resolution in support of birth control). She did meet a major obstacle in the person of M. K. Gandhi, who agreed that population growth was a problem but felt abstinence was the only solution.[5] Although this Gandhian resistance to birth control persisted into the 1950s through such key figures as Health Minister Rajkumari Amrit Kaur, the post-independence climate was nonetheless ripe for Sanger's message when she decided to hold the 1952 Third International Conference on Planned Parenthood in Bombay. Part of the reason she chose India for the conference was the birth control advocacy of Lady Dhanvanti Rama Rau. Often referred to as the "Margaret Sanger of India" (a title that flattens out Rama Rau's longer history of social and feminist work in India and also mistakenly implies that India came to eugenics and birth control belatedly), Rama Rau was involved in a range of work for the rights of women and the poor over her long lifetime. Family planning advocacy was her enduring cause, however; she founded the Family Planning Association of India in 1949 and was the cofounder, with Sanger and

Elise Ottesen-Jensen of Sweden, of the International Planned Parenthood Federation in 1952. Although it was to become her life's work, Rama Rau stumbled upon the cause of birth control seemingly by accident during a 1949 tour of a Bombay slum. In a scene not unlike the famous opening of Paul Ehrlich's 1968 *Population Bomb* (where he describes being in a crowded street in Delhi and viscerally experiencing what overpopulation means), Rama Rau is overwhelmed by the "deplorable conditions" she encounters in the slums of Bombay and renders them in the most alarmist of terms.[6] Describing the *chawls* as "plague spots, poisoning the environment of the open spaces of the city" she reserves her greatest shock and pity for the children she sees "[swarming] about the huts, naked, undernourished, uncared for."[7] Remarking that "more were being born every day into these squalid conditions, to live like maggots in a pile of refuse," Rama Rau decides that family planning was of "pivotal necessity" to "the gigantic task of social and economic improvement" facing the newly independent nation.[8]

I pause here to consider how very different Rama Rau's view is from the positive eugenic view with which I began. Instead of a concern with right reproduction, she views the problem as uncontrolled fecundity. And, as her unflattering description of slum dwellers ("maggots") and slums ("piles of refuse") attests, Rama Rau's birth control crusading was primarily focused upon differential fertility—the population problem is a problem of the prolific poor. What's more, the slums themselves are painted in a kind of parasitic relationship to proper national development, attaching themselves to and "spreading" alongside legitimate "building projects."[9] Instead of thinking of population in terms of national resources to be preserved and fostered (as expressed in the "Children are our future" sentiments of Sanger's speech and the figure of Mother India "beget[ting] glories from [her] endless womb" of Naidu's poem), population becomes a problem to be solved. Children are transmogrified from "glories" into "maggots," not only feeding on and thus contaminating the rightful aims of national development projects but also signifying that perhaps the project of development is already rotten. Instead of calling the project of national development into question, however, the children themselves become the hitch in national progress. Such a reconfiguration allows Rama Rau, while describing the experience of concurrently planning a conference on family planning and a conference on child welfare, to write with no sense of irony: "It was important that the subject of family planning should receive more publicity than the Conference on Child Welfare."[10] Children have become burdens to be avoided rather than resources to be protected.

I begin this book on twentieth-century eugenic feminism in the United States and India with Margaret Sanger and Dhanvanthi Rama Rau for a couple of reasons. The first is to draw attention to what changes with the crucial event of Indian independence in 1947, arguing that the focus on positive eugenics notable in Sanger's radio broadcast and in pre-independence Indian nationalist feminism is largely supplanted in the post–World War II era of development by the negative eugenics of population control. That is, the qualitative focus on making the best kind of people is replaced by a quantitative numbers game that nonetheless retains the idea of differential fertility (after all, the fear evoked by "the population bomb" is that of the world being decimated by overly reproductive brown, black, and yellow people). This dialectic between positive and negative eugenics is at the heart of the different iterations of eugenic feminism I trace throughout this book. If positive eugenics emphasize better breeding to make the "finest men and women possible," in Sanger's phrase, then negative eugenics is concerned with controlling the reproduction of those deemed unfit. While positive or negative aspects of eugenics are emphasized at different points in the histories of eugenic feminism in the United States and India, these positive and negative projects are nonetheless inextricably linked. In using a transnational analysis to demonstrate these troubled linkages, I show how movements for birth control and reproductive rights (which have been central to liberal feminism) can be aligned with far less emancipatory discourses. After all, as historian Sarah Hodges reminds us, "unlike the American or European historiography of birth control, the uneasy legacy of population control is not part of any emancipatory narrative" in the postcolonial world.[11] This is not to say that movements for reproductive justice are irredeemably compromised and thus should be abandoned. Instead, I argue that to avoid becoming eugenic, a truly global postcolonial feminist reading practice must work within this positive–negative dialectic as opposed to plotting an emancipatory future based on a logic of political purity.

The second reason I begin with Sanger and Rama Rau is to highlight the important continuities between what Sanger advocates in the pre-independence 1930s and what family planning activists such as Rama Rau take up in the post-independence 1950s. Specifically, the focus on the relationship among fertility, national development, and modernity remains, even if translated into a neo-Malthusian fear of population outstripping resources. In this sense, the two seemingly opposed figurations of children are simply different sides to the same eugenic coin. The distinction is that if the promise of birth control in mid-1930s India is one of perfecting the future national population, the fear of overpopulation post-independence is that population will destroy national development. Focusing on what changes and what stays the same between these two moments, moreover, highlights the continuities and discontinuities between eugenics and population control in the United States and India, and illuminates how (as Hodges proposes) "a maternalist eugenics [in India becomes] subsumed into the agenda of U.S.-led neo-Malthusian international population control policies" after Indian independence.[12]

In charting these connections, *Eugenic Feminism* suggests that both U.S. and Indian nationalist feminisms launch their claims to feminist citizenship based on modernist constructions of the reproductive body as the origin of the nation. It traces the workings of eugenic feminism in the United States and India from the late nineteenth through the twentieth century, beginning with the start of U.S. overseas imperialism (1898) and ending with Indira Gandhi's period of Emergency rule (1975–77). *Eugenic Feminism* is consequently framed by two national crises: the first entailed by the closing of the frontier and the funneling of U.S. imperial ambitions overseas, the second entailed by the betrayal of Indian nationalism in the Emergency. I begin and end with different moments of national crisis, at junctures where the very meaning of the nation is up for grabs, in order to think through how nationalist feminism reimagines itself in relation to the nation in times of upheaval. I similarly focus on reimaginations of the nation, tracing the rise of U.S. imperialism and developmentalism alongside the growth and realization of anti- and postcolonial nationalisms in India. This time period also quite neatly maps onto the birth of eugenics in the late nineteenth century and ends with the notorious excesses of Indira Gandhi's population policies. In the epilogue I take up the aftermath of the process of liberalization begun under Indira Gandhi's regime, bringing the story of eugenic feminism to the present day by considering the outsourcing of reproductive labor to India in relation to what has been called the "new" or "liberal" eugenics of new reproductive technologies. Instead of understanding eugenics as falling out of favor after the Nazis took it to its logical conclusion, I draw a line from eugenics to population control to argue that both marry concerns about the maintenance of national stock and of national borders, positing a fundamentally modern understanding of the relationship among biology, science, and the nation-state.[13] Asserting that nations can be won or lost on the basis of population rather than territory, right reproduction enters the public domain as a responsibility of governments and citizens alike. That imperial and postcolonial nationalisms alike answered eugenics' call speaks both to its widespread appeal and to the complicity between these seemingly oppositional nationalisms; nonetheless, no matter who brandishes it, the science of population always rests on anxieties about the "unfit" (however defined) undoing the nation, as the twin fears of "race suicide" and "overpopulation" attest.

It would be possible to trace the workings of eugenic feminism in a variety of national sites, but I focus on eugenic feminism in the United States and India for a couple of key reasons. First, even though there is much scholarship on the relationship between British and Indian feminisms, less attention has been paid to the ways in which U.S. and Indian feminisms developed in discursive relationship to each other throughout the twentieth century. Of course, this focus necessarily includes an engagement with British as well as U.S. articulations of empire, as the development of Indian feminism is split as it travels between British and U.S. imperialisms. In taking up the relationship between U.S. and Indian feminisms, I trace the prehistory of what Inderpal Grewal theorizes as "transnational connectivities": the ways in "which subjects, technologies, and ethical practices were created through transnational networks and connections of many different types."[14] Indian immigration to the United States before the 1965 Immigration and Nationality Act may have been negligible (particularly after the Immigration Act of 1917 banned it altogether), but India nonetheless held an important place in the U.S. national imaginary. Although the so-called Hindu craze of the late nineteenth and early twentieth centuries romanticized India as the site of spiritual enlightenment, for some U.S. observers India represented gender relations gone astray. In turn, Indian nationalist feminists positioned themselves in relation to U.S. feminisms (particularly in the wake of the scandal surrounding Mayo's 1927 *Mother India,* the topic of my third chapter), arguing for an alternative Indian feminist modernity that predates that of the West. Despite the different ways U.S. and Indian feminists resolved the issue of women's inclusion in the nation, therefore, both were engaged in shared and competing conversations about the nature of the "eugenic feminist woman" who would serve as the foundational citizen-subject and reproductive agent of the nation. In focusing on the United States and India I thus bring to light an unexplored, but foundational, chapter in the evolution of U.S. and Indian feminisms.

Second, by focusing on nationalist feminist preoccupations with reproductive bodies in the United States and India, *Eugenic Feminism* submits that developmental regimes of population control in India must be traced to technologies of U.S. imperialism and eugenics in the first part of the twentieth century. The international eugenics movement may have developed differently in different national contexts, but its post–World War II incarnation as population control displayed a remarkably similar neo-Malthusian logic around the globe. Population control linked national reproduction to modernity, positing population limitation as the means to jumpstart economic development. Unsurprisingly, then, the first large-scale population control programs based on such reasoning—and packaged under the more palatable label of "family planning"—had particular purchase in modernizing postcolonial nation-states. India led the way with the first explicit governmental program in 1951 (the National Family Planning Programme), and in 1953 launched the earliest population control experiment (the Khanna Study) in concert with the Harvard School of Public Health and with funding from the Rockefeller Foundation. If India presented the globe with the problem of overpopulation, the United States offered the solution by way of development and population control aid. Thus even as reproductive control in India was understood as a crucial component of national development, the inspiration (and often funding) came from a U.S.-led developmentalism that was one of the key forms U.S. hegemony took in the second half of the "American century."

At first glance, feminism, with its longstanding investments in women's reproductive rights, would seem at odds with a movement explicitly concerned with dictating and controlling reproductive behaviors.[15] However, the reliance of feminists such as Sanger and Rama Rau on eugenic notions of reproductivity shows that these discourses are not always as discrete as we might think. For one thing, eugenics may have inspired observers concerned with the "rising tide of color," but it also captured the imagination of many radical thinkers who saw perfected reproduction as the way forward to a utopian future.[16] In this sense, the reliance of certain strands of feminism on eugenic thinking is hardly surprising. Nonetheless, in examining the relationship between eugenics and feminism (and in formulating my central concept of "eugenic feminism"), I want to be clear that I am not accusing feminism writ large as being eugenic. Rather, I am pointing to a specific kind of maternalist feminist investment in biological reproduction, and biological reproduction as the means of progress and improvement, as the platform for women's rights within the state. As such, it is through feminist investments in nationalism (which, I propose, work according to a racialized reproductive mechanism) that feminism becomes dangerously tied to eugenicist thinking. I thus trace the strain of feminism that is mediated by nationalism to show its persistent reliance on a eugenic reproductive logic as the means of national and feminist improvement. In doing so I suggest, contrary to the often-repeated truism that anticolonial national liberation movements fail in part because of their inability to recognize feminist concerns, that feminist concerns were articulated to infelicitous ends.

In concentrating on the ways in which nationalist feminisms leverage eugenic thinking to install feminism within the state, I am necessarily telling a selective story. Beginning this introduction with two hegemonic feminist figures—Margaret Sanger and Dhanvanthi Rama Rau—is thus very much to the point. As is now well known through the works of Angela Davis, Linda Gordon, and Dorothy Roberts (to name just a few feminist scholars who have excavated Sanger's links to eugenics movements), Sanger can be considered a heroic crusader only if we ignore the ways in which she became increasingly aligned with movements for eugenics and population control.[17] Forwarding Sanger as a champion of "choice," moreover, relies on a liberal feminist emphasis on individual rights and disavows her biopolitical concerns with improper reproduction on a domestic and global scale. While less critical work has been done on Dhanvanthi Rama Rau, she similarly represents a very particular engagement with issues of birth and population control. As is perhaps unsurprising given her initial impressions of Bombay slums, Rama Rau's birth control advocacy eventually led her to support compulsory sterilization under Indira Gandhi's regime.[18] Her organization, the Family Planning Association of India (FPAI), ultimately backed down from that position in favor of a system of (often coercive) incentives and disincentives, but during the second year of the Emergency (1976) the FPAI was nonetheless responsible for sterilizing eighty thousand people.[19] Focusing on such individuals, therefore, underscores a crucial point about eugenic feminism as I am formulating it here: it is always in some way in service of the nation-state. Hence I concentrate on hegemonic nationalist feminism throughout this book precisely because of its investment in making feminist right reproduction part of state and nation building.[20]

Nonetheless, I want to underscore the troubling elisions the emphasis on such figures entails. Taking up Sanger and Rama Rau as *the* representatives of the U.S. and Indian birth control movements, for instance, ignores the ways in which the birth control and eugenics movements in both sites were always riven with internal fissures and contestations. In the U.S. context, feminist scholars of color have exposed how a narrow liberal feminist conception of reproductive rights as concerned only with access to birth control and abortion fails to address sterilization abuses of poor women, particularly poor women of color. They have also shown how reproductive rights in this guise are linked to population control overseas (again, Planned Parenthood and the International Planned Parenthood Federation are paradigmatic here), as well as to larger structures of neoliberal globalization in the form of development. Such scholarship has powerfully demonstrated that real reproductive justice would address the racism of an environmental movement that scapegoats indigenous peoples, immigrants, and the poor; the imperialism of regimes of national security; and the coercions of population control. Finally, the focus on Sanger and Rama Rau has the danger of painting the communities targeted for reproductive control as merely passive victims. Much excellent work has been done on the ways in which such communities, both domestically and internationally, have contested state regulation of their reproductive bodies.[21]

The Indian context is similarly marked by contestations. While it is true that the energies of nationalist feminists like Rama Rau were absorbed into welfarist departments of the state in the 1950s and 1960s (the "first phase" of the modern Indian women's movement, which was largely marked by faith in the newly independent government to solve the problems of gender inequity), during the "second phase" of the 1970s and 1980s Indian feminists launched powerful critiques of the ways in which the developmental state insisted on viewing women only in terms of a bourgeois domesticity that went hand in hand with population control.[22] In this sense, the modern feminist movement in India coalesced around the failures of development (some coming from within the discourse of development itself, such as the groundbreaking 1974 report of the Commission on the Status of Women, *Towards Equality*), and in response to coercive population policies, particularly those enacted by Indira Gandhi during the Emergency (1975–77). Accordingly, in the 1980s there were powerful protests against the introduction of injectable contraceptives (Depo-Provera and NET-EN) into the Indian market, and in the 1990s against the population control consensus advanced at the 1994 conference on population in Cairo.[23] My point is that if one of the narratives of Indian feminism is that it is coopted by nationalism in the years following independence (an argument I explore in depth in chapter 4), in the 1970s and 1980s the Indian feminist movement is defined by activism directed toward changing state policies. While in this sense the second phase is nonetheless engaged with the state, the most recent phase of the Indian feminist movement (beginning roughly with the Shah Bano case in 1986) is marked by antistatism.[24]

There is thus a powerful history of feminist critiques and contestations of state control of women's and men's reproductive bodies in both of the national contexts I take up. Nevertheless, *Eugenic Feminism* opens up a different conversation about how hegemonic feminism uses eugenic discourse to launch claims to citizenship and national belonging, arguing that both U.S. and Indian nationalist feminisms leverage women's reproductive labor into citizenship rights within the nation-state. That is, they use the logic that because women reproduce the nation they should have full rights within the state. Nonetheless, if eugenics is founded in the desire for "more children from the fit, less from the unfit," then eugenic feminism enacts this ambition by creating a feminist subject fit to reproduce the sovereign nation.[25] This subject is always created in contradistinction from the nation's "others;" eugenic feminism shapes national identity in negative terms, returning repeatedly to phantom and figural others to define them as precisely what must be excluded in order for a eugenic feminist subject to advance the nation as a whole. By figuring the eugenic feminist subject as the means of national advance, however, eugenic feminism is also enormously generative, positing purified reproduction as the way to assure a more perfect future.

In making this point, I want to stress that I am not using eugenic feminism as a label to attach to various feminists or feminists movements, but as an analytic through which to chart intersections among nationalism, feminism, race, class, and sexuality. Many of the figures (Katherine Mayo, Indira Gandhi) and historical moments (the 1950s, the Emergency) I analyze are distinctly *un*feminist, and yet using the framework of eugenic feminism allows me to trace the relationship among nationalism, eugenic reproduction, and the brandishing of feminist rhetoric in the name of progress in each. I therefore take up eugenic feminism not only as a historically specific relationship between feminism and eugenic movements but also as a trope within nationalist feminism that insists that difference must be removed in order for feminist advance. I argue that the trope of eugenics is expressed formally in narratives of utopia and nostalgia; thus in chapters 1 and 2 I take up Charlotte Perkins Gilman's utopian novels and Sarojini Naidu's Romantic nostalgic poetry respectively in order to trace the literary logic of utopia and nostalgia, a logic that will be repeated in one form or another in the rest of the book. *Eugenic Feminism* thus builds on important scholarship on eugenics and literature such as Laura Doyle's 1994 *Bordering on the Body,* Angelique Richardson's 2003 *Love and Eugenics,* Daylanne English's 2004 *Unnatural Selections,* and Dana Seitler's 2008 *Atavistic Tendencies.*[26] Each of these works explore how narrative forms grapple with eugenics, as (in English's words), a "central national ideology;"[27] in focusing on the workings of utopia and nostalgia (and in formulating the concept of "developmentalist nostalgia") I uncover the transnational and comparative workings of eugenic narratives subtended by concerns with national development and decline.

If at first glance the pairing of eugenics and feminism seems as unusual as the focus on the United States and India, I hope to show over the next five chapters that such incongruous couplings are precisely the point. Indeed, because the aim of this book is to uncover a logic of eugenic purity at work in a number of likely and unlikely sites—feminism, nationalism, developmentalism—the methodology I must use to do this is necessarily "impure." There are therefore many impure couplings in these chapters, as I mix literary texts and planning documents, poetry and political speeches, utopian works and dystopian propaganda in telling the story of eugenic feminism over two continents and eighty years. I thus use what could be called a hybrid or "dysgenic" approach of placing heterogeneous texts, geographical sites, and historical moments in conversation with one another. One of the results of this methodology is to reveal the strange bedfellows the issue of right reproduction makes, allowing me to consider figures as varied as Charlotte Perkins Gilman, Katherine Mayo, Sarojini Naidu, and Indira Gandhi. As such, even as *Eugenic Feminism* is interrogating nationalist feminist investments in purity (and in reproduction as the means of achieving that purity) it is a deeply feminist project that seeks to question biologistic investments in women's reproductive bodies as the motors of national improvement.

Population, Eugenics, Development

Key to the development of eugenic feminism is a modern view of "population" as a natural phenomenon endogenous to the workings of the state. This modern view of population is a fundamental aspect of the rise in the mid-eighteenth century of what Michel Foucault calls biopower. Arguing that the sovereign's power "to *take* life or to *let* live" is replaced by the "reverse right of the social body to ensure, maintain, or develop its life" Foucault identifies a new politics of controlling the species body as a population.[28] Although the "anatomo politics of the human body" works to increase the utility and docility of individuals through discipline, biopower works on populations, constituting a "new body, a multiple body, a body with so many heads that, while they might not be infinite in number, cannot necessarily be counted."[29] Where discipline individuates, biopolitics massifies, creating a hydra-like beast in need of governmental regulation and control.

Foucault traces this shift in thinking about population through political economy, arguing that although the mercantilists viewed population in positive terms, for the physiocrats and other eighteenth-century economists population begins to signify differently. Because mercantilists viewed population as the source of the nation's productive forces and thus wealth, the nation with the most people is the most powerful. Such a formulation rests on the idea of population as a collection of citizens organized under a sovereign able to deploy them at will. For the physiocrats and other eighteenth-century economists, however, population meant something else entirely. Instead of understanding population as a collection of subjects organized under a sovereign, population becomes its own entity, a new kind of political actor that is both less and more than the sum of its parts. On the one hand, individuals are no longer important as individuals. On the other, population is understood as an independent and natural (if potentially out of control) force that can be acted upon through government regulation of seemingly external factors—the economy, food supply, public health, and so on. Therefore, coincident with the rise of population is that of what Foucault calls governmentality—the power of the sovereign over subjects is replaced by a government acting to produce proper citizens.

With the birth of population as a political actor in its own right comes the "population problem." Reverend Thomas Malthus was certainly not the first to formulate the problem as such; nonetheless his 1798 *Essay on the Principle of Population* popularized the idea that population and natural resources were locked in a death battle. He argued that food supplies increase arithmetically and population expands geometrically, meaning that population will always grow faster. Unless population is brought under control, he postulated, there will be increasing social unrest and civilizational decline. Despite the way this last point links Malthusianism and eugenics, they differ in at least one vital aspect. Although Malthus launched his argument "against the perfectibility of the mass of mankind," painting an essentially dystopian picture of the future, eugenics was an altogether more utopian vision, expressing the modern injunction to scientific improvement and progress in biological form.[30] Malthus may have inspired Charles Darwin, who in turn inspired his cousin Francis Galton (the originator of the term *eugenics*), but in some ways eugenics is Malthusianism's optimistic opposite.[31] Where Malthus saw the inevitability of humanity's decline, Galton viewed the potential for endless progress, understanding eugenics as the humane way to help along the process his cousin had described as "natural selection." Instead of letting nature take its violent course, it could be guided by benevolent human hands. This is why eugenics appealed to social conservatives, progressives, and radicals alike. But, as we all know, eugenics was likewise a violent vision, in which certain peoples and populations were marked out for extinction. At its heart, then, eugenics is both utopian and violent: utopian in that it looks forward to a future in which disease, disability, and conflict arising from racial differences are things of the past; violent in that achieving such a future requires the excision of all those deemed "unfit."

In attempting to plot this utopian future, eugenics depends upon the uniquely modern relationship between populations and states defined by biopower. Despite the fact that, as Alison Bashford and Philippa Levine point out in their introduction to *The Oxford Handbook of the*

History of Eugenics, "writers in the early twentieth century often drew a long genealogy for eugenic ideas and practice, writing about ancient traditions of the withdrawal of aid to weakly children and adults," modern eugenics is distinct in that it posits individual citizens' reproductive behaviors as the express concern of the state.[32] At its heart, eugenics is the biopolitical project par excellence—as the "state control of the biological," it encourages reproduction from some and discourages it from others.[33] The centrality of sexuality and reproduction to the larger biopolitical management of life is suggested by the fact that Foucault comes to biopolitics through volume 1 of *The History of Sexuality,* in which he argues that the twin poles of disciplinary power and biopower come together through strategic deployments of sexuality throughout the nineteenth century. He identifies "four great lines of attack" through which sexuality was harnessed and controlled in the nineteenth century—the sexualization of children, the hysterization of women, the limitation of certain populations, and the psychiatrization of perversion—arguing that in these areas the dual focus on population and individuals converge.[34] As Ann Stoler reminds us in her 1995 *Race and the Education of Desire,* to these we must also add the processes by which colonized subjects were imagined as "savage" and "primitive" in relationship to their bourgeois metropolitan counterparts.[35] Doing so, moreover, allows us to think about the ways in which the figures of the "Malthusian couple" and the "primitive" are united in postwar population control discourse. When population concerns go global in the era of development (a process that this book narrates), the problem is no longer simply about internal populations making the nation uninhabitable, but rather about a global catastrophe caused by overly reproductive people in the underdeveloped world.

In this way, the biopolitical management of life is also linked to the rise of state racism; Foucault asserts that modern "racism is born at the point when the theme of racial purity replaces that of race struggle."[36] Although racism predates biopower, Foucault argues that state racism is both novel and necessary for two reasons. First, racism introduces a break in the biopolitical continuum, accounting for the justification of death within the larger incitement to life. Second, racism justifies the death of the other not simply in terms of safety and protection, but rather by insisting that the death of the other makes the population purer, stronger, better: "Killing or the imperative to kill is acceptable only if it results not in a victory over political adversaries, but in the elimination of the biological threat to and the improvement of the species or race."[37] This idea of progress as a biological imperative (and as a biological imperative that can only be realized through what Achille Mbembe theorizes as a necropolitical stance toward those peoples and populations marked for extinction) is the logic that underpins postwar development.[38] This is not to say that development equals eugenics; however, in tracing a line from eugenics to population control, I suggest that the notion of progress to which development adheres displays a eugenic logic. Like eugenics, development is grounded in a utopian belief in the perfectibility of humanity and by extension the world. At the same time, development (again like eugenics) measures this future perfection against a present that can only be considered lacking. I am not implying that development creates problems where none exist; the problems development purports to solve are very real indeed. By forwarding an idea of progress based upon the specific course of economic development in the West, however, development transposes into economic form many of the biological assumptions that are both eugenics' inheritance and legacy. This is never more evident than when we look at the issue of population. If development is about a transformation in the mode of production that is also understood to be a transformation in subjectivity, then altering reproductive behavior becomes one of the linchpins through which to enact these changes.

Particularly in its modernization theory guise, development (as the constellation of ideological and institutional apparatuses born in Bretton Woods, New Hampshire, in 1944) was premised on the idea that societies move through a series of predictable stages on the way to being deemed "developed." In this, development is implicitly comparative insofar as it naturalizes the paths of industrialization and modernization in the West by parsing them into clear-cut stages divorced from history and politics. At the same time, the discourse of development identifies all other trajectories of development as inherently lacking. Developmentalism thereby retains many characteristics of colonialism while translating explicitly racial hierarchies into supposedly neutral economic ones. Nonetheless, as María Josefina Saldaña-Portillo argues in her 2003 *The Revolutionary Imagination in the Americas and the Age of Development,* development is powerful precisely because of the promise of full-fledged modernity it holds out to all who subscribe to its progressivist creed. Development may be a form of U.S. imperialism/neocolonialism, but it is also a key component of postcolonial nationalisms.

As Saldaña-Portillo asserts, "Development's discursive emergence was thus, paradoxically, *both* a liberatory strategy for decolonizing the world *and* a 'neutral' rearticulation of racialized colonial categories as national difference."[39]

Precisely because of its historical centrality to the postcolonial state, therefore, development is a key form of postcolonial governmentality that becomes a defining idiom not only of postcolonial statecraft but also of postcolonial national identity. As such, it requires national populations to accede to what Saldaña-Portillo terms development's "regime of subjection," wherein the "movement of societies is contingent on the development of the members of these societies into free, mature, fully conscious, and self-determining individual subjects."[40] Development is not just about developing nations into fully modern entities, it is also about developing people into fully modern subjects. The key to this, of course, is destroying "premodern" or "traditional" ways of life standing in the way of complete capitalist modernity. As a regime of subjection, then, development is tied to a notion of individual conversion wherein the subject sheds outmoded practices and beliefs stemming from traditional culture. As Saldaña-Portillo demonstrates, this idea of individual transformation pertains across the ideological spectrum, undergirding U.S.-led modernization theory, Marxist dependency theory, and revolutionary movements alike.

Although many aspects of so-called traditional society are represented in development discourse as barriers to be overcome in the formation of fully developed national subjects, *Eugenic Feminism* focuses on the ways in which development turns its eye to reproductive behavior as the key to transforming subjects and societies. As Matthew Connelly details in his provocative recent history of the global population control movement, *Fatal Misconception,* the alleged population problem pits population against development in a potentially lethal race. With improvements in public health toward the middle of the twentieth century, death and infant mortality rates fell and population numbers began to rise—in some people's view precipitously. As evident in Rama Rau's assessment of a burgeoning population as both a product of and parasite upon development, population growth was understood to be a barrier to national growth rather than a resource to be fostered. Part of this view was based on an instrumental understanding of the relationship between family size and capitalist development. Early theorizations of population and development used "demographic transition theory" to argue that the key to curbing population growth was industrialization: "Fertility would not begin to fall until peasants moved to cities, earned paychecks, and enrolled their children in school."[41] Over time, however, the causal relationship between development and fertility was flipped. The 1950 study of the Rockefeller Foundation, *Public Health and Demography in the Far East,* proposed that reproductive behavior could be reformed in isolation of other variables. Instead of reduced fertility following on the heels of development, development could be spurred by manipulating birth rates. Therefore, proponents of population control "persuaded leaders of newly independent countries to not just choose between capitalism or communism. . . . They presented population control as a means to jumpstart the process. By rationalizing and redirecting reproduction, [national leaders] could make their people modern in a single generation."[42] To reverse the popular slogan, rather than "development [being] the best contraceptive," contraception becomes the best means of development.

If development describes the workings of a capitalist modernity that is also about a transformation in subjectivity, and if reproduction is the key to this new subjectivity, then proper reproduction is what defines modern men and women. In other words, controlling reproductive and sexual behaviors (having the right kind of children, having fewer children) is understood in the logic of development as a vital way to become modern, or to stay "primitive." In this, development's concerns are contiguous with colonialism's deployment of reproduction and sexuality as crucial technologies of empire.[43] Regulating sexuality is part of the larger biopolitical management of populations by the state and as such is a strategy utilized by colonial and postcolonial national governments alike. The mobility of discourses of reproduction and sexuality render them useful to postcolonial governments for their ability (in Laura Briggs's words) "to *produce* change and transition"—that is, regulating sexuality and proper reproduction (both biological and cultural) for the nation was a way to shed the colonial past and chart a brighter national future.[44]

Crucially, then, the first way in which women enter into development is through the issues of reproduction; in the first decades of development planning (in India and globally) women are primarily targeted as either mothers to be protected or victims in need of welfare assistance, and even in this latter incarnation it is their maternal role that is highlighted and policed. In insisting on seeing women only in their domestic roles, development discourse relegates gender problems to the inner sphere of "traditional culture," ignoring how the processes of colonialism and developmentalism have themselves negatively affected women, and imagining gender inequality as crumbling away in the face of development's triumphal march. As forty years of feminist critiques of development have shown, this inability to account for women as productive subjects has had deleterious consequences for both women and for development.[45]

It may be true that the failure to account for women's productive labor has stymied national development, but the larger question for me concerns what happens when development interpellates women primarily in their reproductive roles. Specifically, I am interested in how development discourse strategically borrows from a liberal feminist language of reproductive choice in enacting population policies. As Gayatri Spivak has persuasively argued in relationship to population policies that cloak themselves in the language of empowerment, "control of women—of their bodies through coercive population policy or of their minds through an education that propagates the values underlying global financialization—is too often portrayed as free choice and the development of women."[46] Issues of women's health, education, and economic empowerment may be increasingly at the fore of development policy (as they were not in the earlier decades of development I take up in *Eugenic Feminism*), but the fact remains that the vision of empowerment such development projects forward are, once again, about a conversion narrative of modernization that advances a liberal feminist subject of rights and free choice. What such a logic ignores, as Spivak notes, is the way in which the ultimate goal is to incorporate subaltern women into a regime of global capitalist development that in fact reinforces the very inequalities to which such women are subject.[47]

This easy linkage among a focus on reproduction, development, and feminism allows all kinds of explicitly antifeminist projects to be labeled as feminist. For instance, radical feminist Mary Daly claims Katherine Mayo, a social conservative who used the figure of abject Indian reproduction as a way to police U.S. women into traditional gender roles, as a feminist foremother.[48] Similarly, Indira Gandhi—who rejected the label of feminism and whose repressive population control policies were certainly not feminist by any definition—is not only often read as a feminist simply by virtue of being a woman in power, but also wins a population prize from the United Nations in 1983.[49] In interrogating the ways in which various kinds of repressive projects are enacted in feminism's name, I hope to chart a nonreproductive feminist politics that attends to the specificities of feminist formations in different historical moments, thereby disrupting progress narratives that cannot help but rely on a reproductive logic.[50]

Feminism, Nationalism, Reproduction

Just as eugenics is thinkable only within the context of the nation-state, so too is eugenic feminism.[51] Mainstream accounts of Anglo-American feminism's relationship to nationalism understand it as largely oppositional; feminism must struggle against the state for equal rights under the law.[52] As Mrinalini Sinha rightly points out, however, this narrative disavows the ways in which Anglo-American feminism is "informed by the racial and imperial politics of [its] . . . projects of nationhood,"[53] painting it instead as a progress narrative of incremental advance. In the postcolonial world, the story is rather different. There the relationship between nationalism and feminism is considered symbiotic at best and parasitic at worst. In one view, feminism develops only because of the mobilization of anticolonial national forces. Because the status of women was used as a marker of civilization, the so-called women's question (debates around issues such as *sati,* child marriage, and widow remarriage) was hotly contested within Indian reformist movements from the late nineteenth century onward.[54] Women are awakened to their rights, in this account, through the agency of male reformers rather than by their own devices. In another view, an emergent and independent feminism is subsumed within a larger project of national liberation, and thus the specificities of feminist struggle are lost.[55]

In tracing the workings of eugenics in nationalist feminism, I draw upon the rich body of scholarship in feminist and postcolonial (and postcolonial feminist) studies on the relationship between women and nation in order to advance the debates on feminism and nationalism. Arguing that the nation is always a gendered construct, critics such as Deniz Kandiyoti, Nira Yuval Davis, and Floya Anthias have explored the ways in which women as symbols are deployed to stand in for the nation even as they are denied rights within the state.[56] As symbols of the nation, women's sexuality and reproductive bodies are first recruited for an anticolonial nationalism that relies on positive reproduction for the nation and are then subjected to reproductive control in the service of postcolonial modernity. In each case, as Lata Mani powerfully argues in relationship to turn of the nineteenth-century debates around *sati,* women are not the subjects of these considerations but are rather the "ground" on which they take place.[57] *Eugenic Feminism* builds on this work by considering the manner in which nationalist feminisms similarly use women's reproductive bodies to consolidate their claims to feminist citizenship, focusing specifically on the conjoining of nationalism and feminism to posit that feminism becomes eugenic when yoked to national narratives of pure and impure reproduction (or, put another way, narratives of progress and degeneration) as a means of ensuring future development or warding against possible decline. At issue here is not simply the ways in which women are instrumentalized by nationalist discourse, but rather how nationalist feminisms strategically brandish the reproductive logic of nationalism for feminist ends.

At its heart, then, *Eugenic Feminism* describes a form of reproductive nationalism. Here, I employ Alys Eve Weinbaum's insight in her 2004 *Wayward Reproductions* that "racial nationalism, or more pointedly, nationalist racism, emerges as a form of reproductive nationalism."[58] Glossing Etienne Balibar's important argument that "racism is not an 'expression' of nationalism, but *a supplement of nationalism* or more precisely *a supplement internal to nationalism,* always in excess of it, but always indispensable to its constitution and yet always still insufficient to achieve its project,"[59] Weinbaum highlights the workings of reproduction to demonstrate that "racism and sexism cannot be thought separately because reproduction is a racializing force."[60] Tracing the significance to nationalism of what she terms the "race/reproduction bind" (the commonplace notion that race is biologically reproducible) Weinbaum argues that racialized reproduction is the basis of national belonging and the motor of national futurity. Because the nation is understood as an organic entity that either advances or declines through a reproductive mechanism (both figuratively through metaphors of nations as motherlands, and literally through concerns with national demographics), the nation is always already racialized. This racialized reproductive mechanism is likewise central to nationalist feminism, as Weinbaum considers in her chapter on Charlotte Perkins Gilman (a foundational U.S. feminist figure I likewise turn to in my first chapter). I add to Weinbaum's work, and to the body of scholarship on women and nation in general, by arguing that what Weinbaum calls Gilman's *maternalist racial nationalism* is not simply feminism's sometime unknowing companion, or an instrument used by a masculinist national politics to police women and their reproductive bodies, but can also (as the example of Gilman shows us) be a powerful tool for nationalist feminism.[61] As such, eugenic feminism in the United States is entangled with U.S. imperialism and nativism, expressing fears of national contamination and decline entailed by imperialist expansion overseas and immigration at home.

Weinbaum's theorization of the way the nation is reproduced (and reproduced as racialized) is important to my thinking here, but because her project is transatlantic in focus she does not take up the race/reproduction bind in anticolonial and postcolonial nationalisms. In thinking through the different workings of reproductive nationalism in these contexts, I turn to Partha Chatterjee's consideration of postcolonial national difference in his 1993 *The Nation and Its Fragments*. In opposition to Benedict Anderson's influential paradigm of the nation as an "imagined community," Chatterjee argues that anticolonial nationalisms are founded not on identity with modular nationalisms but on difference articulated through the "inner," "spiritual" sphere of culture as opposed to the "outer," "material" sphere of politics and statecraft.[62] In India this spiritual sphere is explicitly feminized, as women come to represent cultural difference in the inner sanctum of the home. Nonetheless, women's consignment to the inner sphere does not mean that they simply represent a static tradition unchanged by the encounter with British colonialism. Instead, the bourgeois "new woman," discrete from the Westernized woman of the upper class and the "common" woman of the lower classes, comes to function as a sign of both India's modernity and cultural distinctness.

While Weinbaum's concern with "wayward reproduction" in the United States is about the contamination of an already constituted state (even if the constitution of that state is highly contested), in the postcolonial context national reproduction holds out different possibilities and problems. Namely, in the imperialist nationalism Weinbaum discusses, the nation (as racially reproduced) is organized around fears of internal and external contaminations that endanger national futurity. When we look at the incipient postcolonial state, the issue is less racial entrenchment (though that certainly is a concern) than it is the creation and definition of the nation-people. Thus reproduction does not simply threaten national purity; it is also the motor of national re-generation. Postcolonial nationalism therefore creates a particular set of conditions and problems for women in general and for nationalist feminism in particular. Specifically, such a reproductive logic creates a space for women to forward themselves as central actors in the nation on the basis of the fact that they are responsible for reproducing future citizens. While Chatterjee fails to account for the place of feminism within his division of nationalism between the spiritual and the mate-rial (focusing instead on Bengali women's autobiographies), *Eugenic Feminism* addresses how Indian nationalist feminists bring the sphere of the "home" into the "world," demonstrating the ultimate untenability of the separation of the public and private by focusing on a eugenic feminist discourse that is both rooted in, and in excess of, this split.

This is not to say that the race/reproduction bind in incipient Indian nationalism does not serve a repressive function. As scholars such as Paola Bacchetta, Charu Gupta, and Mahua Sarkar have shown (and as I discuss in more detail in chapter 2), despite contestations over the nature of Indian nationalism, Hindu nationalism prevails in the crucial run up to independence.[63] But far from representing continu-ity with the past, as Chatterjee reminds us, the notion that "'Indian nationalism' is synonymous with 'Hindu nationalism' is . . . an entirely modern, rationalist, and historicist idea."[64] Indeed, Hindu national-ism developed alongside and in conversation with political nationalism from the late nineteenth century onward, and (among other strategies) used the regulation of women's bodies, behaviors, and sexuality to as-sert and strengthen communal differences.[65] Women as symbols de-fined Hindu unity in distinction from Muslim difference, with Muslim male sexuality portrayed as a threat to Hindu women, and Muslim female fecundity portrayed as a threat to the nation.[66] Furthermore, non-normative (because non-reproductive) sexuality presented its own problem; as Charu Gupta argues, "in the efforts to regulate homo-sex . . . what was also at stake was the issue of female reproduction and its utility for the nation, in terms of producing good citizens."[67] Finally, in spite of its populist rhetoric, Indian nationalism as practiced was largely elite in character. As three decades of subaltern studies scholar-ship has demonstrated, the nation did not make good on its liberal promises, and structures of subalternity have remained in place (and in some cases intensified) even after independence. This is not to say that there are not competing voices and visions of Indian national modernity, but the Indian eugenic feminist formations I explore are largely in service of middle-class, upper-caste Hindu hegemony.

From Eugenics to Population Control

Looking at the different stakes of eugenic feminism in imperial versus anticolonial and postcolonial sites sheds light on the diverse and interlinked trajectories of eugenic feminism in Britain, the United States, and India. While this book focuses primarily on the traffic of eugenic feminist discourse between the United States and India, such traffic is unavoidably triangulated with British imperialism. Eugenics was born in Britain, after all, even if it developed as an international movement and according to a unique logic in each of the national sites in which it took hold.[68] In addition, if anticolonial debates about reproduction and sexuality helped solidify an Indian national identity, this identity is articulated primarily in response to British colonialism, even if also in conversation with the United States. Finally, examining how eugenics, birth control, and population control regimes developed in each national site is helpful in thinking about the United States and Britain as vying (even if aligned) empires in the first part of the twentieth century. On the one hand, U.S. imperialism turned to the British Empire as a model and guide.[69] On the other, the United States was attempting to establish itself as a world power, and accordingly its expansionist capitalist interests were eager to gain a foothold in British colonial markets. That the United States established itself in these markets through interventions into public health and reproduction speaks to the fact that, as David Arnold has suggested, "the value of medicine as an aid to economic imperialism was most fully recognized by the emissaries of North American capitalism."[70]

Born out of the crucible of Victorian debates on evolutionary thought and heredity, eugenics caught hold in turn-of-the-twentieth-century Britain precisely because it responded to these shifting currents of global power. For one, eugenics spoke to instabilities in British Empire, with some observers citing British "unfitness" as the reason for imperial decline in the face of anticolonial resistance and competition from other empires. Thus while it is commonplace to say that eugenics in Britain was concerned more with class than with race (and certainly class concerns were at the forefront), eugenics was also a racialized discourse in the British context, with particular interest in the miscegenation that empire inevitably brings. Nonetheless, eugenics in Britain was largely a domestic concern, speaking to anxieties over urban poverty, falling birth rates, high infant mortality rates, and social unrest in the guise of labor movements, socialism, and movements for women's suffrage.[71] Specifically, eugenics overlapped with the so-called woman question: feminist Sybil Neville-Rolfe founded the Eugenics Education Society in 1907 (it was renamed the Eugenics Society in 1912 and the Galton Institute in 1989), and women formed the majority of its members.[72] Through linking feminist and eugenic concerns, eugenic feminists in Britain were not merely passive adopters of eugenics but actively helped to craft the terms of eugenic debates.[73]

If feminists were important in shaping the eugenics movement in Britain, in the United States feminism and eugenics are intertwined but discrete movements, with mainstream U.S. eugenics rejecting eugenic feminism's basic premise that racial advance must be achieved through women's liberation and equality. Tracing the history of eugenic feminism in the United States, legal scholar Mary Ziegler argues that "feminists involved in the eugenics reform movement . . . did not defer to traditional eugenic science, but redefined it."[74] U.S. feminists were largely unsuccessful in this attempt, as mainstream eugenics was more concerned with U.S. feminists committing "race suicide" in the face of immigrant fecundity than they were with supporting voluntary motherhood. However, when the focus shifted from the positive eugenics of encouraging reproduction from the fit to the negative eugenics of preventing reproduction from the unfit, birth control became a way to, in Sanger's words, "preserve [the eugenicist's] work."[75] Sanger courted eugenicists, both because of their political and economic clout and because of her own eugenic views, and in the process the overtly feminist content of the birth control movement was sacrificed to the cause of gaining respectability and institutionalization—as solidified in the 1942 name change from the Birth Control Federation of America to the Planned Parenthood Federation of America. By forwarding normative ideas of parenthood (the goal is to plan parenthood rather than prevent pregnancies), Planned Parenthood sidestepped any critique of the family as the site of gender inequalities.

Although feminism and mainstream eugenics were opposed in the United States, in India, as in Britain, nationalist feminists were central to advocating the eugenic cause. Crucially, eugenics in India was not undertaken by the colonial government but was instead a means through which to articulate Indian (and particularly Indian feminist) modernity. That is, the Indian eugenics societies of the late nineteenth and early twentieth centuries were started almost entirely by Indians and were explicitly anticolonial: first, nationalists critiqued the British for not enacting adequate reproductive reforms; second, they forwarded eugenics as the means of revitalizing the nation and ousting the British. By implicating a noninterventionist British colonial state for the failure to adequately address public health concerns (including, but not limited to, reproductive ones), Indian nationalism both rejected British colonialism and set the stage for U.S.–led modernization schemes post-independence.

In making this last point I underscore that British reluctance to take on issues of public health (particularly as pertains to reproduction) differed from the United States and indeed opened up the space for U.S. intervention into India. As Mrinalini Sinha maintains in *Specters of Mother India,* "public health policy was the cornerstone of the expansionist interests of early-twentieth-century U.S. capitalism: it provided the basis for grounding the claims for, and the necessity of, the global dissemination of Western civilization on supposedly more scientific lines."[76] Tracing this dissemination through independence and beyond, I argue that this discourse will reach its fruition and global articulation in the mission of modernization that the United States undertakes through the regime of development in the post–World War II period. If eugenics in India pre-independence is, in part, about an anticolonial discourse that indicts the British colonial state for failing to take on any meaningful reforms, then post-independence Indian nationalism turns to the United States as both a model and a partner for reproductive reform. In this, I'm suggesting that that if we look at British imperial decline in the face of Indian nationalism, partnering with India in the realm of public health and development is one way that the United States asserts its influence in the postwar period. Despite Indian national resistance to the United States through the policy of nonalignment (a policy that allowed India to receive development aid from both the United States and the Soviet Union) and its "mixed" model of state planning for capitalist development, the developmental regime of modernization that India follows is a largely U.S.–based one, as I argue in chapter 4. Therefore if the history of eugenics and birth control in India is triangulated between British and U.S. empires pre-independence, after independence the histories of eugenics and feminism in the United States and India meet up in the developmentalist era of population control.

One way of understanding the relationship between eugenics and population control is to argue it is a simple matter of renaming—eugenics becomes tainted through its association with Nazism and thus must be refashioned as population control. Certainly many U.S. eugenicists turned their money and institutional energies to population control; while one group of eugenicists moved into genetic biology, the population demographers, as Minna Stern notes in *Eugenic Nation,* "merged their interest in salvaging and retooling eugenics with the export of Western-led modernization to the Third World."[77] At the same time, the very interest of eugenicists in "third world" development signifies a crucial difference between eugenics and population control; namely, the optic is no longer national but global as the United States becomes increasingly focused on population growth in poorer countries. At first glance this framework seems less divisive than what came before (just as references to "spaceship earth" seem to index a common humanity equally in danger from, and responsible to, the population problem), but in fact the very language of "three worlds" belies the idea of a shared project. Instead, overpopulation in the third world is understood as both endangering the environmental future of the planet and as fomenting communism and increasing global instability. Thus population control not only concerns differential fertility on a global scale, it also becomes part of a Cold War strategy of resisting communism.

At the same time, population control as a crucial component of national development becomes an important focus for postcolonial governments. This is why, paradoxically, population control in India is more eugenic than the eugenics movements that preceded it—as my discussion of Sanger and Rama Rau notes, with independence the focus shifts from fostering reproduction from the fit to preventing reproduction from the unfit. This shift, fueled by a largely U.S.-led neo-Malthusian mission for population control, also charts a new phase of eugenic feminism. As I survey in my fourth chapter, the typical narrative of feminism in the 1950s (both in India and globally) is that feminism vanishes in favor of a bourgeois domesticity that once again valorizes women's roles within the home. Although I do not necessarily contest that narrative, I do illustrate how it gets worked out in terms of U.S.-led agricultural and population developmental policies, arguing that the Indian "eugenic woman" who is forwarded as the subject of the nation has much to tell us about the feminism of the time. Thus while in India the movement between eugenics and population control is quite direct (and, indeed, is exactly where the energies of much of the U.S. eugenics movements go), post-independence population control is much less feminist than the eugenic feminist formations that preceded it. Therefore the final two chapters of *Eugenic Feminism* trace how modernizing the nation is linked to modernizing gender roles in a logic that is explicitly comparative with the United States. Although my final chapter on Indira Gandhi's period of Emergency Rule (1975–77) focuses almost exclusively on the Indian context, it nonetheless positions population control programs before and during the Emergency in relation to U.S. developmental regimes; after all, this is the era in which President Lyndon Johnson made food aid to India contingent on national population control policies.[78]

Eugenic Feminism and Subalternity

In telling the story of eugenic feminism over two continents and eighty years I focus predominantly on elite formations of eugenic feminism, with an eye to what such narratives violently excise: the subaltern subjects who must be sacrificed in the name of national development. In chapters 1 and 3 I trace the ways in which the imperial nation imagines itself in relation to its internal "others" as a prehistory of development's postwar regime of managing difference on a global scale. Similarly, I trace how Indian nationalism articulates itself both pre-independence (chapter 2) and post-independence (chapters 4 and 5), to think through the fate of subaltern figures explicitly marked out for obsolescence by the project of development. Let me be clear: in trying to unravel this logic my own stance toward subaltern figures who are the objects of development is not one of nostalgia (indeed, I explore the violence inherent in such a stance in chapters 2, 4, and 5). What I am interested in thinking through, however, is how such subaltern figures are strategically mobilized *as figures* by the very discourses that both create them and seek to modernize them out of existence. Given that the entire discourse of modernity produces the very subaltern subjects it seeks to abject and although one must invoke and be responsible to the subaltern, that very discourse of responsibility is always already compromised.

I begin this process in my first chapter by tracing the abjection of Asian women in the writings of Charlotte Perkins Gilman. I start with

Gilman not only because of her foundational status in U.S. feminism, but also because the relationship she charts between the economic and the reproductive is central to the eugenic feminist ideology I delineate throughout this book. In works such as her 1898 *Women and Economics* and 1914 *The Man-Made World,* Gilman offers a revolutionary though troubling critique of the masculinist ideology of separate spheres by locating the most important site of production within the female body, suggesting that "nation building" is literally the work of reproduction and as such should be controlled by the state. I turn to Gilman's three utopian novels (her 1911 *Moving the Mountain,* 1915 *Herland,* and 1916 *With Her in Ourland*) to examine how they depend upon excising race, class, and even gender differences. Concentrating particularly on how Gilman mobilizes the figure of the downtrodden and potentially dangerous Asian woman as eugenic feminism's foil, I argue that she consistently turns to Asia as an "object lesson" in the potential pitfalls of U.S. feminism's advance.

My second chapter turns to nationalist feminist poet Sarojini Naidu. Reading Naidu's political speeches and nationalist poetry from the first part of the twentieth century through to Indian independence in 1947, I argue that Naidu complicates both patriarchal national and imperial feminist discourses by insisting that nationalist regeneration can *only* happen through the agency of Indian women. She posits the new, bourgeois Indian woman as the model for the abstract citizen-subject of the nascent nation, figuring the Indian woman as symbolizing a feminist modernity that predates that of the West. By retreating to a golden, Vedic age as a model for India's future, however, Naidu implicitly privileges high-caste Hindu women over both low-caste and Muslim ones. The subalternity that Naidu seeks to erase in her political speeches resurfaces in her pastoral poems, which both make visible and disavow subaltern women through a Romantic nostalgia that insists subalternity cannot be a part of the modernizing nation. Naidu thereby presages the developmental imaginary I survey in the latter part of this book by illustrating how eugenic feminism aligns itself with a project of development that views both subalternity and gender oppression as part of an unusable past to be jettisoned in the inevitable march of progress.

I elucidate the stakes of eugenic feminism in these opening chapters through Charlotte Perkins Gilman and Sarojini Naidu—two writers who are known for their literary writings as much as for their political ones—precisely because of the place of the literary in relation to their political pronouncements. In both cases (Gilman's utopian novels and Naidu's nostalgic poetry), the literature serves to reveal that which their politics seeks to conceal, namely the paradox of subalternity as both a site of potential and paralysis. Thus Gilman's utopian novels seek (unsuccessfully) to excise subalternity altogether, and Naidu's poems exhibit what I call a "developmentalist nostalgia" for the subaltern that ultimately reveals a eugenic intent. I return to the way the literary grapples with subalternity as both foundational and disavowed in chapters 4 and 5. My discussion of Kamala Markandaya's 1954 novel, *Nectar in a Sieve*, returns to the concept of developmentalist nostalgia to describe how cultural productions such as *Nectar* and Mehboob Khan's 1957 film, *Mother India*, celebrate the peasant mother precisely as a way to posit her as obsolete. This same relation to the subaltern is repeated in Nayantara Sahgal's 1985 novel, *Rich Like Us*, although in this case the obsolescent subaltern is made to serve as a critique of the excesses of Indira Gandhi's period of Emergency rule. In both instances, cultural representations of subalternity supplement (in the Derridean sense) the policy documents and political speeches I survey in these chapters.

While my first two chapters explore the workings of eugenic feminism through two exemplary figures, the rest of the book extends this analysis by applying it to specific historical moments. Chapter 3 marks the transition by taking up a work that is both a muckraking polemic and an event: American journalist Katherine Mayo's 1927 text, *Mother India*. An imperialist attack against Indian self-rule thinly disguised as journalistic exposé, *Mother India*'s sensationalized account of reproductive practices in India caused an international firestorm. I read the controversy surrounding *Mother India* as a crucial moment in the relationship between U.S. and Indian eugenic feminisms. Exploiting Indian subaltern female suffering to justify both the continued British rule of India and the continued exclusion of Indians from U.S. citizenship, Mayo draws on the scientific language of public health to argue that in a new era of global circulation of goods and bodies the United States must strengthen its borders to protect itself from the threat of disease that Indian bodies contain. Imagining India as embodying a sexual threat to be kept in check, Mayo fashions a peculiarly U.S. version of imperial containment to segregate populations and police behaviors. By putting reproduction at the center of the question of sovereignty, however, her argument against Indian sovereignty ultimately rebounds upon U.S. women who similarly fail to fulfill their reproductive duties. I return to Sarojini Naidu as Indian feminism's response to Mayo's attack, looking at the North American tour Naidu undertakes in the wake of Mayo's book. By using experiences of racism in the diaspora to shore up homeland nationalism, Naidu reveals a eugenic stance to minorities in the United States as well as India. The *Mother India* controversy thus exposes how reproductive nationalism becomes both a crucial site of feminist engagement and an exclusionary strategy of containment on both the national and international levels.

If the fervor surrounding *Mother India* was crucial to the formation of nationalism and feminism in colonial India, then my fourth chapter takes up the seeming disappearance of Indian feminism in the years following Indian independence in 1947. I begin this chapter with readings of economic planning documents from the 1930s and 1950s: the 1938 *Women's Role in Planned Economy,* the 1951 First Five-Year Plan, and the 1956 Second Five-Year Plan. I read the WRPE against the five-year plans because, as the lone feminist planning document of its time, it reveals the contours of a feminist modernity that is foreclosed. At the same time, the WRPE contains a eugenic feminist impulse in the way it splits the "Women" of the title into subjects to be developed and those to do the developing. I trace the persistence of this split in the five-year plans. Focusing on how women appear (or do not appear) in the plans, I argue that women enter into development only in their roles as mothers or as victims in need of welfare measures. Against this backdrop, I take up Kamala Markandaya's *Nectar in a Sieve* and Mehboob Khan's *Mother India* to examine how both works refashion the icon "Mother India" into the figure of the self-sacrificing peasant mother. While this would seem to be a revaluation of the position of the subaltern in the nation, in each case the peasant mother serves as the obsolescent handmaiden of development rather than the subject of development. Finally, I consider how U.S. readers and viewers consumed these works as paradigmatic articulations of the new Indian nation, suggesting that both works disarm the potentially destabilizing problem of "third world" development by offering India as a vision of the United States' past.

While chapter 4 looks at the post-independence consolidation of Indian identity both nationally and on the global stage, my fifth and final chapter examines eugenic feminism in a moment of national crisis:

Indira Gandhi's period of Emergency rule (1975–77). Widely understood as a betrayal of the promise of national independence, the Emergency also saw a refashioning of the icon "Mother India" by Gandhi
herself. This chapter considers Gandhi's self-fashioning as Mother India
throughout her political career, focusing specifically on her mobilization
of this language during the Emergency to interpellate Indian women as
mothers united with her in the name of national modernity. I focus on
the sleight of hand required to reconcile this rhetoric with slum clearance and population control policies targeting the nation's poorest and
most vulnerable citizens, arguing that Gandhi's maternalist discourse
presupposes a reproductive, eugenic model as the means of national
futurity. Gandhi thus understands the Emergency as fighting against
the atavistic forces (either in the guise of her political enemies or in the
over-reproductive wombs of the nation's underprivileged) that threaten
to overwhelm and stall India's progress. Alongside this I read Indian
novelist Nayantara Sahgal's fictionalization of the Emergency in her
novel *Rich Like Us*. Sahgal represents the Emergency as an atavistic
return to feudalism that can only be overcome through the agency of
the liberal feminist subject. At the same time, Sahgal recuperates the
subaltern as the subject of the Emergency, thus illustrating the psychic violence required to enter modernity: the shearing away of alterity in the name of progress. In explicitly considering how both Indira
Gandhi and Nayantara Sahgal claim to recuperate and represent the
subaltern—for Indira Gandhi as the national subjects she represents
in her guise as Mother India, and for Sahgal as a critique of Gandhi's
rule—I take up the problem of subalternity that underwrites all of the
nationalist narratives I survey throughout *Eugenic Feminism*.

Finally, I end *Eugenic Feminism* with an epilogue that considers
what a 2007 special issue of *New Formations* calls the "new eugenics": innovations such as gene therapies and new reproductive technologies. While the new eugenics are ostensibly about choice rather
than coercion, this choice is inevitably that of the market, and thus
should be read in relation to the imbrications of nationalist feminism,
imperialism, and developmentalism that I trace throughout the book.
I discuss the 2009 documentary *Google Baby* to make it clear that this
is "coercion" by another name. Tracing how transnational surrogacy is
coded in the language of both liberal feminist and market freedom, I
argue for a non-eugenic reading practice that resists such forces, suggesting that the subaltern figures eugenic discourse obsessively seeks to

manage and abject implicitly represent a challenge to eugenic feminism by refusing to cohere at the level of idealized national and reproductive politics. I return to these figures and to the problem of subalternity to think through what a non-eugenic (because nonreproductive) feminism might look like, arguing that in uncovering the workings of eugenic feminism throughout this book I model a non-eugenic reading practice. By reading these texts not only for what they produce but also for the possibilities they foreclose I hope to disrupt the project of reproductive futurity on which the progress narrative of eugenic feminism depends.

In uncovering this diverse archive of eugenic feminist nation building, *Eugenic Feminism* continues the work begun by antiracist feminist scholars who have excavated feminism's complicity with various kinds of racial projects. By showing how eugenic feminism leverages the power of eugenicist thinking toward feminist ends, however, I am going beyond the usual diagnoses of mere expediency on the one hand and unwitting complicity on the other. Instead, I argue that a focus on eugenic feminism reveals the ways in which narratives of nationalist feminist progress themselves are raced and classed. *Eugenic Feminism* thus shifts analyses of feminism and nationalism to the manner in which nationalist feminisms mobilize a biopolitical rhetoric of national belonging to authorize some feminist subjects on the basis of objectifying others.

1 PERFECTING FEMINISM

Charlotte Perkins Gilman's Eugenic Utopias

IN A 1895 POEM TITLED "The Burden of Mothers: A Clarion Call to Redeem the Race!," Charlotte Perkins Gilman characteristically places women's reproductive powers at the center of nation building. On the grounds that "through [women] comes the race" (8), she insists as long as women are "fettered with gold or with iron" (7) humanity will be "besotted, and brutish, and blind" (14). But while her address is ostensibly to the entire human "race," her model is more national than global. Asserting that "No nation, wise, noble and brave / Ever sprang—tho' the father had freedom— / From the mother a slave!" (22–24), Gilman links the fate of the nation to its mothers: How can a nation rise to glory if half its population is enslaved? If women "[make] the men of the world" (12), then the country where women enjoy the most freedom must be the one with the superior race. Gilman thus enjoins American men to give American women equal rights not for women's sake but for the nation's.[1]

Although Gilman was one of the most influential and prolific feminist scholars of her time, her work fell into obscurity until it was rediscovered in the 1960s and 1970s. The Gilman revival began with the 1968 reprint of *Women and Economics,* the 1973 reprint of "The Yellow Wallpaper," and the 1979 reprint of *Herland.* In particular, Gilman's trenchant critique of separate spheres resonated with a second-wave feminism that took its impetus, in part, from Betty Friedan's indictment of the cult of domesticity in *The Feminine Mystique.* And yet, as critics such as Alys Eve Weinbaum and others have argued, feminist celebrations of Gilman's work overlook the articulation of feminism to racism both in Gilman's time and our own. Just as Gilman was concerned with creating a pure genealogy for the American nation, so too are present-day evocations of Gilman as feminist foremother interested in sanitizing her in the service of an idealized feminist genealogy. Early readings of Gilman's "The Yellow Wallpaper" exemplify this desire, understanding the story as a heroic narrative of a woman's attempt to escape a stifling patriarchy.[2]

Unfortunately Gilman's radical critique of the ideology of separate spheres cannot be untangled from her views on race. Indeed, what is radical about her critique is also what is troubling about it. Gilman does away with the separation between the public and the private by locating the most important site of production within the female body. Because this reproductive economy is always under threat from pollution in the form of racial mixing, however, the national feminist subject Gilman imagines must be protected from miscegenation through a eugenic mechanism. In developing her feminist theory through the idea of eugenic reproduction, Gilman therefore creates a feminist politics that is always already embedded in discourses of race. I thus focus on her racial politics not simply to point out that she was participant in the racist discourses of her time but to argue that her views on race are foundational to her creation of a national feminist subject. She claims women's abstract equality (and even superiority) to male citizens through a eugenic feminism that creates a feminist citizen cleansed of racial otherness.

I'm hardly the first to interrogate Gilman's racial and reproductive politics; her involvement with the eugenics movement and the eugenicism that underlines much of her thinking has been the source of considerable recent critical attention.[3] In adding to the body of scholarship on Gilman and eugenics, my point is not simply to show that Gilman's feminism is indebted to eugenic notions of reproduction, though that is certainly one aim of what follows. Rather, my intention is to chart the economic workings of eugenic feminism that will be repeated, in one form or the other, in the rest of the chapters in this book. Gilman's particular take on feminist economics allows me to elucidate the relationship between reproduction and production in eugenic feminism, demonstrating how her melding of economics and biology both corresponds to and differs from the modes of subjectivity (and subjection) propagated by postwar regimes of development. Looking at how her eugenic philosophy is worked out in terms of domestic and foreign populations alike, I excavate the workings of eugenic feminism in relation to nationalist attachments and xenophobic rejections. I thus examine how Gilman trades in racism against African Americans and figures Asian American immigration as a simultaneously internal and external threat to national development, arguing that despite her belief in the civilizational superiority of an (implicitly white) United States, she ultimately retreats to an imperialist isolationism.

This retreat is suggested by the increasingly isolationist underpinnings of her three utopian novels: her 1911 *Moving the Mountain,* 1915 *Herland,* and 1916 *With Her in Ourland.* I take up Gilman's utopian writing to examine how utopian fiction, with its emphasis on creating ever more perfect worlds, reveals developmentalism's eugenic impulse. If, as Dora Ahmad argues in her recent *Landscapes of Hope,* "utopian novels . . . exhibit a perfect faith in developmentalism . . . merged with the novel pseudoscience of social Darwinism," then examining Gilman's utopian fiction as the purest expression of her eugenic fantasies allows me to investigate utopia as one of the modes eugenics takes.[4] Throughout *Eugenic Feminism* I will return to the interplay of utopia and eugenics, examining its mutation into the antidevelopmental, degenerative dystopia of Katherine Mayo's *Mother India* in my third chapter, identifying it in Indian planning documents of the 1950s and 1960s in my fourth chapter, and investigating strains of utopian and dystopian thinking in representations of new reproductive technologies in my epilogue. I begin with utopia in its most classic form—the utopian novel—to argue that doing so helps illuminate the relationship between eugenics and utopia that is concealed by the generic limitations of the other kinds of utopian projects I consider. Planning documents may project imagined futures, but they are nonetheless constrained by practicalities that are absent in imaginative works. Gilman's foray into utopian fiction, to the contrary, allows her to present a graphic illustration of the consequences of eugenic feminism; worlds in which raced, classed, and even gendered differences are utterly excised. Concentrating particularly on how she mobilizes the figure of the downtrodden and potentially dangerous Asian woman as eugenic feminism's foil, I argue that Gilman consistently turns to Asia as an "object lesson" in the potential pitfalls of U.S. feminism's advance. I focus on this abjected Asian other at the heart of U.S. nationalist feminism, finally, to suggest the centrality of that figure both to Gilman and to those versions of U.S. feminism that measure their own freedom in contradistinction from various oppressed "other" women.

Primal Rapists and "Infuriated Virgins"

Gilman's 1900 work, *Concerning Children,* opens with a characteristic statement of her worldview: "According to our religious belief, the last, best work of God is the human race. According to the observation of biologists, the highest product of evolution is the human race. According to our own natural inner conviction, this twofold testimony is quite acceptable: we are the first class."[5] Blending religion and biology, Gilman argues that because humans are "the first class," the continued evolution of the race is paramount to a religious duty. As Gilman hastens to remind us, however, "humanity is superior to equinity, felinity, caninity; but there are degrees of humanness."[6] While the overall goal of the human race is its evolutionary development, only certain members of certain races are equal to the job: to be human may be "first class," but some races are more human than others.

By describing the races in terms of "degrees of humanness," Gilman both draws upon and reworks theories of social evolution ascendant at the time of her writing. Evolutionary theory, particularly as popularized by Herbert Spencer and his U.S. follower William Graham Sumner, was a dominant intellectual trend in turn-of-the-twentieth-century United States. Amid the failure of Reconstruction, the turmoil of labor struggles, the growth of consumer culture, the overseas expansion of U.S. imperialism with the Spanish–American War, and the burgeoning women's movement, social evolution offered a way to make sense of social unrest in the present as well as to predict a more perfect future. Linking biology and culture into a scientific theory of change, social evolutionary theory provided reformers with a blueprint for progress. This blueprint was furthermore connected to a discourse of civilization that advised making the world over in white reformers' own image, understanding civilization as "a precise stage in human racial evolution—the one following the more primitive stages of 'savagery' and 'barbarism.'"[7]

Despite civilization discourse's dependence on an explicitly racialized hierarchy, African American intellectuals of the era likewise reasoned "along . . . civilizationist lines for the race's development and potential."[8] The project of racial uplift appealed to the idea of civilizational evolution to insist that uplift was simply a matter of work and time, thereby abandoning egalitarianism for a highly classed language of intellectual and cultural achievement. This is not to say that African

American mobilization of civilization discourse was uncritical; reformers such as Ida B. Wells and Anna Julia Cooper used the language of civilization to indict white hypocrisy and assert the sanctity of black womanhood.[9] As Gail Bederman demonstrates in relation to Wells's anti-lynching campaign in the 1890s, for instance, the very mobility of civilization discourse proved effective in illustrating the savagery of white racial violence against blacks, thus subverting civilization discourse's very terms. In general, however, as Kevin Gaines argues in *Uplifting the Race,* "the reformers' biologism posed a feeble challenge to racial and sexual stereotypes, remaining imprisoned within an anti-black bourgeois morality."[10]

The ease with which the language of civilization turned into that of eugenics in the discourse of racial uplift speaks precisely to the problems of this biologism. "Race conservationists" such as T. Thomas Fortune and Nathan B. Young argued for racial purity as a means of asserting black autonomy, while others like Charles Chestnutt and Pauline Hopkins advocated an embrace of racial mixing.[11] African American support for birth control also occasionally veered into eugenic territory. Leaders such as George S. Schuyler and W. E. B. Du Bois rightly viewed access to birth control as a social justice issue and opposed sterilization (which, as Dorothy Roberts notes, was "the chief tool of eugenicists"), but at times this support for birth control was leveraged in favor of differential fertility.[12] Margaret Sanger used some of Du Bois's less savory pronouncements in her 1938 proposal for the "Negro Project," and, as Daylanne English among others has recently explored, there were strains of eugenicist thinking in Du Bois's writings.[13] Similarly, New Negro women writers such as Angela Weld Grimké, Nella Larsen, and Mary Burrill also weighed in on the issues of birth control and eugenics, launching stringent attacks on the racial politics of eugenics while nonetheless remaining within its basic vocabulary.[14] In making this point I am not suggesting that these varied figures occupy a singular place on the political spectrum; rather I am pointing out, as English writes, that "many intellectuals and artists (white and African American, reactionary and progressive) envisioned a better social and political future achieved through aesthetic and reproductive means."[15]

In taking up evolution and the project of civilization with a missionary zeal, Gilman leveraged these debates about racial improvement or decline to both feminist and racially problematic ends. She rejected the rigidity of the social-Darwinist orthodoxy, adopting instead Lester

Frank Ward's "reform Darwinism" to transform evolution into an agenda for action. While the rather gloomy theories of Spencer and Sumner argued that social progress advances through natural processes over which humans have little control, Ward suggested that society could be best developed through natural evolution ("genesis") combined with social evolution ("telesis") guided by the human hand. Following Ward, Gilman advocated a conscious program of evolutionary advance, saying it is "the business of mankind . . . to carry out the evolution of the human race."[16] In a chapter of her autobiography appropriately titled "Building a Religion," Gilman describes evolution as a "long, irresistible ascent" and names this ascent "God."[17] But her progressivist creed presents a problem: evolution may be the "business of mankind," but (as her notion of "degrees of humanness" indicates) clearly not all humans are equal to the task. If civilization discourse understands different races as occupying different evolutionary states, then in Gilman's estimation only those at the vanguard of civilization can be entrusted with the sacred duty of guiding evolution.

Though the elitism of Gilman's evolutionary religion was in step with many of the racial and class commonplaces of civilization discourse, her particular innovation was to argue that rather than being naturally ordained, gender inequality was a perversion that stymied the evolution of the species as a whole. She once again turns to Ward to diagnose this problem, using Ward's "gynecocentric" theory that "the female sex is primary and the male secondary in the organic scheme" to contend that women are the originators and conservators of race traits (a view that reversed social Darwinist orthodoxy).[18] Echoing British and U.S. eugenic feminist beliefs that the key to eugenic advance was to allow women to choose their mates, Gilman hypothesized that under natural social relations women are in charge of sex selection and accordingly choose their mates based on qualities such as physical prowess and intelligence.[19] Over the course of time, however, this natural relationship has been overturned; instead of competing against each other, men simply began to imprison the women they desire. Consequently, women have adapted to the need to attract a man who will support them and their offspring. Gilman thus adopts an antifeminist position and uses it for feminist ends. She argues that women *are* evolutionarily inferior because they have developed according to the designs of men, not nature. Accordingly, they have developed excessive sex traits (such as physical weakness and a smaller size) that are detrimental to the race as a whole.

Gilman forges her particular brand of eugenic feminism from precisely this feminist use of an antifeminist argument. In contradistinction from mainstream eugenicists like C. W. Saleeby (who used the term "eugenic feminism" to argue that feminists of eugenic stock should attend to their reproductive duties above all else), Gilman promoted education and greater rights for women as key to improving the genetic makeup of the United States.[20] She wrote at some length about eugenics in her journal *The Forerunner,* initially in a reformist mode that tried to forge an alliance with mainstream eugenics while maintaining a feminist stance. In a series of articles written in 1915, for instance, she argued that increasing women's economic opportunities and access to education served eugenics by leading to "an improvement in quality" of the population overall.[21] Her attempt to redefine eugenics was largely unsuccessful, however. As Linda Gordon states in her groundbreaking study of birth control in the United States, *The Moral Property of Women,* "every eugenic argument was in the long run more effective in the hands of antifeminists than feminists."[22] Thus against feminist arguments that women's education and economic advancement would improve the race as a whole, mainstream eugenicists countered that educated women reproduced less and therefore contributed to racial decline. This in turn fed a conservative "race suicide" logic that combined antifeminist and anti-immigrant rhetoric. Coined in 1901 by sociologist (and Gilman mentor) Edward Alsworth Ross and popularized in a 1905 speech by Theodore Roosevelt, the term *race suicide* pitted the declining birthrates of so-called native (that is, Anglo-Saxon) Americans of "good stock" against the fecundity of immigrants, arguing that an implicitly white United States would be overwhelmed by "non-native" peoples. Within this climate, feminist calls for voluntary motherhood were ridiculed as selfish and unnatural. Gilman refused this antifeminist position; she may have accepted the basic premise of race suicide that the more developed the race the lower the birthrate but countered by emphasizing quality over quantity.[23] However, her piecemeal rejection failed to change the direction of eugenic debates.

Gilman's support for birth control proved to be another sticking point, because since the late nineteenth century mainstream eugenicists in the United States had viewed birth control as the means by which educated women committed race suicide. Gilman's engagement with contemporaneous debates on birth control was complex (and changed throughout her long lifetime), but she ultimately supported it, and her involvement in the fight to pass birth control legislation in the 1930s was the last campaign of her life.[24] While her initial objections drew from nineteenth-century social purity arguments that birth control would simply sanction men's unreasonable sexual desires, she always supported birth control to prevent the reproduction of those deemed unfit. Going even further, she openly proposed the sterilization of certain groups, arguing in a 1916 *Forerunner* article that "human life is . . . far too sacred to be allowed to fall into hideous degeneracy. If we had a proper regard for human life we should take instant measures to check the supply of the feeble-minded and defective persons."[25] Although the categories "feeble-minded and defective" were often used to describe women who refused to conform to gender norms, Gilman's unflinching use of such rhetoric suggests her eugenic concerns outweigh her feminist ones (or, more accurately, they are one and the same). Unlike free love advocates such as Victoria Woodhull, therefore, her support for birth control was "not only designed to guarantee social equality for women but also . . . to prevent racial decline."[26]

The problem of racial decline is made ever more striking by the fact that Gilman attributes women's degraded state in the present to an act of racial violence in the evolutionary past. Turning to the racially charged figure of the primal rapist to create an origin story for women's subordination, Gilman describes the initial distortion of sexual relations in her landmark 1898 text, *Women and Economics*. Through a prologue poem that playfully rewrites the Fall, Gilman casts primal man as Eve and argues that once he eats from the "Tree of Knowledge" he becomes entirely governed by lust and gluttony. Instead of competing against other men, primal man realizes "it was much cheaper and easier to fight a little female, and have it done with, than to fight a big male every time. So he instituted the custom of enslaving the female; and she, losing freedom, could no longer get her own food nor that of her young."[27] Primal man sins, then, in two ways: first, he disturbs the natural evolutionary order by usurping primal woman's role as the sex selector, thereby forcing women to evolve according to what men desire rather than what nature requires. Second, primal man disrupts women's relationship to production, a relationship that for Gilman springs from women's vital role in biological and social reproduction. Because women are confined to the home, they can no longer provide for themselves and their children and are forced to rely on men. Reversing the bromide that men produce and women consume, Gilman instead posits man's "never dying hunger" and woman as "she who helps and saves."[28]

The consequences of the primal rape are similarly twofold. First, by raping primal woman and interfering with the natural course of sex selection, primal man pollutes the forces of civilization that women (as the race type) embody with his unrestrained masculinity—a masculinity that is linked with gluttony, drunkenness, and lust, and resonant with the racist stereotypes of Gilman's time. Paradoxically, the second consequence of the primal rape is that it civilizes men. Because women entrapped in the home can no longer support their families, men are forced to provide for the women they've imprisoned and any subsequent children they might have. Over the course of time, this productive industry exerts its civilizing influence on men and spurs their evolution. But even if the primal rape is an enabling violence that civilizes men, by relegating women to the private sphere of the home, primal man "confined her to primitive industry."[29] Thus restricted, women remain racial primitives. If men develop and women do not, then all heterosexual unions are equivalent to race mixing in that they combine members of the species existing at different—and, Gilman feels, incompatible—stages of development. By arguing that women's present evolutionary inferiority developed from an act of racially coded sexual violence, Gilman seeks to reinstate women at the vanguard of civilization for reasons that are as racially motivated as they are feminist.

Arguing that men represent the pinnacle of development while keeping women at a lower level, Gilman declares, "We have made a creature who is not homogeneous, whose life is fed by two currents of inheritance as dissimilar and opposed as could be well imagined. We have bred a race of psychic hybrids, and the moral qualities of hybrids are well known."[30] Gilman refers to white men and women as "psychically" different in order to suggest that men and women represent different levels of development even if part of the same race. Lest the racial connotations of hybridity escape her readers, however, Gilman explicitly references nativist and racist fears of miscegenation to argue that the failure to uplift white women to their proper evolutionary place results in pathological reproduction.[31] Gilman likens the marriage of "any man of a highly developed nation . . . to the carefully preserved, rudimentary female creature he has so religiously maintained by his side" to that of an "Anglo-Saxon" with "an African" or "Oriental." Cast in Darwinian terms, the key to advancing the race is to allow women to assume their rightful places as sex selectors and resume their evolutionary advance.

Furthermore, even if men have become more civilized than women over time, the fact remains that this process was spurred by an originary act of violence that must be read within the racial climate of the late nineteenth and early twentieth centuries. As Bederman argues, Gilman's portrait of the primal rapist as a "savage" and a "primitive" knowingly borrows from a powerful racist vocabulary, "making all men, including civilized white men, the evolutionary descendants of the original primal rapist—a figure indelibly coded Negro and therefore unmanly."[32] Gilman thereby seeks to reinstate women at the vanguard of civilization for reasons that are as racially motivated as they are feminist, asserting that women's present evolutionary inferiority actually developed from an act of violent miscegenation. In mobilizing the figure of the "black rapist," a phantom that Ida B. Wells was in the process of very publicly denouncing as apocryphal, Gilman was undoubtedly leveraging the race politics of her time and overwriting the real histories of sexual violence against African American women and the lynching of African American men. After all, Gilman publishes *Women and Economics* only four years after Wells's two British tours (in 1893 and 1894) had made lynching part of the national conversation.[33] Though in general Gilman's views on African Americans are complicated, her stance on lynching and the threat of sexual violence it supposedly contains is revealed in a 1912 article, "Should Women Use Violence?" There she states, "If the dangerous negroes of the black belt knew that every white woman carried a revolver and used it with skill and effect there would be less lynching needed."[34] Here, as elsewhere, Gilman leverages a racialized threat of sexual violence against white women as one plank of a larger feminist argument. That she perceived white southern women at risk of being raped by African American men is further stated in a 1904 article in which she writes that in the South "women suffer most frequently from masculine attack . . . by men of a lower grade of civilization."[35] In painting African American men as sexual predators and not-so-subtly evoking the black rapist in her scene of the primal rape, Gilman denies African American claims to civilization by implying all rapists are black and all raped women are white.

Indeed, *Herland* is utopian precisely because it allows Gilman to rewrite the primal rape and narrate an alternative history of white female achievement unconstrained by male oppression. The novel describes a remote and socially advanced all-woman society from the perspective of three American male explorers: the sociologist narrator Vandyke Jennings (Van) and his two friends, Jeff Margrave and Terry O. Nicholson. In a reversal of imperialist tropes of exploration and discovery, the men enter Herland in the hopes of being received as saviors by a sex-starved female populace, but instead it is they who are tamed and reeducated. Descended from a single race-mother who was able to reproduce spontaneously, the mothers of Herland are far more advanced than the American men who discover them. Gilman thus proposes the race and gender isolation of *Herland* as the solution to the problem of miscegenation posed by the primal rape. While Herland begins as a "bisexual" society, "of Aryan stock, and . . . in contact with the best civilization of the old world" due to an accident of fate the male population is lost.[36] A volcano cuts off the only means of ingress and egress to the nation while the men are away at war, thus isolating the women and slaves from the rest of the world. Seeing their chance, the slaves kill the remaining old men, old women, and mothers in an attempt to seize power. The "infuriated virgins" who remain refuse to submit to the slaves' attempted conquest of them and their country, and instead "[rise], in sheer desperation, and [slay] their brutal conquerors" (194). Founded on a repudiation of racial or sexual contamination, Herland is set for the careful evolutionary and eugenic work of consciously improving the land and people, without the barriers of racial difference, or racially coded gender difference, to stymie their progress. *Herland* thus demonstrates that free of the interference of men, white women would easily surpass them and reach a new pinnacle of civilization.

Although Gilman describes her first utopian novel, the 1911 *Moving the Mountain,* as a "baby utopia, a short-distance utopia" (37) that tries to offer practical solutions to a recognizable if radically altered real world, *Herland* is the fullest expression of her utopian vision. In realizing this vision, as Dohra Ahmad notes, Gilman departs from the utopian conventions of her era by depicting Herland as a utopian world removed in space, not time (other turn-of-the-twentieth-century utopian novels, most notably Edward Bellamy's *Looking Backwards,* rely on a temporal conceit). Gilman's utopia, however, must operate by exclusion precisely because its developmentalist vision depends upon describing itself in relation to some kind of less developed outside. Part of this is the repudiation of difference at *Herland*'s core; Gilman's civilized Herlanders must both define themselves against and project outside their boundaries the very "savagery" they overcame. In addition, the fact that Herland is a geographically isolated utopian land in an otherwise recognizable early twentieth-century world allows Gilman to offer Herlander solutions to real-world problems in *Herland*'s sequel, *With Her in Ourland*. This insistence on contemporaneity between Herland and the world of her readers, furthermore, highlights the extent to which the origin myth of "infuriated virgins . . . [slaying] their brutal [slave] conquerors" also calls up the United States' not-so-distant slavery past, making *Herland* into what Ahmad calls a "feminist version of *Birth of the Nation*."[37] Just as the foundational premise of *Herland* is the repudiation of the primal rape, the mechanism that accounts for Herland's ever-increasing perfection is that of eugenic reproduction; reproduction is the very mode through which both eugenics and *Herland*'s utopia work.

No place for women of color

The Milk of Human Production

The key to the Herlander's utopian society is that they have organized their productive forces around what Gilman names "mother-power." The Herlanders are the superior race because they have made the values of maternity the values of society at large, thus restoring women to their natural relationship to production. In a chapter from her 1911 *Man-Made World* Gilman proposes that women are the first productive subjects: "Industry, at its base, is a feminine function. The surplus energy of the mother does not manifest itself in noise or combat, or display, but in productive industry. Because of her mother-power she became the first inventor and laborer; being in truth the mother of all industry as well as all people."[38]

In this formulation, the biological duties of childbirth become the model for all forms of production. Although Gilman uses the phrase "as well as" to link motherhood and industry, the relationship is more than simple analogy. Women's economic duties stem from their biological ones, rendering them primary actors in economic and evolutionary development. In one of her stranger (if more telling) metaphors, Gilman describes production as a natural, biological process, saying, "Socially organized human beings tend to produce, as a gland to secrete."[39] By insisting that it is as natural for people to produce as for a gland to secrete, Gilman privileges women's production by suggesting nothing so much as lactation. Unfortunately women's natural relation to production has been perverted, resulting in what Gilman terms the "sexuo-economic relation": namely the fact that women must rely on sex relations to fulfill their economic needs. Under the sexuo-economic relation women are forced to pour all of their notable creative energy into their immediate families instead of society at large. To twist Gilman's phrase, they have been reduced into secreting glands instead of producing members of society, with the result that the individual has been valorized at the expense of society: "The sexuo-economic relation in its effect on the constitution of the individual keeps alive in us the instincts of savage individualism which we should otherwise have outgrown."[40] Here, the sexuo-economic relation itself is figured as a primitive survival, unnecessarily "keeping alive" a "savage individualism." Although antifeminists of Gilman's time argued that "the endeavor of women to perform . . . masculine economic functions marks a decadent civilization," Gilman insists that to prevent women from performing such duties amounts to savagery.[41]

As her metaphor of the secreting gland implies, Gilman's larger project in *Women and Economics* is not simply to argue that women should be fully participant in a male domain of production. Walter Benn Michaels may succumb to the temptation to read Gilman as "relentlessly bourgeois" and ultimately liberal in her understanding of the market economy, but such an assessment underestimates the radical dimension of her project.[42] Gilman does not critique a sexist economy in favor of a gender-blind system that would allow women to become abstract and unsexed economic subjects as well as full-fledged producers; her point is to redefine production as reproduction. In proposing this, however, she is not simply arguing that women should be allowed to enter the public sphere as workers. Instead, she abolishes the separation between the public and the private by locating the most important site of production within the female body, thus not simply allowing for state control of the reproductive but actively insisting upon it.

Gilman's theory of mother-power remains necessarily abstract in her economic writings, but in *Herland* it becomes the very mode of production. The Herlanders are able to convert their desire for motherhood into work by redirecting the energy that would have become a child into other forms of production. The description of this rather mystifying process suggests that not only does all productive work stem from the need to fulfill the wants of children, but that the desire for children *is itself* the source of all productive industry. As one of the Herlander mothers explains:

> Before a child comes to us there is a period of utter exaltation—the whole being is uplifted and filled with a concentrated desire for that child. . . . Often our young women, those to whom motherhood had not yet come, would voluntarily defer it. When that deep inner demand for a child began to be felt she would deliberately engage in the most active work, physical and mental. (207)

Resonating with Gilman's formulation that the human injunction to work is like the glandular injunction to secrete, the desire to have a child is a "deep inner demand" to create something with the body. The fact that the two processes are so easily substitutable suggests that childbirth is simply another form of work, even if exalted. While the most important work is "the direct care and service of the babies," such "service" extends to all forms of productive industry. Importantly, this ability to redirect the desire for a child into other forms of industry is expressly linked to a eugenic project of controlling population. The fact that all of the women of Herland are able to parthenogenically reproduce initially ensures their survival, but eventually the pressure of population threatens to overwhelm their bounded geographical space. Their solution is neither a cutthroat "struggle for existence," nor "predatory excursions to get more land from somebody else, or to get food from somebody else" (205), but rather to limit their population.[43] Here Gilman prioritizes the purification of a domestic population over imperial or colonial projects. Additionally, because the abilities to work and to have children are merged and naturalized as automatic biological processes, those who are judged unfit for childbearing nonetheless cannot help but labor for the greater good.

By locating the source of all industry in mother-power, moreover, Gilman argues that the ultimate product of any society is its children. In a perhaps unintended reversal, Gilman commodifies people just as she biologizes industry, turning people into products to be perfected or rendered obsolete. While the Herlanders revere and depend upon the products of motherhood ("All that they ate was fruit of motherhood, from seed or egg or their product" [198]), they are most significantly "Conscious Makers of People" (205). Gilman's description of how these "half-adored race mothers . . . [built] up a great race through the children" is unabashedly eugenicist in both the positive and negative senses. While right reproduction is elevated to the level of a national religion, this goes hand in hand with prohibiting reproduction from the unfit. Because the children are all descended from one mother, racial difference is not an issue, but similarly no difference in opinion or habit is allowed because such dissent would interfere with the upward advancement of the race. The Herlanders thus made it their "business to train out, to breed out, the lowest types" (217) by not allowing a woman who exhibits morbid or criminal traits to have children. If such a woman insists on having a child anyway, they do not allow her to raise it, entrusting the unlucky child instead to special educators. Gilman explicitly uses metaphors of cultivation to describe babies raised in professional "baby gardens," saying that they "compared with the average in our country as the most perfectly cultivated richly developed roses compare with—tumble weeds" (208). By using botanical metaphors, Gilman insists on the inherent naturalness of engineering reproduction, likening it to a process as benign as cultivating roses. But the very idea that the nation is reproducible, and perfectible through the very mechanism of reproduction, is what enables a bio- and necropolitical project that marks out certain populations for life or for death in the interests of national futurity. Roses versus tumbleweeds indeed.[44]

Thus not only are children the most important product of society, *as products* they indicate the level of that society's civilization. In Gilman's reckoning, savage labor produces savage people and products, while civilized labor produces civilized ones. For instance, we first learn of Herland when the men discover a rag of "a well-woven fabric, with a pattern, and of a clear scarlet that the water had not faded. No savage tribe that we had heard of made such fabrics" (153). At this moment Gilman presages a shift from the biological to the economic, even though in her model these two categories are firmly melded. A focus on nonbiological markers of civilization is crucial in that it allows Gilman to both borrow from and disavow a racist discourse. At the same time, however, it also points to the way that Gilman marries biological and economic language in making her claims about social evolution. Even while translating civilization into a question of its products, certain products (such as the "well-woven fabric") are metonymically linked with the high level of civilization that for Gilman only the white race can obtain. I call attention to this because it allows us to glimpse the continuities and discontinuities between Gilman's explicitly civilizational stance and the developmental worldview that will define the post–World War II time frame I turn to in the fourth and fifth chapters. While the idea that "no savage tribe that we had heard of made such fabrics" loses its specific racial taint in the discourse of development, development nonetheless recapitulates the idea that the level of cultural attainment is directly reflected in what a society is able to produce. "Savage" gets replaced with "un" or "underdeveloped," but in both cases the hierarchal ordering is linked both to mode of production and to what a society can produce.

Situated at the pinnacle of white civilization, it would seem the Herlanders are perfectly poised to make over the rest of the world in their own image. But as *With Her in Ourland* demonstrates, *Herland* finally fails to move beyond the double bind of women's underdevelopment on one hand, and miscegenation on the other. *Ourland* charts the views of Van and his Herlander wife, Ellador, as they journey throughout the world diagnosing its ills. Theirs is originally an imperial project of bringing Herlander civilization to all corners of the globe; after touring the outside world Ellador leaves with her "mind . . . full of the great things that can be done here, [with] all the wisdom of Herland at work to help" (384). Ellador imagines her work as a kind of white woman's burden, a benevolent imperialism confident that its greater "wisdom" can reform a "savage" (272) planet. At this point, most readers jump to the conclusion that the Herlander's drive to perfect the globe is a simple expression of Gilman's imperialism. I suggest, however, that the final message of the sequel is one of radical isolationism. *Ourland* ends with Ellador and Van deciding to return to Herland without letting the rest of the world know of its existence. Although this decision is presented as temporary—Ellador says they can return to the outside world "later—much later" (382)—the novel does not present this return as a truly viable option (certainly it is not one Gilman revisits, despite the fact that she has nineteen years of creative output after *Ourland*). Despite her original optimism about U.S. imperialism (Gilman supported the Spanish–American War, for example),[45] in the end Gilman's evolutionary vision is too vulnerable to corruption by otherness. Ultimately, Gilman considers the eugenic side of evolution more important than the civilizing project of bringing "great things" to all corners of the earth. To control the potential problem of miscegenation, the Herlanders choose to remain apart from the world, arguing, "They must preserve their own integrity and peace if they were to help others" (386). Gilman's imperial desires are thus undone by her need for racial purity. As one critic puts it, "For Gilman, real cultural imperialists, those sustained by a sure sense of the superiority of their civilization and race, stay at home."[46]

The irony here, of course, is that the Herlander's "integrity and peace" has already been disturbed. The arrival of the men and the Herlanders' subsequent dedication to recreating a "bisexual" society radically alters the evolutionary path to which they have been so unswervingly wed. Although the men must undergo a process of rehabilitation and reeducation, eventually they are deemed fit enough to marry their hosts. But while Van's marriage to Ellador and Jeff's marriage to Celis are successful (if somewhat frustrating to men used to U.S. modes of masculinity and femininity), Terry is not sufficiently reformed and tries to rape his wife, Alima. Not surprisingly, the Herlanders exile Terry for his mortal sin, in a plot twist that facilitates the sequel by requiring Van and Ellador to accompany Terry home. Terry's attempted rape echoes both the primal rape and its repudiation by the "infuriated virgins" of Herland, marking Terry's irredeemably inferior level of civilization. Terry's atavism, however, also works to highlight the fact that Van and Jeff *have* been reformed and thus can be folded into the Herlander's civilizational project. At *Herland*'s end Celis is pregnant (presumably by Jeff, not parthenogenis), and *With Her in Ourland* similarly closes with the birth of Ellador and Van's son.

Rather than derailing Gilman's utopian project, however, I suggest that these marriages and births resolve the problem of racially inflected sexual difference by reintegrating right-minded white American men into the civilizational fold. Thus if, as Dohra Ahmad proposes, the turn-of-the-twentieth-century utopian novel's emphasis on progress makes it the developmentalist form par excellence, then *Herland* is instructive for how it deals with the problem of difference. It is not alone in confronting this issue, as most utopias of the era typically resolve the formal problem of narrative stasis through a romance that assimilates the stranger-narrator into the utopian society being described. In this sense, turn-of-the-century utopian novels are developmental romances in which the underdeveloped (and often somewhat skeptical or hostile) subject must be dragged into utopian modernity, a process that also requires abandoning all nostalgia for the previous order. In *Herland,* however, this strategy is complicated by the fact that the U.S. men who "discover" Herland introduce sexual difference, which has the potential for undoing the careful eugenic work of generations. Although the

Herlanders are eager to put themselves back on the path to a "bisexual" society, one could imagine that they would be bothered by the potential horrors lurking in these white men's gene pools. Nonetheless, what is modeled here is a process of development whereby some subjects answer development's call and others reject it and thus must be expelled: Van and Jeff can be assimilated, Terry cannot. I suggest that this kind of assimilative relation to difference, in which only some are viewed capable of civilization and the others must be excluded, is a key strategy that gets enacted both in Gilman's "real-world" utopias, *Moving the Mountain* and *With Her in Ourland,* and in the later narratives (both literary and otherwise) *Eugenic Feminism* surveys.

"Compulsory Socialization": Gilman and Immigration

The reason that Gilman's utopian vision cannot survive outside of Herland (even if two of the male explorers can eventually be incorporated into it) is that it depends upon erasing the distinction between the nation and the family. Resonant with Gilman's larger critique of separate spheres, Herland is utopian precisely because the nation is all one family, racially identical and organized around the common cause of eugenic improvement. Women must enrich the public sphere with their intellect and morality, while the tasks formerly accomplished by women in the private sphere of the home must become specialized occupations performed by society at large. As *Herland* teaches us, however, precisely because separate spheres are eradicated the racial makeup of the nation becomes vital; if the entire nation is to be managed like a family, then the "fitness" of each member is a cause for national concern.

In refiguring the entire space of the nation as "domestic" (even as she denaturalizes and expands the conventional understanding of domesticity through her theory of mother-power), Gilman's logic evokes what Amy Kaplan has termed "manifest domesticity": namely, the palliative role the ideology of domesticity played in the consolidation and expansion of U.S. empire. Although Kaplan describes how the "outward reach of domesticity" girds up (even as it undoes) an imperialist expansionism, Gilman's project, coming at a later national moment, collapses separate spheres as a way of suggesting the very dangers of imperialism. In this sense the domestic space of the nation can undermine the nation's imperial designs; Gilman uses a discourse of domesticity to contest an imperialism that would make the nation different from itself. After all, even as Gilman tropes sexual difference as racial difference in *Herland, Ourland,* and *Women and Economics,* in many of her other writings she closes racial ranks. Women's degraded evolutionary and social status may be the result of racialized gender violence, but because white men represent the highest expression of evolution, white women must be allowed to join them in their evolutionary struggle. Ultimately, Gilman bridges the gap between the utopia she imagines in *Herland* and social change in the real world by shifting the locus of difference from gender to race.

In doing so, the issue of assimilability becomes key. The male explorers to Herland may be considered racially different from, and inferior to, the women of Herland ("No combination of alien races, of color, caste, or creed, was ever so basically different to establish as that between us, three modern American men and these three women of Herland" [248]), but they are nonetheless assimilable. While the explorers originally discover Herland during a scientific expedition "up among the thousand tributaries and enormous hinterland of a great river; up where the maps had to be made, savage dialects studied, and all manner of strange flora and fauna expected" (151), they become the objects of study in an ironic reversal that marks them as savage. The Herlanders do to the men exactly what the men thought they would do to the less civilized races they would surely encounter: the women create maps from the men's accounts, they study their language, and they quiz them about plant and animal life in the United States and other parts of the world. After a process of reeducation, the men are "at last considered sufficiently tamed and trained" (209) to remain in Herland (with the exception of rapist Terry), but it is a Herland that must be carefully sheltered and separated from outside influences. The real mark of difference is the "poison-arrow savages" who live in the forests beneath Herland. The men are assimilable, but with the "poor savages far below" (277) the Herlanders have "no contact" (277).

The racial ideology that we can glimpse at the margins of *Herland* is more fully expressed in Gilman's nonfiction writing and other utopian novels that directly critique race and gender relations in the real world of her readers. During the decade in which she penned her utopian novels, Gilman wrote extensively on the issue of immigration, particularly in the *Forerunner*. It is unsurprising that she would take up immigration, because not only did it affect her vision of U.S. evolutionary progress, it was also one of the touchstone topics of her day.

As immigration increased at the turn of the century, so too did anti-immigrant sentiment. The problem, of course, was not just the uptick in immigration in absolute terms; it was the national origins of the new immigrants. By 1910 Eastern and Southern Europeans equaled 70 percent of immigrants entering the country, and though Asian exclusion acts from 1882 onward had slowed Asian immigration to the West Coast, this was nonetheless the era of the "Yellow Peril," which painted Asian American immigrants as dangerous threats to U.S. national unity.[47] Indeed, as Susan Lanser argues in her groundbreaking 1989 article "'The Yellow Wallpaper' and the Politics of Color in America," Gilman penned her famous 1898 story while living in San Francisco, and the "yellow" color of the paper can be read as a veiled reference to fecund "yellow" immigrants overrunning, and thus destroying, the terms of U.S. feminism itself.

Even though Gilman's views eventually become openly nativist, it is important to note that this is a revision of her earlier, entirely more positive view of what immigration could do for the burgeoning United States. In this, Gilman's increasing nativism mirrored that of many other Progressives. She was initially supportive of unrestricted immigration, but as immigration from Asia and Eastern Europe increased she became less and less sanguine about the promise of unrestricted immigration to the United States. Because her view of immigration was ultimately assimilative, she was afraid that the latest immigrants were too foreign to "melt" into the body of the United States. Furthermore, she worried that the newest immigrants came from patriarchal cultures and thus would drag down U.S. womanhood as a whole. These concerns, while mirrored by many Progressives, also interacted with eugenic concerns about the relative fitness of the U.S. population. As Alison Bashford argues, "U.S. historians in particular have shown the influence of eugenic arguments on the shape of the famous 1924 Immigration Act and more generally on linked histories of territorial governance, population management and U.S. nationalism."[48] Indeed, it is possible to read Gilman's eventual support for birth control in this light.

This view was in the process of crystalizing when in 1914 she wrote an article titled "Immigration, Importation, and Our Fathers." In it, Gilman argues that those people "intelligent enough to know about another country . . . strong enough to break home ties and old customs; and competent enough to pay the passage" should be allowed to immigrate to the United States, provided they are "of *assimilable stock.*"[49]

Lest there be any doubt about what "stock" is "assimilable," Gilman goes on to say, "Our imported millions of Africans and their descendants constitute a problem . . . and many millions of Hindus, even if free immigrants, would make another problem."[50] In explaining this seeming contradiction between immigration open to all "intelligent" and "competent" enough to reach the United States and immigration restricted on the basis of "stock," Gilman turns to the idea of "national psychology":

> The American nation consists of certain Ideas, Ideals, Qualities, Modes of Conduct, Institutions. Blood does not of itself constitute Americanship. There are Americans hailing from all countries but they agree in those qualities which make America.
>
> This national psychology is what must be shared for true citizenship, and it is the sense of an alien, an irreconcilable psychology, which makes the American citizen of whatever stock, shrink from the overwhelming flood of unassimilable characteristics.[51]

If being American is not a question of biology or "blood," if race and nation are not identical, then "national psychology" becomes a question of culture or development. Given Gilman's reliance on social evolutionary theory and civilization discourse, however, culture and development are always racialized. As Gilman argues through her mouthpiece, Ellador, "All that 'America' means . . . is a new phase of social development, and anyone can be an American who belongs to it" (318). At the same time, she insists, "The human race is in different stages of development, and only some races—or some individuals in a given race—have reached the democratic stage" (323). Once again, Gilman disavows an overtly racist language in making her nativist argument while nonetheless retaining the racial implications of civilization discourse. The phrase "irreconcilable psychology" is therefore a shorthand for those races who are not evolutionarily advanced enough and are therefore "unassimilable." We can read Gilman's many contradictory statements on race through this lens. On the one hand, Gilman condemns the genocide of native peoples and of race prejudice in no uncertain terms. On the other hand, as we follow the logic of these condemnations through, we come to realize they stem from her evolutionary religion. Slavery is wrong because it saddles the burgeoning United States with an African American population that slows the evolution of the entire nation. Even as Ellador condemns slavery and anti-black racism, calling it "silly, wicked and hypocritical" (323), Gilman's way out, as penned in her 1908 "Solution to the Negro Problem," is to segregate African Americans into labor armies until they are developed enough to rejoin the project of U.S. democracy. In anticipation of that time, African Americans must remain separate from the rest of the population, lest they "retard the progress" of the (implicitly white) nation as a whole.[52]

Prefiguring the sentiments of "Immigration, Importation, and Our Fathers," Gilman's most expansive vision of how immigration should be regulated and controlled appears in her 1911 *Moving the Mountain*. In it, Gilman describes a 1940s utopian United States transformed by American women "waking up" and taking control of the nation. The novel is told from the point of view of John, an American man rescued by his sister Nellie after being lost in Tibet for thirty years. As he and Nellie enter a reformed United States she explains to him how immigration now operates, describing the port of entry at Long Island as "an experiment station in applied sociology" (54). Recognizing that immigration is impossible to curb altogether, Nellie describes how the government has "discovered as many ways of utilizing human waste as we used to have for the waste products of coal tar." Evoking the logic of naturalization as what Priscilla Wald calls "the alchemy of the state," Nellie explains that through such government interventions "the grade of average humanity is steadily rising" and that U.S. immigration helps it along through the process of "Compulsory Socialization"—"No immigrant is turned loose on the community till he or she is up to a certain standard, and the children we educate" (55).[53] Just as the image of immigrants as "human waste" reveals her true attitude toward immigration, so too does the idea that immigrants need to be socialized before they are "set loose on the community." Moreover, the immigrants who will benefit from "compulsory socialization" are mainly of the Western European sort. When the immigrants come through the harbor they are confronted with "a great crescent of white piers, each with its Gate. . . . There's the German Gate, and the Spanish Gate, the English Gate, the Italian Gate—and so on" (57). The truncated list implies that only certain kinds of immigrants can be assimilated into America citizens. Once these citizens have arrived, however, "they have to come up to a certain standard before they are graduated. . . . We have a standard of citizenship now—an idea of what people ought to be and how to make them" (57).

The language of "standard" and "grade" recalls the degrees of humanness with which I began. The idea of how to "make" people, however, suggests a eugenicist language of reproduction as well. Not surprisingly, one of the important facets of compulsory socialization is regulating the supposed problem of immigrant fecundity through the logic of development: "We individualize the women—develop their personal power, their human characteristics—and they don't have so many children" (58). Such a formulation resonates with Gilman's theory of the sexuo-economic in which sex differentiation is more pronounced in the lesser (both savage and degenerate) races. It likewise resonates with the contrast between right reproduction and bad fecundity and also proposes a relationship between fertility and development that continues to this day through the idea that "development is the best contraceptive." Once assimilable immigrant women are brought up to the standards of their U.S. counterparts, they too can be trusted to reproduce appropriately.

Returning to the lessons of *Herland,* then, central to the creation of proper citizens is the development of a national feminist subject devoted to the reproduction and management of the nation. Gilman uses the metaphor of the nation as a child to highlight the stakes involved in this. By imagining the national collectivity as a singular organism (an image current in the evolutionary philosophy of Herbert Spencer and the sociology of E. A. Ross, and dependent on the modern view of population as a political actor in its own right), Gilman is able to understand the racial (or in her terms "evolutionary") difference of immigrants as a "disease" attacking the national body. This attack is made to seem even more pernicious as it is directed toward the defenseless body of the nation-child. Gilman gives her most sustained treatment of this metaphor in *With Her in Ourland.* Although the United States is clearly understood to be the most civilized nation Van and Ellador visit, coming from the utopian society of Herland Ellador is nonetheless shocked by the social conditions she finds there, particularly as pertain to women and children. As Gilman's mouthpiece, Ellador calls the United States a "Splendid Child" (314) who is nonetheless a very "dirty child, a careless child, a wasteful child" (316). In order to diagnose and cure its diseases, she and Van decide to serve as the child's "doctor[s]" and "hygienist[s]" (315). Not surprisingly, Ellador's chief complaint with the United States is that it is "swelled" (320) with growth, "stuffed . . . with the most ill-assorted and unassimilable mass of human material that was ever held together by artificial means"; it is "bloated and verminous" (320). Deeming the United States to be an "idiot child" (313), she raises the specter of miscegenation once more, attesting to the obvious eugenic dangers of bringing together such varied citizens into one national body. In order to avoid the problem of the idiot nation-child, Ellador argues citizens need to be fittingly "made" (a process that involves careful selection, breeding, and education) in the same way that parents make children: "Legitimate immigration is like the coming of children to you,—new blood for the nation, citizens made, not born" (324). Thus not only does the nation-child need to be protected from "parasites" and "disease," but it also needs to have a mechanism for its appropriate reproduction in place.

Taking the biopolitical view of the population as a singular entity to be managed and regulated, and using the metaphor of the nation as a child to underscore the importance of proper reproduction, Gilman predictably argues that feminism is the key to national futurity. What the nation-child requires is mothering by women freed from the bonds of unnatural sex distinction and able to realize their full evolutionary potential. Gilman thus evokes the specter of America as an "idiot child" in order to argue that what America needs is mothers of "good stock" (like the mothers of Herland) single-mindedly devoted to reproducing and perfecting the nation with each generation. While such reforms speak to a positive eugenic project, negative eugenics are also important to Gilman's reformed United States. Any person diagnosed with a venereal disease must be registered with the government and not allowed to reproduce, and addicts (even reformed ones) are forbidden from having children. One of these reformed (and childless) addicts bluntly describes how certain sections of society needed to be "amputated" for the good of the whole, saying, "We killed many hopeless degenerates, insane, idiots, and real perverts, after trying our best powers of cure" (259). In speaking of the national body as singular, the wholesale destruction of those deemed unfit is justified through a metaphor of amputation that maintains that some parts of the national body must be sacrificed in order to preserve the whole. Although the reformed addict is presumably referring to the amputation of portions of the domestic U.S. population, this is clearly a logic that applies to immigration as well, charting the ways in which, as Alison Bashford argues, "the explicit nomination of race or nationality gave way to health and fitness (that is, eugenic) rationales for exclusion of individuals."[54] Gilman faces the excision of these social undesirables head on; what *Moving the Mountain* does not address, however, is the disappearance of racialized bodies that nonetheless insistently figure on the margins of the text.

Degenerate Asia

Even while the discourse of social evolution is based upon linear notions of progress, that does not mean that evolution cannot go astray. Indeed, unless properly guided civilization can easily turn into *over*civilization, or degeneration. In the mid- to late nineteenth century the term *degeneration* (originally applied to the decay of nerve tissue) came to signify the process by which whole civilizations and cultures decayed. The concept was most often applied to Asian cultures; Africans may have been thought to occupy a state of uncivilized savagery, but Asians were, in Mariana Valverde's words, "seen as belonging to a civilization long past its prime, to a race that was overly evolved, decadent."[55] Thus if African Americans threatened to dilute the forces of (white) American civilization with their savagery, Asians threatened to pollute it with their decadence. This presented a particular conundrum for proponents of civilization like Gilman who understood the United States as embarked on a precarious civilizational ascent—because Asia represents civilization gone wrong, Asian immigration presents a special threat and warning to the United States.

The beginning of *Moving the Mountain* stages precisely this threat. Far away from the utopian United States it describes, the novel opens with what is meant to be a startling tableau: "On a gray, cold, soggy Tibetan plateau stood, staring at one another, two white people—a man and a woman. With the first, a group of peasants; with the second, the guides and carriers of a well equipped exploring party" (37). As we soon come to realize, these "two white people" are linked not just by their race but by actual blood—they are Nellie and John, long-lost brother and sister. At first this kinship is not apparent. Nellie recognizes John by his "leather belt—old, worn, battered—but a recognizable belt of no Asiatic pattern, and showing a heavy buckle made in twisted initials" (38). Intricately crafted and as enduring as the civilization from which it comes, this belt stands in stark contrast to John's "peasant" dress and his "heavily bearded face" (38). It is the belt, not his white face, that immediately distinguishes him from his surroundings. This is perhaps unsurprising, because during his thirty amnesiac years in Tibet, John lives as a native. Remarking upon his time in

Tibet, John vaguely notes, "I suppose I turned a prayer mill: I suppose I was married," but as the conditional "I suppose" indicates, such details are unimportant. John has been "lost" in Tibet and remembers nothing of his former life until Nellie utters his name and he falls to the ground with a thud that revives his memory. At this point John "wakes up; comes to life; [and] recognizes [him]self as an American citizen" (38).

This chance meeting of a brother and sister on a Tibetan plateau stresses their similarity against the background of "the group of peasants" whose contrast with the "well equipped exploring party" underscores the racial differences so central to Gilman's evolutionist model of society. She puts her characteristic feminist spin on this contrast by aligning femininity with civilization and masculinity with degeneration, making a woman the standard bearer of civilization who calls forth the civilized side of degenerate man. Hence Nellie is allied with the forces of modernity and progress, and John appears as a native in "peasant" dress (38). If Gilman's *Women and Economics* labeled women part savage because of their confinement to the home, then *Moving the Mountain* gives us a utopian United States where women take charge of their own evolutionary future, realizing that instead of "female human beings" (75) they are full "human beings" (74). Accordingly, the U.S. man recognizes the U.S. woman as his superior and cheerfully takes his place at her side. Gilman's play on the theme of degeneration, moreover, suggests that U.S. men's entrapment of women in primitive homes could eventually lead to male degeneration as well as female savagery.

I call attention to this framing narrative to argue that it is not incidental that Gilman chooses South Asia as the site of John's exile—as the site where he de-evolves into a "'child of the day'" in need of a feminist and civic re-education and re-evolution. Taking into account the centrality of social evolutionary thought to Gilman's eugenic feminism, it is absolutely vital for her to portray Asia as the site of evolution gone wrong. Furthermore, because Asia represents degenerate overcivilization, it presents a danger to American modernity; as signified by John's amnesia, it is the place where even the memory of that modernity must be lost. The reason for this is linked to the sexuo-economic relationship taken to the extreme. In *Women and Economics* Gilman uses Asian cultures to represent the "injurious effects" of "excessive sex-distinction": "In the Oriental nations," as she puts it, "the female in curtained harems is confined most exclusively to sex-functions and denied most fully the exercise of race-functions. In such peoples the weakness, the tendency to small bones and adipose tissue of the over-sexed female is transmitted to the male, with a retarding effect on the development of the race" (46). Here is the nub of Gilman's feminist warning: American sex relations too nearly resemble the harem. "Confined most exclusively to sex-functions," gender difference will bring about much the same degeneration that John experiences in Tibet.

John, a specialist in "ancient languages," had gone to India and Tibet "eager for a sight of those venerable races, those hoary scriptures, those time-honored customs" (39). His desire to know Asia, however, results in his own "fall"—John quite literally drops out of his own time and place and becomes one of the very "venerable race" he had sought to study. John is lost during his expedition when he sleepwalks over a "Himalayan precipice" and falls into a Buddhist village. The villagers "mended [his] bones . . .[and] made [him] quite the chief man, in course of time, in their tiny village. But their little valley was so remote and unknown, so out of touch with any and everything, that no tale of this dumb white man ever reached Western ears" (39). Significantly, Asia exists for our narrator as a kind of dream; John spends thirty years in Tibet, but he "[does] not remember one day of them" (40). While Asia is characterized by advanced age (in contrast to John, who in his memory-less state is called a "child of the day" [39]) paradoxically the accumulation of time has translated into a sort of timelessness. Just as John's mind cannot accommodate memories of both his life in Tibet and his life in the United States—as soon as he gains the latter he loses the former—modernity cannot accommodate Asia. Similarly, the only African American John encounters in the novel is contained in the curiously anachronistic space of his uncle's farm in upstate New York (the uncle rejects the changes the United States has undergone and isolates his family on his farm, stubbornly adhering to what has become an antiquated way of life). Upon seeing the unnamed African American farmhand John remarks that he "apparently hasn't aged a day" (278) despite the intervening twenty years. Though we could read this moment as a comment on unequal race relations as a thing of the past (and certainly that is one implication), the present tense of the novel is marked by racial absence rather than equality. Moreover, given Gilman's evolutionary productivist religion the farmhand's utter stasis shows he is unsuited for the utopian modernity Gilman describes.

Just as the Tibetans serve only to present a contrast to the utopian United States John gains, so too does the sole U.S. person of color in the text serve to illustrate a dangerous atavism, thus suggesting that racial bodies are precisely what need to be excised in order for such a utopia to exist.

Despite mobilizing the imperialist trope of exploration in order to place Nellie on the Tibetan mountaintop where she can miraculously meet and save her brother, Gilman once again underscores the danger of the imperial project. It should come as no surprise to learn that the most dangerous product of cross-cultural contact is manifest in children: just as the pathologies of the "oversexed female" can infect the male to the detriment of the entire civilization, so too will contact between civilizations spread the degenerate features of Asians to Americans. Gilman's use of miscegenation as a metaphor for cultural intercourse intimates that real miscegenation presents a much graver problem: Just how did John spend his thirty years in Tibet? He may have conveniently forgotten a "marriage," but the possibility that he sired hybrid children taints his return to civilization. Within the moral economy of the novel, the bonds of marriage and family are held extremely dear, but in this instance they do not even register. Neither John nor Nellie takes the trouble to find out whether he was married, or whether he had any children ("Nellie didn't ask that, and they never mentioned such a detail" [39]). If John can "suppose he was married," then the reader can "suppose he had children," but such children are precisely what must not be brought into the utopian United States. If different races are at different stages of civilization, then some have to be excluded from reproduction in order for the state to advance. This is why Gilman's focus on the space of the nation is so crucial. Why is it a utopian *United States* to which John returns? Although in Bellamy's *Looking Backward* the protagonist, Julian West, falls asleep for 113 years and wakes up in a utopian world, Gilman does not use that convention, choosing instead to place her protagonist in a geography that is characterized as a kind of dream. Though the utopian impulse is necessarily a global one (indeed, the "no place" of utopia is precisely what makes it adaptable to every place), Gilman's utopias are national ones because they are always dependent on defining themselves in relation to some kind of outside from which they must be protected.

Just as Asia threatens the corners of Gilman's feminist utopia in

Moving the Mountain, in *With Her in Ourland* Asian women are similarly positioned as object lessons in feminine degeneration. The Asian women that Van and Ellador meet are objects of pity, too enfeebled by their excessive sex distinction (and, accordingly, their excessive fecundity) to be considered fully human. These are mothers whose enslavement has perverted the institution of motherhood and rendered them unfit for feminist citizenship. Accordingly, Asian women are unable to overturn patriarchy by themselves and must wait for their Western counterparts to save them. As Gilman puts it in "A Human World" (1914):

> In older days, without knowledge of the natural sciences, we accepted life as static. If being born in China, we grew up with foot-bound women, we assumed that women were such, and must remain so. Born in India, we accepted the child-wife, the pitiful child-widow, the ecstatic *suttee* as natural expressions of womanhood. . . . We have done wonders of upward growth— for growth is the main law, and may not be wholly resisted. But we have hindered, perverted, temporarily checked that growth, age after age; and again and again a given nation, far advanced and promising, sunk to ruin, and left another to take up its task of social evolution; repeat its errors—and its failures.[56]

Having offered a veritable laundry list of orientalist stereotypes, Gilman goes on to reaffirm her faith in progress. But her notion of progress is fundamentally unidirectional: once a nation has "sunk to ruin," it cannot help itself; it is up to another nation to try and uplift it. Although something can be done about patriarchal practices in India and China, Indian or Chinese women are inadequate to the "task," with their development left to the white women of the United States to accomplish.

Of course, because Asian civilizations are degenerate, they need to stay separate, patiently waiting for the light from the West. But instead, Asian immigration to the United States means that these evolutionary failures are coming to the United States, bringing with them an excessive sex distinction linked to excessive fecundity. As in Gilman's economic theory, in which women confined to the private sphere of the home end up fostering individual indulgences because their desire to produce has been perverted, if women are compelled only to produce children, then they will overproduce. When Ellador travels to India and China in *With Her in Ourland,* for instance, her first comment is upon the environmental devastation of the land as a result of overpopulation:

Here is intelligence, intellect, a high cultural development—of sorts.... And yet ... they live on [the land] like swarming fleas on an emaciated kitten.... However ... this horrible instance of a misused devastated land must have been of one great service. It must have served as an object lesson to all the rest of the world. Where such an old and wise nation has made so dreadful a mistake—for so long, at least no other nation needs to make it. (298)

Through Ellador, Gilman sketches the lineaments of a degenerate culture. There is "cultural development—of sorts," but it is incorrect development, as the culture's inability to "master" "simple and obvious facts" implies. Human fertility has taken too much precedence over other kinds of fertility because of exaggerated human sex functions. Ellador asks Van for assurance that the rest of the world has "learned how to save its trees—its soil—its beauty—its fertility" (298) instead of placing a premium on human fertility over all others. Whereas in Herland *all* the products of motherhood are revered, whether they be animal or vegetable, Gilman understands Asian societies as having perverted that natural relationship, in a logic that anticipates later figurations of India as the epicenter of the so-called population explosion.[57] The evolutionary purpose they do serve, however, is that of functioning as an "object lesson."

But this meager evolutionary purpose is overshadowed by the problem of Asian immigration. Just as Asia is represented as the site of overpopulation in *With Her in Ourland,* Asian immigration to the United States is understood as potentially overwhelming the "native" population of America. Gilman's friend and mentor E. A. Ross forwards this argument in his 1901 "The Causes of Race Superiority," in which he asserts that while U.S. citizens (and by this he means white U.S. citizens) will have only as many children as will allow them to maintain their standard of living, the Chinese will have more children because they have a lower standard of living. This is the article in which Ross coins the phrase "race suicide" to describe how "the American farm hand, mechanic and operative might wither away before the heavy influx of a prolific race from the Orient" unless "native" Americans take their reproductive duty in hand.[58] Gilman was heavily influenced by Ross's sociology, and she takes his argument one step further in her 1915 "Letting Sleeping Forefathers Lie," in which she argues for barriers to immigration. She does not see the closing of immigration as a betrayal of America's foundational beliefs; rather she argues that when our forefathers "opened wide their gates to the poor and oppressed of all nations" they believed that "accommodations were not bounded and that immigration was."⁵⁹ Calling China a "saturated solution of humanity" and an "unwieldy mass." Gilman warns, "[China] wants to overflow into more thinly settled lands, and fill them up too. So do other nations. The ultimate result would be the occupation of the earth by those races having the largest birthrate; namely, the Oriental and the African" (263). In place of Asia's and Africa's "swarming millions," Gilman advocates the careful and conscious motherhood of Herland. But instead of holding Herland mothers up as an ideal for *all* women to emulate, clearly hers is an exclusionary vision.

Gilman's evolutionary religion thus runs up against an insurmountable barrier. Although despite its obvious racism, her 1908 "Solution to the Negro Problem" was ultimately an optimistic vision of the power of African Americans to "develop" and thus be assimilated into U.S. modernity, Asian degeneracy presents a different problem. In turning to Asia Gilman's developmentalism becomes undone. "Savage" African Americans can be reformed, but degenerate Asians are too far gone to be helped, and in fact pose the danger of the degeneration of the self—as illustrated by John, who "goes native" and can only be pulled back from the brink by Nellie's white feminist reeducation. In fact, by the end of her career Gilman regards her evolutionary project with a sense of defeat. She leaves New York because she is overwhelmed by its immigrant populations, retreating to a mostly "native" community in Connecticut. After a lifetime of fighting for social evolution, she seems forced to admit that white America may perhaps not be at the vanguard of progress after all. She abandons the idea of assimilation, confessing that the First World War "left [her] with principally a new sense of the difference in races and the use of nations in social evolution . . . [which] forced [her] to see that the 'next steps' in social progress in England, America, or France were not those most needed in Uganda or Tibet." Even more alarming than the United States' failure to serve as a model to benighted nations is the thought that the United States itself might not be able to take the next step because of foreign interlopers. The specter of immigration causes Gilman to lament the "rapidly descending extinction of our nation, superseded by other nations who will soon completely outnumber us" (324). Just as Ellador and Van returned to Herland, Gilman retreated to a white enclave in Connecticut, distressed by what she saw as the ceding of America to non-native foreigners. Given that her utopian dream can only be realized in the geographic, sexual, and racial isolation of Herland, her eugenic project ultimately fails. In a racially diverse world, Gilman's feminism will always be undone by the same purifying mechanism through which it constitutes itself, its quest for purity betrayed by the difference it attempts to erase.

2 REGENERATING FEMINISM

Sarojini Naidu's Eugenic Feminist Renaissance

SPEAKING IN LONDON IN 1913, Indian nationalist and poet Sarojini Naidu challenges the notion that Indian women are hostages of tradition, patiently awaiting enlightenment from the West. Instead she traces a feminist genealogy to India's distant past, insisting that "all these new ideas about the essential equality of man and woman and their cooperation in every sphere of life, are not at the least, new to us. Hundred years ago the foundation of Indian civilization was laid on this very basis."[1] Figuring gender equality as the "foundation of [an] Indian civilization" only recently compromised by colonial rule, Naidu rejects an imperial feminist stance that believes Indian women must be rescued from oppressive tradition by colonial modernity. Instead she recasts Indian women as full participants in "the world movement" of global feminism, even going so far as to assert Indian women as the original feminists.[2] Feminism might be a "new idea" in the West but it is not, as she puts it, "new to us."

The manner in which the Indian woman became a contested site for imperialists and nationalists alike has long been noted by postcolonial critics, who interpret the nationalist project in India as either interminably postponing gender inequality in the quest for sovereignty or as subordinating the feminine within a masculinist nation and family. Naidu, however, forces us to rethink these postcolonial genealogies. She insists that national regeneration can *only* happen through a reproductive mechanism whereby India's illustrious past will be reborn as its future, thereby complicating both a patriarchal national discourse and an imperial feminist one. Naidu's claims are radical in that she understands women not only as the spiritual repositories of national culture but also as active agents and origins of a nationalist and feminist modernity. Her rhetoric thus mirrors a larger nationalist project that uses Indian women as signifiers of Indian nationalism's particularity and mobilizes the universalizing discourse of global feminism to construct a feminist teleology in which elite Indian women are more advanced than their Western counterparts. By relying on eugenic reproduction as the mode of national regeneration, however, Naidu forwards an exclusive (high-caste and Hindu) view of which women are nationalist and feminist innovators.

If Charlotte Perkins Gilman presents us with the paradigmatic example of U.S.-based eugenic feminism, then nationalist feminist poet Sarojini Naidu reveals much about its workings in the Indian context. The two women are roughly contemporaneous (although Gilman is nineteen years Naidu's senior), and both partake in the powerful reproductive, evolutionary, and nationalist politics of their time. But whereas Gilman's eugenic utopias are the fullest expressions of her progressivist feminist religion, Naidu mobilizes nostalgic versions of the past that are no less utopic for looking backward as well as forward. Just as Gilman's utopias depend upon a purified genealogy, Naidu's nostalgic renderings of the nation rely upon a sanitized (and, I suggest, eugenic) version of the past as a blueprint for a more perfect future. To be sure, Naidu's politics were far more inclusive than Gilman's, and in comparing the two women I am not suggesting they are the same. Both may have been nativists, but one needs only to think of the different valences of nativism in its U.S. and anticolonial contexts to discern the point at which Gilman's and Naidu's politics part company. Despite their obvious differences, however, I argue that both ground their politics in notions of eugenic reproduction as the means of ensuring nationalist and feminist futures. Naidu may not have been as prominent in the movements for birth control and eugenics in India as women such as Rameshwari Nehru and Rani Laxmibai Rajwade, but her high-profile deployment of reproductive rhetoric nonetheless has far-reaching implications for the relationship between nationalism and feminism in India. Naidu was, moreover, a key figure in the transnational feminist connections between the United States and India, as expressed in her embodiment of "Mother India" during the 1928–29 North American tour she undertook in response to Katherine Mayo's muckraking polemic, *Mother India*. In this chapter I trace the ways Naidu's feminism repeatedly returns to the positive eugenic rhetoric that characterized the eugenics movement in pre-independence India, and take up the implications of her North American travels in my discussion of Mayo's *Mother India* in the next chapter.

Dubbed "the Nightingale of India" by M. K. Gandhi, Sarojini Naidu was a successful poet and politician. Although she began her career as strictly a poet (writing in English after the style of the Romantics) her last book of poetry was published in 1917, after which she wholeheartedly devoted herself to Indian nationalism.[3] In 1925 she was the first Indian woman to be elected president of the Indian National Congress and was appointed the first governor of the state of Uttar Pradesh in independent India. Although she was one of the most visible and vocal Indian female activists of nationalism and women's issues, her legacy is somewhat mixed. A characteristic assessment of Naidu, as Makarand Paranjape remarks in the introduction to his volume of Naidu's selected poetry and prose, is that she "was a minor figure in a major mode."[4] For one thing, because of her close relationships with Gopal Krishna Gokhale and M. K. Gandhi she is often viewed as an accessory to these powerful figures. Her much-commented-upon love of jewelry and colorful saris contributes to the tendency to dismiss her significance as a political figure, leading to a reading (in the words of Parama Roy), of her "putatively frivolous (female) identity as a travesty of Gandhi's more seemly and serviceable Indian femininity."[5]

This assessment of Naidu's "frivolity" and excessive femininity extends to her poetry, which has not survived the test of time. She wrote in a florid style that has been viewed as both derivative and Orientalist, and that represents everything that a later generation of Indian modernist poets rejected.[6] In addition to its outdated language and form, the subject matter of much of her poetry presents a problem to modern readers. While in her political life she was devoted to the advancement of women, her poems are populated with women in subservient postures. Recent critical reassessments of Naidu have focused on the tensions between her feminist and nationalist politics, particularly as embodied in the contrast between her public activism and her poetry.[7] In what follows, I argue that this tension is less a contradiction than it is a residue of her eugenic feminist politics.

I apply the label "feminist" to Naidu cautiously, as she famously rejected the term as too Western. Nonetheless, her activism around issues such as women's education and suffrage is recognizably feminist, even if she locates feminist modernity in the "traditional" Indian past (making her, as the title of a biography by Hasi Banerjee declares, "the traditional feminist"). [8] In any case, Naidu refuses the term *feminism* based on its reference to a Western movement of recent provenance, whereas in her estimation Indian feminism's task is not to work toward a liberation to come but to recuperate the enlightened status women had in the past. Despite gender inequalities in the present, she argues, India has its own tradition of women's equality that simply requires restoration. Asserting a narrative of feminism as indigenous to India, Naidu reformulates imperial commonplaces about the traditional and the modern to posit the Indian woman as the originator of feminist modernity. In harkening back to a past when Indian women were liberated, however, she forwards a specific version of the high-caste, Hindu, liberated Indian woman that undermines both her Romantic celebrations of subaltern life in her poetry and the explicitly anticommunal thrust of her politics.

Chatterjee's "Resolution of the Women's Question" and the Problem of Modernity

In order to parse the way Naidu reconfigures the categories of tradition and modernity, I return to Partha Chatterjee's influential paradigm of postcolonial nationalisms as split between the spiritual and the material, the inner and the outer. Chatterjee locates national cultural difference in the inner sphere of the home, suggesting that the derivative project of modern nationalism takes place in the outer sphere of the world. By locating the primary agent of change in the outside world of the masculine public sphere, however, Chatterjee suggests a traditional ground upon which outside forces work. Within this rhetoric it is easy to discern the figure of a passive femininity acted upon by forceful male agency; the issue of feminist reform is swallowed up by a masculine nationalist agenda invested in preserving gender difference over gender equality. The problem of native patriarchy falls to the wayside, and the subalternization of women within this discourse gets erased.

Such a paradigm cannot account for a woman like Sarojini Naidu, who presented herself as a paragon of traditional Indian womanhood while at the same time actively participating in and redefining the public, modern sphere of nationalist politics. Mrinalini Sinha importantly complicates Chatterjee's argument by demonstrating that the late colonial period saw women asserting themselves as political subjects in recognizably modern ways, as indicated by the emergence of women's organizations such as the Women's Indian Association (WIA), the National Council of Women in India (NCWI), and the All-India Women's Association (AIWC), of which Naidu served a term as president. In Sinha's assessment, this is a unique moment in Indian nationalist feminism (one that is crystalized in the fervor surrounding the 1927 publication of Mayo's *Mother India*) in that it allows Indian feminists to exceed cultural nationalist formulations of women as representatives of nation and community and instead form a political constituency *as women:* "The political demands of women were . . . beginning to be articulated by means of a new set of concepts—equality, rights, representation— that were associated less with the imperatives of enduring cultural or national 'difference' than with a liberal political discourse of women as themselves rights-bearing subjects."[9] Sinha thus offers an important corrective to Chatterjee by demonstrating how Indian female activists reject a cultural nationalist script for what she calls an "agonistic liberal universalism" that contests communal and sectarian identifications in favor of gender.

In taking up the case of Sarojini Naidu, however, I suggest that even as she uses the political language of rights on behalf of India's women, she also mobilizes this discourse for cultural nationalist purposes. That is, insofar as she turns to a language of liberal humanism, she does so to locate its origins in India, using the liberated status of India's women in the ancient past as a means of, in Dipesh Chakrabarty's important paradigm, "provincializing Europe."[10] The most prominent example of this is her well-known rejection of the label "feminist." While she most famously disavows feminism in her 1930 Presidential Address to the AIWC (her "I am not a feminist" speech), she distances herself from Western feminism as early as her 1912–14 sojourn in London, stating in an interview in the London *Forward*, "We have never had a feminist movement (of the kind which existed in Britain) in India. There has never been any need for anything of that kind."[11] In making this statement, Naidu renders feminism superfluous to India for reasons of *British* cultural particularity rather than Indian; India may lack a feminist movement "of the kind which existed in Britain," but only because, unlike Britain, it has no need for one. As Naidu elaborates seventeen years later in her 1930 speech, "To be feminist is to acknowledge that one's life has been repressed. The demand for granting preferential treatment to women is an admission on her part of her inferiority and there has been no need for such a thing in India as the women *have always been* by the side of men in Council and in the fields of battle."[12] Though the British need feminism in order to combat a patriarchal culture that insists on the "inferiority" of women, India has a long-standing history of gender equality.

Against imperialist and patriarchal nationalist views of Indian women as irredeemably stymied by particularity, Naidu forwards the Indian woman as the universal subject of both nationalism and feminism. In doing so she participates in a larger nationalist strategy of what Vasant Kaiwar and Sucheta Mazumdar describe as "revers[ing] the signs of Orientalism, while retaining its grammar, thereby claiming a universal significance without vacating . . . locational specificity."[13] Naidu's approach is unique, however, in that she claims the originary status of Indian feminism as much for global feminism as for Indian nationalism, proclaiming the "'indivisible kinship of women the world over.'"[14] Despite this "indivisible kinship," the relative youth of feminist movements in the West implies that imperialist feminism is the derivative and belated discourse rather than the other way around. As Naidu states in a 1914 speech at the Lyceum Club in London, "'The Women's movement which is recent in Europe was realized in India 4000 years ago when the basis of social culture was comradeship and equal responsibility between men and Women.'"[15] This pronouncement is characteristic of the speeches and interviews that she gives during her time in London, where she repeatedly insists on the "absolutely unbroken tradition" of feminism in India.[16] Saying that Indians need to "regain [their] lost inheritance," Naidu proclaims it may be "overlaid and obscured but still so real that it has prevented the raising of any thing like sex barrier I find in England. We are not pioneers but reawakeners of [a] women movement which is welcome by men in India."[17] Giving a nod to the groundbreaking work of British feminist "pioneers," Naidu argues that no such ground needs to be broken in India, because equality is an inheritance shared by all Indians alike.

Asserting gender equality as native to India participates in a larger nationalist discourse that harkens back to Vedic times to demonstrate India's heroic past. As Uma Chakravati argues in her important 1989 essay, "Whatever Happened to the Vedic *Dasi?*," "reaction to the attacks by Colonial writers ensured that Indian women were almost built up as superwomen: a combination of spiritual Maitreyi, the learned Gargi, the suffering Sita, the faithful Savitri and the heroic Lakshmibai."[18] In turning to this "golden age" nationalist narrative of the Indian "superwoman," Naidu borrows from the colonial truism that the status of a culture's women represents the level of that culture, citing in her 1917 lecture, "The Soul of India," that the "highest proof of [her] country's civilization" is the fact that in Vedic times "[India's] womanhood enjoyed a freedom and franchise unknown in the modern world."[19] Time and again Naidu compares Indian and Western feminism to conclude that Indian feminist roots are the deeper and stronger ones, suggesting that Western feminists have something to learn from Indian feminists rather than the other way around. Although much imperial feminism of the time was based on a missionary ideal of saving colonized women from oppressive tradition, thereby making feminism another kind of Western import, Naidu insists that feminism is indigenous to Indian soil.

Naidu ascribes a recognizably modern and liberal form of feminism to ancient India's women to make her argument; this is a feminism marked by "equal responsibility," "freedom," and "franchise." This strategy is particularly important when we turn to the campaigns for women's suffrage, of which Naidu was at the forefront. When in 1917 the secretary of state for India, Edwin Montague, and the viceroy, Lord Chelmsford, embarked on a tour of India with the aim of gathering information about including more Indians in the process of government (which ultimately resulted in the Government of India Act of 1919), Naidu served as spokesperson for the delegation of women who met with Montague and Chelmsford to petition for the franchise on the same basis as men. In 1918 she presented a resolution on women's suffrage to the Eighteenth Session of the Bombay Provincial Council and to the special session of Congress held in Bombay. Although there was wide support in India for women's enfranchisement on the same basis as men (it was backed by the Indian National Congress, the Home Rule League, and the Muslim League), ultimately the Southborough Franchise Committee decided against granting franchise to women.[20] An incensed Naidu traveled to London as a representative of the WIA with Annie Besant in 1919, where she presented a memorandum to the Joint Select Committee arguing that the "primal right of franchise is a human right and not a monopoly of one sex only."[21] Ultimately the Government of India Act of 1919 did not enfranchise Indian women, instead punting the decision to the provincial councils, which approved it in separate measures passed between 1921 and 1930.[22] Despite this victory, the number of women eligible to vote was nominal at best. When the second campaign for women's suffrage in the 1930s attempted to remedy this problem by increasing the number of women voters, Naidu was likewise at the vanguard of that effort, representing the three women's organizations at the Second Round Table Conference in London in 1931. Although this second campaign did increase the number of women voters, it did so at the expense of women as an independent political constituency, instead dividing them along class and communal lines. Despite women's increased representation, this was not viewed as a victory by Indian suffragists (including Naidu) who had argued against reservations in favor of universal adult suffrage, which was granted with Indian independence in 1947.

In speaking on the issue of suffrage, Naidu adopts different discursive strategies, at times emphasizing women's difference from men as moral and cultural arbiters and at others emphasizing a universalist rhetoric of rights. Though the two strategies would seem to be at odds, Naidu resolves this tension by understanding suffrage (and, indeed, women's equality) as both traditional and culturally specific, painting (in her 1918 speech to the Bombay Provincial Council) a picture of "ancient India" in which "the influence of women in bringing about political and spiritual unity" was "far reaching."[23] Once again Naidu insists that India's women have always played an important role in political life; in asking for the franchise, Indian women are simply asking for what has always been theirs. As Naidu argued in front of the Joint Select Committee (in response to their claim that Indian women were not ready for the franchise), "So far from demanding an alien standard of emancipation, she desires that her evolution be no more than an ample and authentic efflorescence of an age-long ideal of dedicated service whose roots are hidden in the past."[24] Even while Naidu cloaks her demands for equal citizenship rights for women in a language of feminine "service," the implication is clear: women must be allowed to exercise their historic rights.

By suggesting that, unlike their Western counterparts, India's women have always been liberated, Naidu attempts to dismantle the opposition between the "traditional" and the "modern" that structures the imperial project. In doing so she claims for India an alternative modernity that depends upon a mixture of the modern and the ancient: what Banu Subramaniam labels in the context of the contemporary Hindu nationalist turn to Vedic science as "archaic modernity."[25] This archaic modernity supports the nationalist project by contending that rather than colonialism bringing modernity to India, India's indigenous modernity has been disrupted by colonialism, thus necessitating a return to the modern past that can only be resumed by Indian self-rule. Naidu thus uses and subverts a developmental narrative to compare Indian nationalism to that of the West. This is most marked in her 1917 "The Soul of India" lecture, in which she asserts that "[India's] earliest record . . . holds in fine perfection of achievement those principles of national freedom and international federation which we are wont to consider the monopoly of our modern age."[26] For Naidu, the very principles that signify modernity in the present age ("national freedom" and "international federation") were the hallmarks of ancient India, thus challenging a modernization theory narrative that would pit tradition against modernity.

In insisting that India's women have always been modern, Naidu's is not simply an argument that metaphorically elevates women's status within the home to women's larger status in the nation—she argues that "not only was it [the ancient Indian woman's] sweet privilege to tend the hearth-fires and sacrificial fires in the happy and narrow seclusion of her home, but wide as humanity were . . . her compassionate service, her intellectual triumphs and her saintly renunciations."[27] Naidu contests a separate spheres ideology to argue that women are not merely, as the title of the lecture claims, "the soul of India," but they are also important actors in the public life of the nation. In this formulation Indian nationalism depends upon Indian feminism rather than the reverse. As she commands Indian men in her 1906 speech to the Social Council of Calcutta, the "Education of Indian Women":

> Restore to your women their ancient rights, for as I have said it is we, and not you, who are the real nation builders, and without our active cooperation at all points of progress, all your congress and conference are invalid. . . . Educate your women, and the nation will take care of itself for it is true today, as it was yesterday, and will be to the end of human life that the hand that rocks the cradle is the power that rules the world.[28]

In a formulation that recalls Chatterjee's, Naidu locates the true heart of the nation within the women's sphere——a sphere signified by the typical maternal symbol of the cradle. At the same time, however, she does not figure women in merely passive postures of support. Women are "the real nation builders" whose "active cooperation" has the ability to either enable, or *disable,* the national project. In a reversal of Chatterjee's argument that the women's question is resolved (or, as

Himanji Bannerjee puts it, "dissolv[ed]") within national politics, here Naidu instrumentalizes nationalism for her feminist project: "Educate your women and the nation will take care of itself."[29]

Thus while the typical view of Naidu is that she simply parroted nationalist commonplaces (even if she did so with her own unique rhetorical flair), I am suggesting instead that in claiming modernity for India's women she is rewriting the terms of nationalism itself. As such, it is important to note that Naidu distinguishes herself from her mentor Gandhi, whose famous mobilization and embodiment of femininity maintains a separate spheres ideology even while recognizing the profound potential of the "'female' strengths of nonviolent resistance."[30] As Ketu Katrak demonstrates, even while Gandhi radically revalued qualities traditionally associated with women (such as passivity and a devotion to serving others), he did not challenge patriarchal relations in the home or in society. While Naidu teeters between asserting women as different from but equal to men, and asserting a common humanity, even in her cultural feminist guise her strategy is quite different from Gandhi's.[31] In preserving the idea of tradition she completely reconfigures the categories of tradition and modernity to make women central to the nation, while also retaining a selective view of which women can be entrusted with the project of national futurity.

Naidu's National Time and the Oriental Renaissance

Yet Naidu's narrative of Indian feminism's roots is not as simple as it may seem. If it were, why would the issues of women's education and suffrage even need to be debated? The problem, as attested to by imperialist and nationalist discourses alike, is that India's glorious past has deteriorated into a less than perfect present. As Naidu frames the dilemma in the memorandum on suffrage she presented to the Joint Committee in 1919:

> I do not for one instant deny that the story of her [Indian woman's] progressive development has suffered severe interruption and shared in that general decline—I had almost said decadence—that befalls a nation with so continuous a chronicle of subjection to foreign rules but of recent years the woman of the Indian renaissance, largely owing to the stimulus of invigorating Western ideas and influences has once more vindicated herself as not wholly unworthy of her own high social and spiritual inheritance. And already she is beginning to recover her natural place and establish her prerogative as an integral part of the national life.[32]

"Foreign rule," rather than oppressive tradition, has caused women's decline. This does not mean, however, that Naidu entirely rejects Westernization; after all she was an open admirer of British civilization, and she wrote and spoke primarily in English.[33] Indian women's oppression may be the problem of "subjection to foreign rules" (despite Naidu's commitment to Hindu–Muslim unity, her use of the plural here implies subjection to Muslim as well as British rule), but at the same time "Western ideas and influences" are not wholly pernicious. Rather, she seems to argue that "Western ideas and influences" are so consonant with the values of India's past that they simply serve as reminders of what India has lost; through Western example, Indian women can reclaim their "natural place." In arguing for the essential kinship between Western modernity and the "high social and spiritual inheritance" of contemporary Indian women, Naidu does not figure the women's sphere as a counter to Western modernity but rather installs it as the originator of an Indian modernity that has somehow gone astray.

Given the explanatory power granted to theories of evolution and degeneration from the mid-nineteenth century onward, Naidu's seems a curious strategy. Even as she stops herself from labeling India "decadent," that is clearly what her account implies; India is a great civilization in a state of decline. That she blames this on colonialism does not free her from the bind of a developmental narrative in which once a civilization has fallen, so there it must remain. To resolve this problem, Naidu turns to the idea of the Aryan model of history and the Oriental renaissance to suggest that the key to future glory lies in the immemorial past. As Vasant Kaiwar traces in "The Aryan Model of History and the Oriental Renaissance," in its earliest nineteenth-century articulation the Aryan model of history used linguistics, philology, archeology, and biology to posit a master civilization that originated in an Aryan homeland and dispersed throughout Europe and Asia. Within this schema, classical Greece represented the highest expression of Aryan culture and India signified its degeneration and decay. Similar to the civilization discourse upon which so much of Gilman's thinking draws, such an account depends upon a theory of history "in which categorically different peoples each develop their own history, not according to material circumstances and interactions between social classes and empires or nations, but according to some genetic or cultural potential laid down at the outset."[34] Linking history and civilization to some notion of "essence" allowed for a transhistorical theory of culture in which Indian languages and philosophies, once translated into European languages, would enable a revitalization of European culture; thus the Oriental renaissance would complete the work of the Italian renaissance. But this celebration of Oriental cultures is short-lived. Although the Aryan theory of history and the Oriental renaissance originally worked to unite diverse races through the assertion of a common heritage, by the mid-nineteenth century "the unholy trinity of biology, philology, and history worked against the German romantic exaltation of India," reverting instead to the by now familiar narrative of Indian degeneracy and decline.[35]

Though originally developed by English and German Orientalists such as William Jones and Max Muller to both trace and rationalize the ascendance of Western civilization, Indian nationalism appropriated the Aryan model of history and the idea of an Oriental renaissance to fashion a narrative of a heroic past unfolding into an equally glorious future. First, by claiming the common roots of Aryan Indian and Western civilizations, the Aryan model of history asserted cultural parity between colonizer and colonized. Second, it allowed nationalists to claim Hindu spirituality as what would not only enable the rebirth of Indian greatness but also help to revitalize the West. Finally, although it may have been marshaled as a secular theory of culture by nationalist leaders such as Nehru, for Hindu revivalist movements like the Ramakrishna movement and the Arya Samaj, and especially for the more right-wing Hindu Mahasabha and Rashtriya Swayamsevak Sangh (RSS), the Aryan theory of history was instrumental in formulating a Hindu nationalism. As Sucheta Mazumdar writes, "[These Hindu nationalist movements] promoted the notion of an organic, all-encompassing Hinduism and energized the concept of *Hindutva* which embraced a unitary notion of nation: race-people-culture-religion-history-civilization."[36] Of course, as I explore in greater detail in what follows, this unitary notion of the nation was forwarded at the expense of religious and other minorities in the subcontinent.

In embracing the idea of the Oriental renaissance Naidu takes the central metaphor of rebirth literally, positing biological reproduction as the way in which the past can be made to live in the future. In her hands the Oriental renaissance becomes not just a theory of history but a biopolitical project of reproducing and perfecting the population in readiness for national sovereignty. This logic is best illustrated in her ode, "To India," collected in her first book of poetry (her 1905

The Golden Threshold), and recited publicly in December 1904 at the Eighteenth Session of the Indian National Congress.[37] The poem's address is that of a daughter imploring a "slumbering Mother" (11) to "Arise and answer for thy children's sake!"(8). The required answer is a reproductive one: Mother India needs to shake off her "gloom" (2) and "Beget new glories from [her] ageless womb" (4). Naidu makes women's reproductive work central to nation building by evoking past greatness and future "splendors" (10) in distinction from a present defined by "darkness" (5). In making this argument one might contend that Naidu paints a picture of degeneration similar to Gilman's. Quite to the contrary, however, Naidu's degeneration metaphor is equated with only a momentary "sleep," as she implores Mother India to "rise, regenerate" (2). In place of the senility Gilman's protagonists found in Asia, Naidu sees timelessness. Mother India's womb is "ageless" (4), and despite her "immemorial years" (1) she remains "young" (1). Even as national progress is predicated on a developmental movement forward, Naidu injects a recursive sense of time that she attributes to the timelessness of the reproductive mechanism itself. Provided that Indian women do their reproductive duty, the past will be reborn as the future.

This circular notion of time (in which, moreover, women are the primary agents of change), disrupts a modernist teleology of the nation. In Benedict Anderson's famous formulation, even as the nation grounds itself in a mythic past, it can only begin to envision itself as modern through a historical temporality that replaces a religious, messianic one, what Anderson calls (through Walter Benjamin) "homogeneous empty time." Unlike older notions of temporality characterized by "simultaneity-along-time," this new form of national "simultaneity is, as it were, transverse, cross-time, marked not by prefiguring and fulfillment, but by temporal coincidence, and measured by clock and calendar."[38] Accordingly, the nation as a modern construct must work through a linear, developmental teleology that relies on a genealogical notion of generation based on biological reproduction. I am suggesting, however, that Naidu's recursive national time (which, at its base, depends on a kind of "archaic modernity") works differently. In painting India's women as the reproducers of a "traditional" sphere that is uniquely modern, she both endorses the idea of Indian women as the keepers of tradition and subverts it through her alignment of the traditional past with the modern future.

In foregrounding reproduction as the key to national progress, therefore, Naidu does not simply leverage women's symbolic status within the nation in order to argue for women's rights (although that is certainly part of her strategy). Instead, Naidu reverses the symbolic valences of femininity and masculinity within the nation: *men* are ruining national progress by oppressing women. Although, as Anne McClintock attests in one of the more well-known versions of this logic, typically "nationalism's anomalous relation to time is . . . managed as a natural relation to gender" whereby women represent the forces of tradition and continuity and men represent innovation and change, Naidu (like Gilman) argues that women are the true innovators.[39] In order for women to successfully reproduce the nation their historic rights must be restored to them so that they can then return to their natural positions at the forefront of national modernity. Women's constancy, or atavism, in this case represents the progressive force: women, not men, are "forward-thrusting, potent and historic."[40] Because Indian women have always been "modern" in the sense of active participation in the political life of the country, they need to be allowed to return to their roles in the public sphere in order to properly reproduce the nation. In making this argument Naidu identifies Vedic Indian women as uniquely suited to modernity; the atavistic trace that women represent is of a precolonial modernity that is more suited to India than any that Europe could offer. Naidu thereby mobilizes the familiar nationalist idea that the regeneration of the nation must be through women; not only does women's liberation lie in women's hands, so too does the fate of a (largely masculine) nationalism. As she puts it, "It is not from [men] that you'll get the impetus to wipe off the stain from our national history, but rather from the womanhood of India. . . . Let the womanhood of the country wake and work. Let us strengthen the hands of our men."[41] On its face, this sounds like a typical instrumentalization of women in the service of nationalism. But the address is of a "woman speaking to women" (54), and it is clear that they are the only possible agents of national change.

Moreover, by using the figure of *re*birth not only does Naidu make women into the innovators of a nationalist modernity, she also troubles a straightforward notion of reproduction as the motor of national futurity. To avoid degeneration (which would result from a purely generational reproductive model—for instance, this is the logic upon which Gilman's descriptions of decadent Asian cultures rely), Naidu argues that women's reproductive powers are timeless, as are Indian women themselves. Hers is not simply a teleological model of generation; if the women of India's past and of India's future all share a common mother (that is, Mother India) then the model instead is one of contemporaneousness over time. In a 1915 speech called "The Ideal of Civic Life," Naidu characterizes the renaissance as "not a new spirit but a spirit reborn and revitalized in the past that held exactly such ideals and dreams that taught by precept and example, such principles as you wish to fulfill in your life for the service of your country."[42] The figures of mythic Hindu Indian women (such as Gargi, Maitreyi, and Savitri) that Naidu mobilizes once and again are not simply the ancestral mothers of contemporary women, but potentially their sisters. The women of today hold the same "ideals and dreams"; they simply need to be allowed to give birth to the new spirit that would regenerate the nation.

Women's "Immemorial Birthright" and "The Degenerated Descendants of Ancient Heroes"

In figuring reproduction as the mode of national regeneration, Naidu participates in a larger nationalist strategy formulated in response to colonial perceptions of Indian men as effeminate. With its picture of a vibrant masculinity given to conquest and expansion, the Aryan model of history served as a powerful corrective to colonial stereotypes about unmanly Hindu men.[43] It also assigned women a vital role in helping men regain their Aryan/Hindu masculinity, a theme that finds one of its most coherent articulations in the writings of Bengali nationalist Bankim Chandra Chatterjee. His 1882 novel *Anandamath*, from which the nationalist cry *"Vande Mataram"* ("Victory to the Mother") is derived, is one of the first to extensively mobilize the imagery of the nation as a mother who needs to be rescued from the ravages of colonialism. But this is not to relegate women solely to symbolic roles within the nation. In *Anandamath* the female protagonist, Shanti, dresses as a man and engages in revolutionary action at her husband's side; in this model women are responsible for remasculinizing effeminate and degenerate men. Though for Bankim women's energy is an active force in the nation, for Hindu reformist nationalists such as Dayanand Saraswati and Vivekananda women are most powerful in their reproductive roles as mothers. Thus Dayanand's injunctions about sexuality and child care practices were primarily designed to help

India's (Hindu) mothers birth healthy, vigorous sons worthy of ruling an independent nation.[44]

The eugenics movement in India likewise connected individual reproductive control to the larger nationalist project of self-governance.[45] In this respect Indian eugenics focused on birth control, though not necessarily on sterilization of those deemed unfit; the eugenic societies that formed in India in the 1920s and 1930s (the Indian Eugenics Society, the Sholapur Eugenics Education Society, the Eugenic Society in Bombay, and the Society for the Study and Promotion of Family Hygiene, to name just a few) were mostly concerned with bringing eugenic education and birth control to their members.[46] Unlike in the United States and Britain, therefore, the eugenics and birth control movements in India were virtually inseparable. The ease with which contraceptive methods and devices were disseminated helped this fusion; whereas anti-obscenity laws restricted their distribution in the United States and Britain, in India contraceptive information was printed in newspapers and contraceptive devices were openly available to the public.[47] Arguably this openness came from the prevailing view that Indian poverty was caused by overpopulation, although it was not until 1931 that the census revealed a substantial demographic increase. Even if this were the reason the colonial government allowed for the circulation of contraceptive devices and information, the fact remains that eugenics in India was a nationalist project undertaken by Indian reformers rather than the colonial state, and as such functioned as a site of nationalist critique of the colonial government.[48]

Given the varied terrain of late colonial Indian nationalism and the mobility of eugenic discourse, eugenic and birth control arguments found purchase in a number of communities and places on the political spectrum. For instance, Imam Hossain, a Muslim, introduced a resolution on population control in India's Council of State in 1935, even though differential fertility was often framed in terms of Muslim fecundity.[49] Similarly, Muslim women's rights campaigner Begum Sharifah Hamid Ali turned to eugenic reasoning in her report "Marriage, Maternity, and Succession," arguing that "those who ought to practice birth control cannot afford it and those who should not . . . do so assiduously."[50] Like Naidu, Ali was a member of the National Planning Committee's Sub-committee on Women and one of the authors of *Women's Role in Planned Economy,* to which I turn in chapter 4. As the only Muslim member of the subcommittee she urged the other members to consult

Muslim law and registered her dissent when they ignored her recommendations. Although these Muslim reformers were speaking from a solidly middle-class position, B. R. Ambedkar, nationalist and Dalit advocate, also presented a measure in support of birth control in the Bombay Legislative Assembly in 1938.[51] Most radically, the Self Respect Movement in Southern India supported birth control as part of a "broader radical agenda of self-emancipation," with leader Periyar E. V. Ramasamy "[linking] birth-control with the sexual freedom of women, and [trying] to free female sexuality from its Brahminical Hindu connotations."[52] The variety of these positions shows the mobility of the charged issue of eugenic reproduction in taking on the social issues of the day.

Despite these varied voices, however, mainstream eugenic discourse in India too often borrowed from a specifically high-caste Hindu discourse. Narayan Sitaram Phadke's 1927 *Sex Problem in India* (which included a foreword by Margaret Sanger) argues, for instance, that "it need never be supposed that the ancient Aryans were ignorant of the first principles of Eugenics and that India will have to learn them anew at the feet of the Western scholars. . . . Even in the Vedic and Puranic times our ancestors had realized the value of Eugenic principles with remarkable fullness of vision and depth of anxious insight."[53] Phadke, like Naidu on feminism, asserts that eugenics is indigenous to India and belated in the West. He indicts colonialism for India's current eugenic decline, suggesting that "the degeneration of our race is aggravated by our political subjugation."[54] By tracing this genealogy, eugenicists like Phadke and Pyare Krishnan Wattal used the Aryan model of history to distinguish themselves from an international eugenics community that by and large insisted that Indians remain objects of research rather than fellow researchers.[55] Unsurprisingly, however, this genealogy was anti-Muslim and naturalized and erased structures of subalternity.[56]

Finally, because of its emphasis on reproduction as the mode of nationalist regeneration, eugenics in India opened up a powerful space of engagement for feminist involvement in nationalist politics. Despite the prominence of male eugenicists such as Phadke, Radhakamal Mukherjee (the chairman of the National Planning Committee's Sub-committee on Population, whose report I examine in chapter 4), Aliyappin Padmanabha Pillay, and Gopaljee Ahluwalia, nationalist feminists were among the strongest proponents of eugenic reforms, making, in Sarah Hodges's estimation, "some of the most enduring contributions to institutionalizing eugenic sensibilities in twentieth-century South Asia."[57] Thus while feminist eugenics in the United States could be differentiated from the mainstream eugenics movements, in India nationalist feminists were central to advancing the eugenic cause. Not only did Indian feminist concerns with eugenics mark them as modern, thereby constituting an appropriate response to British perceptions of Indian women as oppressed by backward tradition, Indian feminists also came to eugenics through some of the heated social issues of the late colonial period—such as the debate on child marriage I take up in the next chapter. Indian nationalist feminists seized upon the issue of eugenics to place reproduction at the center of nationalism, putting maternal health and child welfare at the center of the national agenda and ensuring that such components would figure in the plan for the postcolonial state.

We must, therefore, situate Naidu's recourse to reproductive rhetoric within this larger context. Even though she was not at the forefront of eugenic and birth control activism, she certainly supported birth control; Margaret Sanger cites her approvingly in her autobiography, and Gandhi acknowledges in his famous 1935 birth control debate with Sanger that both Naidu and Rabindranath Tagore disagreed with his anti-contraceptive stance.[58] Regardless, as Sarah Hodges details, nationalist feminist involvement in eugenics was most concerned with arguing for the importance of women's reproductive health to the incipient nation, using the logic that "only healthy mothers could produce strong children, . . . and only a health race . . . could hope to wrest from foreign rulers the right to self-government."[59] In this, Indian eugenic feminism of the era was less concerned with sterilizing the unfit—lobbying for legislation to get rid of those deemed dysgenic—than it was with installing women's reproductive work at the center of the nation, a project of which Naidu was undoubtedly a part. In tracing the linkages between Naidu's feminist rhetoric and the larger discourse of the Indian eugenics movement, my point is that we cannot separate them—Naidu's recourse to a maternalist rhetoric can only be read in relation to the larger eugenic politics of her times. That in her guise as one of the drafters of the 1938 report of the National Planning Committee, *Women's Role in Planned Economy,* Naidu explicitly argued for eugenic measures to be implemented in independent India, furthermore demonstrates how the brandishing of eugenic rhetoric leads to eugenic policy.

In installing reproduction at the center of nationalism, Naidu gives her formulation of women's reproductive work her own feminist bent;

women need to be returned to their ancient, liberated status in order for the nation to once again advance according to its predestined development. She defines this movement as a repetition instead of a simple forward motion, stating in a 1917 lecture titled "The Voice of Life": "History will always be made to repeat itself exactly as by your will power you can make yourself repeat certain things. The whole basis of civilization is the evolution of our will power."[60] Given the correct national will, national history can be repeated and India can once again ascend to greatness. In making this statement Naidu links national regeneration to Hindu doctrines of reincarnation, saying that the idea that history can be made to repeat itself is "the real power of the Hindu race, the peculiar teaching of the Hindu race."[61] Expounding on this theme two years earlier in a speech titled "The Sunlit Lamps of India," Naidu argues Hindu spirituality is what distinguishes India from the fallen civilizations of Greece and Rome, which "could not be re-vitalized after centuries because they were not spiritual."[62] Because women are the keepers of spirituality they are the key to national regeneration, but this regeneration can happen only if men restore them to their ancient rights. Using herself as the example of liberated womanhood, Naidu importunes her male audience that "it is your duty which you have not recognized to fulfill the task of giving the women those very opportunities which you yourselves had, which are necessary for their equipment, fully to realize all these hidden virtues that lie within their souls."[63]

The problem with national development is that men have fallen from their historic duties to, and respect of, women. While this may hurt women, the true consequence is for the nation. In an argument that echoes Gilman's 1895 poem "The Burden of Mothers: A Clarion Call to Redeem the Race!," Naidu contends that as long as women are enslaved the race cannot be free. However, she takes it one step further. While Gilman asserts that "No nation, wise, noble and brave / Ever sprang—tho' the father had freedom— / From the mother a slave!," Naidu argues that it is *impossible* for men to be free if women are enslaved.[64] This is so, Naidu believes, because freedom is an inheritance passed through the maternal line. While women simply need to have it to pass it along, if they are denied it then they will not be able to give it to their sons. As she states in her 1906 speech on the "Education of Indian Women," "Does one man dare to deprive a human soul of its immemorial inheritance of liberty and life? And yet, my friends, man has so dared in the case of Indian women. That is why you men of India are to-day what you are: because your fathers, in depriving your mothers of that immemorial birthright, have robbed you, their sons, of your just inheritance."[65]

In this formulation, the problem with present-day men originates in the faults of their fathers who dared "deprive" their mothers of their "immemorial birthright" of "life and liberty." Women need to be free in order to give birth to sons who can develop into men worthy of leading the nation. Women are naturally bestowed with "liberty and life"—it has to be wrested from them in an act that is essentially a "robbery." Men, as it turns out, are not so lucky. If both men and women were equal recipients of this "immemorial inheritance," it would seem that men would have life and liberty regardless of their mothers' status. And yet by depriving the mother you deprive the son; because women are naturally born with this inheritance it must be stolen from them, but men can receive it only through the maternal line. Thus Naidu locates the dilemma of India's subjection to foreign rule firmly in the hands of a native patriarchy that denies its sons freedom by oppressing its mothers, ultimately making a people who are unfree and available for colonial domination. Against a narrative that insists colonialism is the result of enervated, effeminate men, Naidu argues that excessive masculinity in the form of native patriarchy is actually the cause.[66]

This critique of Indian men is most pronounced in relation to Naidu's somewhat curious stance toward *sati* (the practice of widows immolating themselves on their husbands' funeral pyres). At a 1906 speech to the Hindu Reform Association in Secunderabab, she argues that *sati* should be abolished because today's men do not deserve such a sacrifice: "'Men of [Ancient] days had sufficient worth in them and if women performed *sati*, they did it out of love and regret for their men. But do men of our days deserve *sati*? . . . They are not men at all. They can be called the degenerated descendants of ancient heroes.'"[67] Naidu implies that the men have grown less worthy, and thus are oppressing women who, if left alone without masculine interference, would be able to rise to their previous level of civilization. Here Naidu does not hesitate to use the word *degenerate,* because it is the men who have degenerated, not the women. By not "honoring women" the Indian man has only hurt himself, leaving the Indian woman unchanged: "her destiny in the future as an unbroken historic tradition from the past."[68] What is remarkable about this, of course, is that Naidu seemingly does not condemn *sati* as a practice; she merely condemns the degenerate men who are not worthy of such a sacrifice.

Stranger still is that Naidu mounts her argument about *sati* within the context of a speech attacking other religious customs such as child marriage, dowry, and unnecessary financial expenditure on religious events.[69] She turns to the troubled topic of *sati* in response to being told that her stance against such customs is offensive to the male leaders of the community. *Sati* seems a peculiar rejoinder, as not only was it a central issue for late nineteenth- and early twentieth-century reformers of the women's question, it was also (along with child marriage) an issue that for Western observers most symbolized the abject position of Indian women.[70] But Naidu takes *sati* in another direction entirely. Rather than condemn the practice, she contends that women are still equal to the sacrifice even though the men have degenerated. In making this point she evokes at once a discourse of continuity and change; the women of today are continuous with the women of yesteryear (streaming back in an "unbroken historic tradition from the past"), but the men have changed and grown less worthy. Once again she adopts and reverses a typical narrative of women's constancy and men's changeability. While such a narrative is normally mobilized to project men as the innovative force in society, Naidu argues that masculine innovation is in fact decadence. Women's constancy keeps them modern, even if the overall society has degenerated. Rejecting a colonial discourse that uses *sati* as an example of Indian women's degraded status, Naidu uses a nationalist discourse that insists, in Gayatri Spivak's phrase, "the women wanted to die."[71] Even so, she turns this nationalist discourse against itself by arguing that *sati* in the present *is* unacceptable, not because women are oppressed but because men are oppressive, and thus unworthy of such an exceptional sacrifice. Naidu therefore mobilizes *sati* as a signifier of women's superiority, indeed of women's modernity, in an attempt to reconstitute the Indian woman as an agent rather than a victim.

Against Naidu's political pronouncements on *sati* stands her representation of it in "Suttee," a poem published in her first volume of poetry, *The Golden Threshold*.[72] The romanticization of the *sati* that we can glimpse in her Secunderabad comments is in full bloom here, as the poem relates the lament of a widow in language that seems to belie the notion that the wife is her husband's better half. As is typical of Naidu's poetry it is a first-person lyric utterance addressed to the lost husband, wherein the wife states that without him she is nothing. He is the "tree of [her] life" (5) "life of [her] life," and she is merely the "blossom" (8) that will surely die now that "the tree is dead" (8). Here, *sati* is rendered as an inevitable and natural outcome of the husband's death—any question of violence or volition is erased. Naidu ends the poem with the line "shall the flesh survive when the soul is gone?" (12), forwarding a dualistic notion that the man is the soul, and the woman merely the flesh, the body, soulless herself. At the same time, however, the poem suggests the equality between the husband and wife, the interconnectedness of their beings. She says that death "sever[s them] like a broken word" (10) it has "Rent . . . in twain who are but one" (11). Thus the wife is willing to make this sacrifice because she has lost an equal half. This suggests that the *sati* is taking place at a moment when man and woman are equal. Following from Naidu's use of *sati* to signify *male,* not female, degeneration, it is significant that the husband is his widow's equal. It is not the widow's sacrifice that is remarkable; rather it is remarkable that her husband is worthy of such an act.

Naidu's maternalist feminism thus has its distinct limits; in making the argument that women should be free because freedom is an inheritance passed through the maternal line, Naidu suggests that women are only central to the advancement of the nation in their reproductive roles: as she says in her 1918 speech before the special session of Congress in Bombay, "Woman makes the nation, on her worthiness or unworthiness, weakness or strength, ignorance or enlightenment, her cowardice or courage lies folded the destiny of her sons."[73] In this statement it would appear that women are valued purely for their ability to birth sons upon whom they can bestow the gift of freedom, thus rendering Naidu's feminism a hostage of her nationalism.[74] I argue instead that she instrumentalizes nationalism for her feminist project (a point that comes into focus when we consider that she launches this argument in support of women's suffrage). Because Naidu reconfigures nationalist politics through a renaissance model in which India's future can only be awakened and fulfilled by India's women, her focus on reproduction is crucial to her configuration of Indian women's power and ultimately Indian women's citizenship rights within the incipient nation.

The Problem of Subalternity

Naidu's maternalist feminism therefore depends upon on a racial theory of history that, in its most conservative mode, posits a master Aryan race that came from the north and conquered the indigenous inhabitants of the subcontinent. Such a theory sanctions not only the continued subordination of lower-caste and tribal groups, but it is also distinctively anti-Muslim. Because the Aryan invasion preceded the Muslim one, nationalist narratives that conjure a Vedic golden age were implicitly (and sometimes explicitly) anti-Muslim—if the Mughal invasions had not happened, then the social relations depicted in Vedic texts would never have been disrupted. In its most Hindu nationalist formulation, the Aryan theory of history posits all racial intermixing—by Aryans first with the Dravidian, "indigenous," inhabitants of India, and later with Muslims and other "foreign" elements (including the British)—as the cause for Aryan/Hindu racial decline. Indeed, the latest version of the Oriental renaissance mobilized by Hindu fundamentalist movements in present-day India is often used to incite communal violence (as witnessed in the razing of the Babri Masjid in 1992 and the anti-Muslim Gujarat riots in March 2002).

At the moment when Naidu is writing and speaking, however, the Aryan theory of history need not represent such a purist impulse. In fact, Naidu herself passionately believed in the cause of Hindu–Muslim unity, understanding both religions as absolutely central to Indian nationalism.[75] In this paradigm syncretism becomes a peculiarly Aryan legacy, with India's strength located in its blend of religious, linguistic, and regional differences. Even this most liberal articulation of the Aryan theory of history, however, cannot escape the racialism at its core. Ultimately, the Aryan theory of history's focus on an originary narrative of an Aryan master race was, in Vasant Kaiwar's words, "all about . . . race and blood, corruption and pollution through miscegenation."[76] Even a model that posits India's syncretic culture as its particular strength depends upon a racial logic in which miscegenation is simply coded positively instead of negatively. Liberal appropriations of the Aryan model of history, such as those by Jawarhalal Nehru as well as by Naidu, thus constitute "a superficial response because many of the deeper notions that underpin the right-wing discourse remain unquestioned."[77] Moreover, because reproduction is always racialized, Naidu's insistent focus on women as the reproductive regenerators of the nation reveals the deeply racial project in which she is involved, whether intentional or not. To continually enjoin India's women to perform their proper reproductive duties as mothers is to interpellate a certain group of India's mothers as those who must reproduce and reinvigorate the nation through heterosexual reproduction.

To be clear, in interrogating Naidu's use of the Aryan model of history and Oriental renaissance I am not accusing her of harboring anti-Muslim sentiment; indeed, Hindu–Muslim unity was one of the causes to which she was most committed. What I mean to suggest instead is how pernicious such models are, because within their confines Naidu can only figure Muslims and Hindus in certain ways. In her 1917 speech on "Hindu–Muslim Unity," for example, she repeatedly calls attention to Muslim conquest, opening her speech with the image of the "Islamic army . . . cool[ing] their swords in the sacred waters . . . of the Ganges" and referring to them as "Muslim conquerors."[78] Although she goes on to say that the "Islamic invaders . . . became the children of India as the generations went by," that Muslims are not indigenous to India is fore-grounded from the outset. Naidu cites Muslim military prowess in a lau-datory way, arguing that Muslim masculinity will complement Hindu spirituality (adding to "the mystic genius [of Hinduism] . . . the virility of manhood"), but even so she is simply putting a positive spin on nega-tive stereotypes of pathologically masculine Muslim men.[79] These are minor moments in what is largely an exhortation to "Hindu–Muslim Unity" based on the essential similarities of Hinduism and Islam and on the fact that both groups have made their home in India (a basis of belonging she extends to Parsis and Christians as well), but they are worth mentioning for what they reveal about Naidu's symbolic uni-verse. Naidu may paint a positive picture of Islam in general (saying, for instance, that Islam is necessary to India because Muslims brought democracy to the subcontinent, a concept that was otherwise lacking), but in discussing Muslims in India she nevertheless remains within the language of alterity.

Even more relevant to my discussion here, however, is the fact that in speaking on Hindu–Muslim unity Naidu largely uses the language of "brotherhood." When her topic is "womanhood," the context to which she repeatedly turns is that of liberated Vedic women. Her speeches and writings are routinely peppered with references to Gargi, Maitreyi, Sita, and Savitri as the examples whom modern Indian women should emulate, therefore privileging a Hindu model of womanhood. When she does mention Muslim women (and certainly they do not escape her notice) it is most often through a comparative logic. In a 1917 speech called "The Ideals of Islam," she argues that Islam values woman "not merely . . . as wife and mother but as citizen," but this conception is subordinated in the next breath to an "Ancient Hindu India [that] laid the foundation of her civilization on the position and responsibility of women."[80] Thus even when she tries to fold Muslims into her recursive, regenerative nationalism, the "golden age" she evokes is Hindu and thus prior. In a 1915 address titled "Women in National Life," for example, when she importunes Muslim and Hindu men to restore the women of their communities to their rightful positions, the logic she uses is tellingly different for each. She says to Muslim men that "unless and until you give to your women all those equal privileges that form the highest and noblest teaching of your great nation-builder and Prophet you will not attain that regeneration of your race that renaissance of Islamic glory."[81] Although this seems to imply the liberated past of Muslim women, this is immediately contrasted to her injunction to the Hindu community: "Oh friends, Oh brothers, Oh sisters, look back to the past and look forward to the future, and let your future draw its diffused inspiration, its highest vitality, just from those living traditions that are our greatest inheritance."[82] Regeneration may be necessary for an Islamic renaissance, but it is not figured as an "inheritance" of living traditions, as a restoration of relations already existing in the past. I look to these examples because Naidu explicitly addresses Muslim women in them; in the bulk of her speeches and writings, however, the renaissance model she uses is simply a Hindu, Vedic one.

Finally, no matter the care with which Naidu deploys the "golden age" narrative, figuring an Islamic golden age in addition to a Vedic one (even though, strictly speaking, the Vedic age to which she harkens is prior to an Islamic golden age in India), the fact remains that she deploys a rhetoric being mobilized elsewhere for explicitly anti-Muslim purposes. As Mahua Sarkar explores in her important recent study of how Muslim women in colonial Bengal are rendered invisible in both late colonial nationalist discourse and in later theorizations of Indian women in the colonial period, mainstream nationalist deployments of the model of liberated Aryan womanhood always work to erase "figures of the poor, low-caste, and Muslim women."[83] In a chapter examining late nineteenth- and early twentieth-century vernacular periodicals and newspapers concerned with women's issues, Sarkar shows how recourse to the "golden age" narrative by even the most liberal and educated sections of the Bengali Hindu middle class creates the Muslim as the other. She argues that in "explain[ing] the 'fall' of Aryan/Hindu 'civilization' from its glorious days in a supposed classical antiquity to a period of medieval backwardness . . . Muslims are introduced . . . as agents of this tragic downfall."[84] The demise, moreover, is then mobilized to explain women's deteriorated position in the present, thus allowing social practices oppressive to women to be blamed on Muslim conquest. A further consequence of this narrative is that it masculinizes the Muslim-as-other, thus obscuring Muslim women.

Finally, even putting to one side the problem of attempting at once to use a "golden age" argument and to argue for Hindu–Muslim unity, the other issue with Naidu's (and Indian nationalism's in general) use of the Aryan theory of history is that it excludes subaltern women in general—not just Muslim women. Specifically, by repeatedly turning to a narrative of liberated Vedic womanhood, Naidu privileges high-caste Hindu women as those who will regenerate the nation. As Uma Chakravarti has persuasively argued, "The myth of the golden age of Indian womanhood as located in the Vedic period . . . foregrounded the Aryan woman (the progenitor of the upper-caste woman) as the *only* object of historical concern. It is no wonder then that the Vedic *dasi* (woman in servitude) . . . disappeared without leaving a trace of herself in nineteenth century history."[85] Of course, as Chakravarti demonstrates, this problem is not just one of historical record—positing the Vedic, Aryan woman as the original feminist subject of India silences contemporaneous subaltern women's claims to representation within the nation. Insofar as the Hindu "new woman" is understood to be the bearer of national modernity, it is at the expense of subaltern critiques of, or claims to, modernity. Thus the upper-caste new woman becomes emblematic of an Indian modernity that "competed against both colonial modernity and rival subaltern modernities in India."[86]

The agency of the modern Indian women is thus purchased at the price of the subaltern woman who will disappear not only from the historical record but also from the historical present. If new women represent Indian modernity in contrast to subalterns who embody degeneration, then such subaltern women must be written out of the nationalist narrative through the process of modernization that is the new woman's legacy. And if further, as Sinha argues in "Gender in the Critiques of Colonialism and Nationalism," "the modern Indian woman was also always the subject of modernity, the transmitter of the fruits of modernization to all other women in India" (494), then part of the way this exclusion and eventual erasure will happen is through the agency of the Indian new woman who will develop her subaltern sisters. For Naidu, this legacy is almost genetic in its connection to the liberated Vedic women of India's past. As Indian feminism turns its modernizing eye on the subaltern as the subject of development, then, it seeks to rid the nation of subaltern subjects who would serve as reminders of less glorious versions of India's past, present, and future. Thus emerges the eugenic mechanism within Indian nationalist feminism: in order for the future to resurrect the glorious past, the present must be cleansed of subaltern women who represent degeneration instead of rebirth.

The Problem of Nostalgia

If Naidu's political writings present us with a recursive temporality in which the past offers a template for the future—thus presenting an alternative modernity that is both universal in its pretensions and particular in the challenge it represents to the notion of modernity as the sole legacy of the West—then I suggest the Orientalist portrayals of picturesque natives and submissive women in her poetry offer a different temporality altogether. As James Cousins parses the problem in a 1917 essay in the *Modern Review:*

> It is curious to observe that while in both her private and public life, Mrs. Naidu has broken away from the bonds of custom, by marrying outside her caste, and by appearing in public platforms, she reflected in her poetry derivative and dependent habit of womanhood. . . . In her life she is a plain feminist but in her poetry she remains incorrigibly feminine: she sings so far as Indian womanhood is concerned, the India that is, while she herself has passed on into the India that is to be. . . .[87]

In Cousins's estimation, Naidu's contradictory representation of women is a temporal as well as feminist issue. Naidu's "feminism" derives from her flouting of "bonds of custom" implicitly aligned with a traditional past—her out-of-caste marriage and her visible movements in the public sphere of politics. Contrary to this, her "feminine" celebrations of women's "dependent habit[s]" are a tacit (if contradictory) acknowledgment of the "India that is," a recognition that is "incorrigibl[e]" precisely because it is romanticized. In distinction from Cousins's clear puzzle-ment at this incongruity, I argue that this temporal disconnect is very much to the point of Naidu's larger vision of Indian womanhood. Her politics may present women's liberation in the past as a model for the future, but she nevertheless must account for the problem of inequality (coded as degeneration) in the present; by presenting this problem in the language of Orientalist nostalgia, rather than "singing the India that is" she is elegizing an India that is in the process of passing away.

In reading Naidu's poetry as nostalgic, I suggest that the nostalgia at work in her poetry is markedly different from the nostalgic evoca-tions of a golden age in her political speeches and writings. In the first instance, her golden age narrative (as problematic as it is) is a form of anti-imperial nostalgia that seeks to recover a narrative of the past as a roadmap for the future. The form of nostalgia she uses in her poetry is less about recuperating a usable past than it is about insisting on the past-ness of certain aspects of the present. That is, when Naidu indulges in nostalgic portrayals of subaltern subjects in her poetry it is precisely her nostalgia that relegates such subjects to the past, thereby maintaining that they have no place in the nation's future.[88] Reworking Renato Rosaldo's theory of "imperialist nostalgia" into what I am call-ing "developmentalist nostalgia," I argue that the very nostalgia with which Naidu portrays subalterns (particularly subaltern women) in her poetry reveals a eugenic impulse—not only are such figures not part of a usable past, but they are also part of an unusable present.

In using the term *nostalgia* I register that in both cases the past (and the present in the process of becoming past, as in Naidu's poetry) is an imagined one. In Susan Stewart's famous formulation: "Nostalgia, like any form of narrative, is always ideological: the past it seeks has never existed except as narrative."[89] Originally a seventeenth-century neolo-gism used to describe a physical malady experienced by Swiss soldiers stationed away from home, in the nineteenth and twentieth centuries *nostalgia* comes to reference the temporal problem of longing for an imagined and irretrievable past. This longing is not only the individual ailment of personal desire, it also refers to the collective fantasies of po-litical life: as Maya Nadkarni and Olga Shevchenko argue in reference to postsocialist nostalgic practices, "The power of nostalgia is precisely its susceptibility to being co-opted into various political agendas, which nostalgia then cloaks with an aura of 'inevitability.'"[90] Despite the "vari-ous political agendas" nostalgia has been made to serve, it is most often associated with conservative, antiprogressive projects of maintaining (or, more precisely, reverting to some earlier version of) a status quo. This is not to say that nostalgia is necessarily antithetical to radical political projects: as Alastair Bonnet argues in his 2010 monograph, *Left in the Past*, "anti-imperial nostalgia" challenges colonial understandings of the "backwardness" of colonized cultures by "[providing] a transgression of, and a challenge to, monolithic visions of modernity."[91] By characterizing Naidu's use of golden age rhetoric as a form of anti-imperial nostalgia, I thereby reference the ways in which she mobilizes nostalgic versions of an Indian past to contest an imperial modernity and to chart a different way forward. As such, Naidu's is what Dipesh Chakrabarty terms a "decisionist" relationship to history, one that "uses 'tradition,' but the use is guided by a critique of the present . . . thus represent[ing] a freedom from history as well as a freedom to respect the aspects of tradition considered useful to building the desired future."[92] We have already seen the ways in which this discourse is deeply problematic on the basis of the usable past it constructs, but it nonetheless has a distinctly liberatory political intent. This is true even though, as Chakrabarty argues, it remains firmly tethered to a future that "will be" rather than those "futures that already 'are.'"[93]

If Naidu's turn to the Vedic past as a way of contesting imperialism in the present is one form of nostalgia, the nostalgia she indulges in her poetry, what I am calling "developmentalist nostalgia," is rather different. I borrow from Renato Rosaldo's imperialist nostalgia—which he defines as a nostalgia that "[mourns] the passing of what [the imperialists] have themselves transformed"—to argue for a developmentalist nostalgia that similarly seeks to memorialize the ways of life being rendered obsolete by the onward march of national modernity.[94] I make this connection not to create a facile equation between the civilizing project of imperialism and the modernizing project of nationalism but rather to suggest, borrowing Rosaldo's words, that both forms of nostalgia "[attempt] to establish one's innocence and at the same time talk about what one has destroyed."[95] While anti-imperial nostalgia looks to the past in order to chart a different possible future, developmentalist nostalgia is an attempt at temporally distancing certain aspects of the present and thereby relegating them to the past. That is, by viewing parts of the present as anachronist, developmentalist nostalgia argues that they have no place in the future. I explore this logic more fully in my discussion of development and nation building

in 1950s India in chapter 4, but I turn to Naidu's deployment of it in
her poetry as an early articulation of developmentalist nostalgia in this
pre-independence moment. If, as I argued earlier, the modern "new
woman" as the subject of development is tasked with developing her
sister in conformity with a predetermined model of Indian womanhood (thus foreclosing alternative subaltern modernities), then the nostalgia of Naidu's poetry is her way of establishing her innocence, of
preserving that which will be destroyed.

In contrast to the liberated Vedic women of Naidu's speeches, defined by such modern qualities as "freedom and franchise," the world
of her poetry is populated by bucolic scenes of subaltern labor and lan-
guishing, subservient women. In some sense, the antimodern thrust of
her poetry simply participates in a form of Romantic nostalgia—after
all, Naidu stylized herself after Romantic poets such as Scott, Shelley,
and Wordsworth. Her poems are also explicitly Orientalist, participating in any number of Western fantasies about India: beautiful
women secluded in harems, picturesque natives cheerfully performing
manual labor, lovers in the throes of all-consuming passion. Naidu is
not wholly to blame for propagating this Orientalism, as it was the
poetic stance suggested to her by her mentor, Edmund Gosse. As he
recounts in his preface to her second collection of poetry, the 1912 *The
Bird of Time,* when she first submitted a youthful sheaf of poems to
him he was dismayed by what he saw as their imitativeness, saying,
"The verses which Sarojini had entrusted to me were skilful in form,
correct in grammar and blameless in sentiment, but they had the dis-
advantage of being totally without individuality. They were Western
in feeling and in imagery; . . . this was but the note of the mocking-bird
with a vengeance."[96] He advised her to throw these poems away, and
to become "a genuine poet of the Deccan."[97] Perhaps unsurprisingly,
he is quite specific about how the "individuality" of a "genuine" Indian
should express itself, directing Naidu to her topics by requesting "some
revelation of the heart of India, some sincere penetrating analysis of
native passion, of the principles of antique religion and of such mysterious intimations as stirred the soul of the East long before the West
had begun to dream that it had a soul."[98] In short, he directs her to the
imaginary of the Oriental renaissance as that which will fulfill Western
longings for a premodern, authentic past that has been lost.

In successfully delivering up the portrayals of India that Gosse requested, Naidu reveals her own nostalgia. As Makarand Paranjape

rightly argues, "In a period of almost exponential social and technological change, she could see vanishing before her eyes a way of life which
the West had already lost and now pined for."[99] Although I agree with
this assessment, I suggest that Naidu is not simply recording "vanishing" ways of life (because, after all, despite the optimism with which
nationalists such as Naidu viewed the project of national modernity
and development, the transformation of everyday life has not been as
thoroughgoing as anticipated), but by viewing them through the lens
of nostalgia she is in fact contributing to their vanishing. That is, even
those figures that have a kind of "past-ness" (such, as I've already discussed, the couple in "Suttee"), they are decidedly not the ones that Naidu
mobilizes in talking about the rebirth of the past. They are understood
as cultural relics to be admired, perhaps, but of little use in the modernizing nation.

Therefore, because Naidu's modernizing feminist project seeks to destroy the subaltern through the process of modernity that new Indian
women represent, her poetry allows her to indulge in romantic celebrations of subaltern ways of life she believes are fast passing away. Although
the rhetoric of her speeches is universal, Naidu's poetry reveals that
her romanticization of Indian culture and especially Indian women
ultimately erases the suffering of the subaltern classes. As Paranjape
attests, "The 'folk' in her folk songs . . . are all made to deny the hardship and toil of their occupations, hide their dispossession and mar-
ginalization, and celebrate their lowly and oppressed state."[100] "The
Palanquin Bearers," arguably her most famous poem, is paradigmatic
of this tendency.[101] As the title states, the menial laborers who "bear
along" their passenger are the ostensible subjects of the poem. Yet it actually focuses on the passenger who "sways like a flower in the wind of
our song . . . skims like a bird on the foam of the stream . . . [and] floats
like a laugh from the lips of a dream" (2–4). The bearers materialize
only as the labor that propels their passenger, but even the political
asymmetry of these positions is erased. They "gaily . . . glide and . . .
sing," as they "bear her along like a pearl on a string" (27). The female
passenger is rendered weightless by the pure charm of the description,
and the lilting anapests that naturalize the movement of the palanquin
through space. Collected in a section of *The Golden Threshold* titled
"Folk Songs," "The Palanquin Bearers" is representative of Naidu's
picturesque images of peasant life. This is a world in which the weav-
ers' work functions as metaphors for the stages of life, and the fishermen

claim (as they do in her poem, "The Coromandel Fishers"), "The sea is our mother, the cloud is our brother, the waves are our comrades all."[102] This is not a world in which the lowest rungs of society are fighting for their livelihood; rather they function as a picturesque backdrop for a poet's musings.

As we saw in her poem "Suttee," Naidu specifically romanticizes women's traditional roles. Her poem "The Pardah Nashin" describes the life of the woman in purdah as "a revolving dream / Of languid and sequestered ease" (1–2).[103] In her political life, Naidu believed it was necessary for the practice of purdah to eventually be eliminated, although she advocated that it be done gradually. But in her poem the only injury that can happen within the confines of purdah is the ravages of time. While the purdah woman's days in seclusion are as "guarded and secure" (9) as "jewels in a turbaned crest" (11), and "secrets in a lover's breast" (12), the days nonetheless accumulate. "Time lifts the curtain unawares" (13), and even the protection of purdah cannot "prevent the subtle years" (17). Within Naidu's larger preoccupation with time, the inexorable march of days is used here to show that the purdah woman is part of a social order that is passing (while, similarly, her reproductive ability declines). Even as Naidu uses a backward-looking discourse of national time to picture the national future, only certain kinds of archaisms (archaisms that, we have seen, are of the most modern kind) are allowed; purdah is not one of them.

In painting this picture, to be sure, Naidu celebrates a traditional way of life that she understands as moribund—as being rapidly swept away by modernity. At the same time, by transforming women into paradigmatic national subjects, she insists on the modernity of India. She is therefore on the side of the force destroying traditional life. Naidu imagines the body of the nation as endowed with an Indian feminist agency that stretches into the immemorial past. Where Gilman sees an enervated and degenerate womanhood, Naidu pictures a mythic feminine energy that will not only renew India but all of the "nations that in fettered darkness weep."[104] She creates an Indian feminist subject that is at once modern and traditional, insisting that this subject is the model for the abstract citizen of the emergent nation. Even as she bemoans a way of life that is passing, she harkens even further back to a past in which the liberated upper-caste Vedic woman was the ultimate national and feminist subject.

While most critiques cite this seeming contradiction between Naidu's poetry and political ideology, I argue that it is in Naidu's poetry that the residue of her feminist politics resides.[105] She speaks out against *sati* and purdah, but romanticizes them in her poems. She celebrates a way of life she understands as passing but in doing so she paints a picture of the very kinds of subjects her feminist rhetoric must not—because it cannot—acknowledge. In this sense, Naidu's poetry does not represent a break from her political espousals at all, but is rather a consistent expression of the problem of her archaic modernity in which only certain aspects of the past can be made to serve the future. In making this argument she recodes the nationalist configuration of women's constancy and men's innovation, arguing that once masculine interference is removed women can resume their traditional roles at the forefront of modernity. As we have seen, however, harkening back to the liberated women of Vedic times installs a eugenic ideology at the center of this argument; only certain kinds of nationalist feminist subjects are to reproduce and be reproduced. It is the task of these "new women," moreover, to modernize their subaltern counterparts out of existence. Because the future can only be fashioned from certain versions of the past, Naidu's poetry, invested in the Romantic desire to celebrate the antimodern, seeks to preserve those aspects of traditional national life that the modernizing nation must destroy. Naidu's nostalgia for the subaltern exposes her eugenic intent, because such nostalgia insists that the subaltern cannot be a part of the modernizing nation.

3 "WORLD MENACE"

National Reproduction, Public Health,
and the *Mother India* Debate

"Whenever India's real condition becomes known," said an American
Public Health expert now in international service, "all the civilized
countries of the world will turn to the League of Nations and demand
protection against her."

—Katherine Mayo, *Mother India*

THE CONTROVERSY SURROUNDING the 1927 publication of
Katherine Mayo's *Mother India* was arguably the most important pre-
independence event between U.S. and Indian feminisms. An imperialist polemic against Indian self-rule thinly disguised as journalistic
exposé, *Mother India*'s portrayal of the subcontinent as a cesspool of
perverse reproductive practices and contagious diseases defined U.S.
views of India for decades to come. Claiming to reveal "the truth about
the sex life, child marriages, hygiene, cruelty, religious customs, of one-
sixth of the world's population,"[1] its lurid subject matter led, in part,
to its immense popularity. Reprinted nine times within its first year of
publication and forty-two times by 1937, it was the basis of a Broadway
musical (Madame Nazimova's *India*), and there was even an attempt
to make it into a Hollywood film.[2] As controversial as it was popular,
Mother India generated a flurry of responses. Conferences were ar-
ranged to discuss its allegations and protests staged to refute them; all
in all, more than fifty books and pamphlets were published in reaction
to Mayo's claims.[3] Official British and U.S. public opinion was largely
positive (there is even evidence that Mayo was enlisted by the British
imperial propaganda machine, if unwittingly), while for Indian nationalists rallying against *Mother India* became a galvanizing cause.[4]

Despite *Mother India*'s international political reach, Mayo's stated purpose in writing it was domestic. She opens chapter 1 by proclaiming she is "merely an ordinary American citizen seeking test facts to lay before [her] own people" (13). Why, however, would India be a matter of U.S. concern? As Mayo sees it, India is a site of dangerous cultural practices that in her vision not only inhabit India but could also travel to and infect the rest of the world. Rewriting the icon "Mother India" as the pathologized figure of a diseased body politic, Mayo articulates the United States' international role as one of protecting women at home and abroad. What makes her argument so persuasive, however, are the insistent connections it draws between public health concerns and sexual habits. Naturalizing all of India as Hindu (a tactic not only in keeping with U.S. nomenclature of the time, but also exploitative of Hindu–Muslim communal tensions), *Mother India* argues that Indians are unfit for self-rule because primitive and debased Hindu sexual practices destroy the bodies of India's women and deplete the bodies of India's men. Through a chain of associations that link biology and culture, *Mother India* latches on to the explosive issue of child marriage to paint Indians as "broken-nerved, low-spirited, petulant ancients," whose "hands are too weak, too fluttering, to seize or to hold the reins of government" (32). Understanding the circulation of culture through a model of contagious disease, *Mother India* figures India as a "world menace"—a public health problem that should elicit more fear than sympathy.

I turn to the international firestorm caused by Mayo's *Mother India* to argue that its dystopian vision of national reproduction is the dark double of the utopian eugenic reproduction upon which both Gilman's and Naidu's feminisms depend. Even though Gilman and Naidu understand eugenic reproduction as under threat from unfit subjects of various kinds, for each a notion of eugenic national progress nonetheless obtains. In contradistinction to this, Mayo focuses on the ways nationalism is imperiled by dysgenic reproduction. This obsession with national degeneration, however, reveals an investment in eugenic reproduction at least as strong as Gilman's or Naidu's. But Mayo takes this investment in a very different direction, turning her stance on national reproduction into an explicitly antifeminist "race-suicide" argument of the kind with which Gilman takes issue. In bringing her recognizably conservative politics to one of the key eugenic debates in India—child marriage—Mayo attempts to fashion herself as a crusader on behalf of oppressed Indian women. What she does not reckon for is that Indian nationalists and nationalist feminists had already made marriage reform a site of critique of the colonial government.[5] Moreover, as Mrinalini Sinha details in her powerful recent monograph about the *Mother India* controversy, *Specters of Mother India,* Mayo's explicit desire to support British imperialism in India backfires. Although she intended to prove that Indians were unworthy agents of modernity in desperate need of British intervention, her critique ultimately recommends the United States as the more effective modernizing imperial power. In other words, Mayo's conservative and antifeminist project of impugning Indian sex and marriage practices as a way of undermining Indian feminism and bolstering British imperialism fails on both counts. Certainly Sarojini Naidu, whose 1928–29 North American speaking tour I turn to at the end of this chapter, contests Mayo's account on precisely these terms by presenting herself as the true embodiment of Mother India.

Furthermore, just as Mayo's use of the figure Mother India (a figure that intimates both nationalist aspirations and the material problems of national reproduction) exceeds the spatial boundaries of India and becomes a U.S. problem, so too does the larger question of national reproduction. Her obsessive attention to Indian reproductive practices reveals a larger preoccupation with national reproduction *in general.* Because Mayo's argument against Indian self-rule rests on what she perceives as India's inability to reproduce itself, she ties national reproduction to sovereignty. By putting reproduction at the center of the question of sovereignty, however, Mayo troubles reproductive practices at home as well as in India; the sexual and cultural promiscuity of the U.S. "new woman" renders her particularly susceptible to India's threat. For Mayo, this danger emanates both from Indian immigration and the "Hindu craze"—U.S. popular attraction to Hindu spirituality and culture. Whereas Gilman figures the abject Asian woman as a foil to white feminist agency, Mayo uses the specter of dysgenic Indian reproductive practices as a means of disciplining U.S. women into their proper eugenic roles. Mayo's argument against Indian sovereignty thus rebounds upon U.S. women who do not fulfill their reproductive duties; the "world menace" that India represents is ineluctably linked to U.S. "new women" who threaten national reproduction through their susceptibility to India's exotic charms.

I argue that Mayo maps the domestic issue of immigration onto the international terrain of imperialism—in this case British imperialism in India—to solidify a nativist nationalism.[6] Insisting on the racial

and cultural difference between Anglo-Americans and Indians (and by
extension arguing for Indian unfitness for nationhood or U.S. citizenship), Mayo adopts a language of global modernity to expose the United
States and India as dangerously inhabiting the same time and space.
As such, her imperialism is riven with intense anxiety; even as her project is meant to strengthen both British imperial and U.S. commercial
interests in India, her writings reveal a deep uneasiness with global
markets and their ability to bring distant peoples and cultures into contact. Imagining India as embodying a sexual threat that must be kept in
check, she fashions a peculiarly U.S. version of imperial containment to
segregate populations and police behaviors. This containment strategy
is as applicable at home as it is abroad: not only must the Indian threat
be neutralized and U.S. borders policed, U.S. women's sexuality must be
controlled and channeled into reproductive work for the nation.

By forwarding reproductive nationalism as an exclusionary strategy
of imperial containment on both the national and international levels,
and by intervening in contemporaneous debates about U.S. and Indian
"new women," the *Mother India* controversy reveals the complicated
circuits of eugenic feminism between the two countries. I thus use a
eugenic feminist analytic to parse out the relationship among eugenics, feminism, sexuality, and empire within the debate, suggesting that
the argument Mayo brandishes in support of British imperialism will
reappear in a greatly sanitized form in the discourse of postwar development. Mayo leverages national reproduction in service of strategies
of containment just as the Cold War discourse of development turns
to population control as a means of fighting communist contamination
on a world scale. This is not to level out the important differences between these two moments; for one thing, while Mayo uses the specter
of pathological reproduction to contest India's fitness for nationhood,
the independent Indian government will turn to population control as
a component of modern nation building. Similarly, the overtly racist
and imperialist language of *Mother India* is disavowed in the supposedly neutral language of development and modernization brandished
by the U.S. and Indian governments alike. Nonetheless, I point to these
continuities to propose the mobility and centrality of eugenic reproduction to imperial, national, and developmental regimes of subjectivity,
suggesting, furthermore, that the problematic of dysgenic reproduction
that Mayo traces sets the terms of eugenic feminist debates between the
United States and India in the pre-independence era.

"Hinduism Invades America"

Part of *Mother India*'s aim was to combat what Wendell Thomas's 1930 book names an "invasion" of Hindu beliefs and practices onto U.S. soil.[7] While U.S. interest in Hindu spirituality can be traced back at least to Emerson, Thoreau, and Whitman, following Swami Vivekananda's address at the 1893 World Parliament of Religion fascination with mystical India became widespread. This late nineteenth- and early twentieth-century Hindu craze encompassed Hindu religious movements (such as Vivekananda's Vedanta Society and Yogananda's Yogada Sat-sanga Society of America), popular lecture tours by Rabindranath Tagore and Lala Lajpat Rai, and Hindu-influenced religious movements such as Theosophy.[8] This surge of interest in Hinduism can also be read as a version of modernist Orientalism (as, for instance, in T. S. Eliot's use of the Upanishads in *The Waste Land*), as well as part of larger pre-occupations with the meaning of U.S. culture in the face of immigration and industrialization.[9]

In addition to India's cultural lure, for some U.S. citizens India's struggle against British imperialism was a reason to make common cause. Indeed, although the U.S. government officially supported British imperialism, many prominent Americans were against continued British rule of India, among them Andrew Carnegie and William Jennings Bryan.[10] This pro-India movement was, in part, an offshoot of the Anti-Imperialist League's opposition to the U.S. acquisition of the Philippines. Some of this faction opposed British imperialism in India based on antiracist principles, but pro-India sentiment was also linked to an anti-imperialism motivated by racist fears of incorporating non-white peoples into the national body. In this guise, anti-imperialism was aligned with isolationist calls for immigrant exclusion. In addition to these U.S.-based anti-imperial efforts, Indian nationalists in the United States actively sought assistance for their cause. In 1914, Indian nationalist Lala Lajpat Rai traveled to the United States to enlist help in establishing Indian self-rule, and in 1917 he founded the Indian Home Rule League of America.[11] The Friends for the Freedom of India was launched just two years later in 1919, and counted Taraknath Das, Sailendranath Ghosh, Robert Mores Lovett, and Oswald Garrison Villard among its prominent members.[12] Alongside these more genteel movements, the revolutionary Hindustan Ghadar Party was formed in San Francisco in 1913 and was a force until the Hindu–German conspiracy scandal of 1917–18.[13] In short, U.S. fascination with Hindu spirituality often translated into support for Indian nationalism even if (as I will discuss) it was accompanied by exclusionary immigration and naturalization laws for diasporic Indians living and working in the United States.[14]

Mayo attempts to disrupt the idea that India and the United States have a shared anti-imperial mission by insisting on the racial divide between Indians and Anglo-Saxon Americans, asserting instead a racialized discourse of British and U.S. imperial solidarity.[15] Toward this end, in 1921 she and Moyca Newell founded the British Apprentice Club to offer hospitality to cadets in the British merchant Navy docked in New York City. Mayo furthermore appeals to conservative gender politics in positing this racial and imperial kinship by exploiting the gendered nature of the U.S. pro-India movement and the Hindu craze. Many pro-Indian anti-imperialists (Agnes Smedley and Margaret Sanger to name just two) united domestic feminist concerns with the fight against British imperialism. That such concerns participated in a racialized hierarchy of womanhood (particularly in the case of Sanger) is undoubtedly true, but nonetheless U.S. feminism was linked to Indian nationalism in the minds of many U.S. observers. In taking on women's issues in India, Mayo attempted to discredit precisely this kind of support by revealing it as hypocritical. Painting Indian women as helpless victims of native patriarchy, she connects saving Indian women to containing male nationalists, thus exposing feminist support for Indian nationalism as aligned with patriarchy. Using as an alibi for her antifeminist agenda her stated concern for India's oppressed women (a concern that, despite her overt politics, was received as "feminist" in many quarters), Mayo accuses feminist supporters of Indian nationalism as betraying their own sensibilities.[16] In focusing on the issue of national reproduction and its supposed perversion in the Indian context, moreover, Mayo further discredits U.S. feminists by linking them to dysgenic reproduction both at home and abroad.

With its eye to the scandalous and sensational, *Mother India* returned to the stock themes of Mayo's earlier work. Although stylistically *Mother India* and Mayo's other writings can be situated within the muckraking tradition of the late nineteenth and early twentieth centuries, thematically they bolstered the very institutions the muckrakers attacked. Her first three books addressed the issue of state police reform, valorizing the Philadelphia police force and ignoring altogether the brutality with which employers had used that force to break strikes.[17] Not only does Mayo reveal her conservative views toward labor in these works, she also articulates her race and gender politics, populating her narratives with "raving mobs" of immigrants, defenseless white women, and murderous and licentious African American men.[18]

Mayo's books before *Mother India* established her imperialist credentials as well. Her 1924 *The Isles of Fear: The Truth about the Philippines* attacked the Wilsonian policy of Filipinization and strenuously argued against Filipino independence. As in *Mother India,* Mayo uses *The Isles of Fear* to paint a picture of irredeemably atavistic natives in need of the civilizing influence of the West. One of Mayo's particular targets in *The Isles of Fear* was the 1916 Jones Act, which was a first step toward Filipino governmental autonomy. Indeed, her indictment of this act was effective enough to attract the attention of the British government. A British edition of *The Isles of Fear* was published in 1925, with an introduction by government official and imperial spokesman Lionel Curtis. In his introduction, Curtis cautions readers that it "cannot be wise for us to ignore the examples and warning afforded in their [the Americans'] more daring experiments."[19] Not coincidentally, Curtis was also one of the architects of the Government of India Act of 1919, which was similarly a step toward developing self-governing institutions.[20] As both Manoranjam Jha and Mrinalini Sinha's archival research has uncovered, Mayo's work on the Philippines led British officials to believe she might be useful in enlisting U.S. public opinion in favor of their imperial project in India. Concerned about the growing tide of U.S. support for Indian nationalism, the British propaganda machine encouraged Mayo to do with India what she had done with the Philippines.

In fact, coming in the midst of shifts in the relationship between British imperialism and Indian nationalism, most notably the 1919 Government of India Act, Mayo's assault on Indian nationalism had immediate political effects. When the formation of the all-white Indian Statutory Commission to examine political reforms in India (known as the Simon Commission) was announced in November 1927, *Mother India* was thought to have influenced the debate about the racial composition of the commission. Free copies of *Mother India* were given to members of Parliament before the commission was discussed and were widely thought to have been prejudicial.[21] Mayo was also incorrectly credited by the international press with the passage of the 1929 Sarda

Child Marriage Restraint Bill, a tribute that obscured the work of Indian women's organizations in the campaign.[22]

Despite this seeming imperialist feminist victory, the *Mother India* controversy enabled new terms for Indian feminism. As Mrinalini Sinha argues in *Specters of Mother India,* Indian feminists used the *Mother India* controversy to wrest a place for Indian women as subjects, not only objects, of debates around Indian womanhood. Furthermore, they were able to fleetingly construct a political identity *as women* rather than as representative of their communities. Therefore one of what Sinha terms the "unpredictable outcomes" of the *Mother India* debate is that its obsessive focus on dysgenic reproduction among various communities in India (though its harshest critiques were reserved for Hindus) both forwarded the existing eugenic debate in India about child marriage and helped to forge a more inclusive Indian feminist identity. Although (as I discussed in the previous chapter) this identity falls apart in the second women's suffrage campaign of the 1930s, this is nonetheless a moment in which a more expansive vision of Indian feminism becomes momentarily available. Thus Mayo's attempt to discredit both U.S. and Indian feminism in some senses has precisely the opposite effect.

A Democracy of Disease

Mayo responds to the Hindu craze by rewriting the terms of the debate along pseudo-scientific lines. She repeatedly insists that *Mother India* "[leaves] untouched the realms of religion . . . politics . . . and the arts . . . [and confines its] inquiry to such workaday ground as public health and its contributing factors" (12). By focusing on what she believes to be the material conditions of everyday life in India, Mayo seeks to counter U.S. fascination with Hindu spirituality and culture. Her emphasis on "brass tacks" instead of "poetic theory" allows her to arrive at the conclusion that "'spiritual' Hinduism, disentangled from words and worked out in common life, is materialism in the grossest and most suicidal form."[23] Brandishing a biopolitical rhetoric that opposes U.S. developmental regimes of public health to the hygienic horrors of life in India, Mayo attempts to disrupt the idea that Hindu philosophy could trump U.S. modernity. The problem is not U.S. materialism (as U.S. proponents of Hindu spirituality would have it), but rather a Hindu materialism named spirituality. Mayo thus remaps the coordinates of the spiritual and the material by arguing that in India religiously mandated material practices lead to public health problems. Consequently U.S. modernity, with its emphasis on hygiene and public health, is more spiritual in its ability to foster and support life. *Mother India*'s focus on public health thus proposes that far from a spiritual utopia, India is a democracy of disease.

In painting this parody of democratization, Mayo presents us with a distinctly dystopian landscape. It is dystopian (rather than anti-utopian) in that, as Dohra Ahmad puts it, it portrays a world that is "patently bad."[24] An anti-utopia (such as Aldous Huxley's *Brave New World*) presents a world that is horrifying because it works too well, thus revealing utopia's violent underside. Here, however, Mayo's muckraking gives us a dystopian picture of India as a way of commenting on social conditions in the real world. In this, it shares with Gilman's utopias an interest in social change. But while Gilman's imaginative fiction creates the fantastical Herland to remark on gender relations in the world of her readers, Mayo uses the supposedly objective and scientific language of public health to similarly indict what she understands to be a public health nightmare. Thus her degenerative, dysgenic, dystopia of unequal sex relations taken to the extreme is in some senses the photonegative of Gilman's utopias. Moreover, if Gilman's vision is always exclusionary, Mayo's is similarly concerned with the cultural contact that globalization brings, thus using the discourse of closeness and contagion to argue for containment.

The global magnitude of India's profligate spreading of contagions is boldly stated in a chapter titled "World Menace." Speculating that cholera and malaria in India are caused by the custom of the "village tank"—a stagnant pool that serves the water needs of the village—Mayo argues that such tanks lead to the "democratization of any new germs introduced to the village, and its mosquitoes spread malaria with an impartial beak—though not without some aid" (366). This "aid" comes in the form of Hindu religious practices that can exacerbate, or even cause, a public health crisis. As Mayo expresses it, this is a perennial problem in many colonial sites. Even though the British are building proper wells, "exactly as in the Philippines, the people [in India] have a strong hankering for the ancestral type, and, where they can, will usually leave the new and protected water-source for their old accustomed squatting- and gossiping-ground where they all innocently poison each other" (369). Typically, the problem is presented as "ancestral" religious habits trumping the advances of modern science and hygiene. The true crisis, however, is not that these habits prevail but that they coexist with modern science, thus the "democratization" of germs, not populations.

If democracy is signified by the spread of germs, not the spread of the abstract rights of citizenship, then modernity's global circulation of goods, bodies, and practices makes India's condition worthy of global interest and perhaps even intervention. In a telling passage, Mayo renders this problem universal by transplanting it to Europe:

> In ordinary circumstances, in places where the public water supply is good and under scientific control, cholera is not to be feared. But the great and radical changes of modern times bring about rapid reverses of conditions; such, for example, as the sudden pouring in the year 1920 of hundreds of thousands of disease-sodden refugees out of Russia into Western Europe. (370)

The movement of refugees from Eastern to Western Europe (a movement that extends even further west to the United States) illustrates the vulnerability of all "healthy" populations from "diseased" ones; the implication of this passage is that populations must be manipulated in order to prevent disease. Thus "scientific control" is never enough—the real problem of modernity is the speed at which populations can move and public health situations "reverse." Taking a biopolitical view of populations as singular (and unpredictably dangerous) entities necessitating both internal and external strategies of containment, *Mother India* forwards Indian public health as a problem for the United States. Even as India would seem to be of little importance to the "average American," Mayo addresses *Mother India* to her fellow U.S. citizens in an attempt to rewrite contagious disease in India as a global problem of local concern (11).

In focusing on the problem of contagious disease, *Mother India* supports a specifically U.S. version of developmentalist imperialism. The science of public health was one of the forms the U.S. civilizing mission took, with the related purposes of creating healthy workers and establishing markets for its goods. While, as Laura Briggs perceptively demonstrates in *Reproducing Empire,* U.S. imperial interest in tropical medicine and public health borrowed from British imperial models, particularly in relation to prostitution policy, the United States was nonetheless at the forefront of the modernizing discourse of public health. As such, Mayo's focus on public health was intended both to bolster the legitimacy of British imperialism in India and to pave the way for U.S. commercial interests (although, as we shall see, her stance toward this second mission was ambivalent at best). By bringing what Sinha calls "the aggressively modernizing discourse of an early-twentieth-century U.S. imperialism to bear on the debate about the nature of the colonial state in India," however, Mayo ends up asserting the United States as the proper modernizing power, which was certainly not the British government's intention in getting Mayo involved.[25] Mayo's connection to the Rockefeller Foundation (which was at the forefront of public health projects in the United States and abroad and was one of the most important agents of U.S. expansionist interests) is particularly telling in this regard. Mayo used the contacts she had forged with the Rockefeller Foundation through her work in the Philippines to assist her in her India project. She traveled to India with letters of introduction from the foundation, and her intended focus on cholera in India was suggested to her by them.[26] Despite these connections, Mayo later disavowed any official affiliation with the Rockefeller Foundation, as her relationship with them would cast doubt on her purported impartiality.

Nonetheless, Mayo's spotlight on public health uniquely marries her domestic and imperial concerns. As Nayan Shah argues in his study of public health, immigration, and the racialization of the Chinese in San Francisco, public health was a form of "'imperial domesticity'" that sought "to manage and reform the 'foreign' within the nation" as well as "to civilize the 'lower races' within the United States and abroad in China and India and, later, in the U.S. imperial territories of the Philippines and Puerto Rico" (106).[27] The notion of public health therefore performs a kind of spatial metonymy whereby all "unhealthy" spaces require the same treatment regardless of their global location. Certainly the Rockefeller Sanitary Commission's extension of their hookworm campaign in the U.S. South to the territories of the British Empire with the 1913 chartering of the Rockefeller Foundation illustrates this point.[28] That issues surrounding the control of sexuality and reproduction were crucial to a public health agenda is furthermore demonstrated by, as Laura Briggs carefully traces, the U.S. adoption of the British Contagious Disease Acts to regulate prostitution in Puerto Rico and the Philippines.[29] Importantly, one of Briggs's points is that the regulation of colonial sexuality is just as much about regulating domestic sexuality, a fact that the *Mother India* controversy certainly substantiates. Characterizing India as a public health problem allows

Mayo to paint a global modernity that is terrifying in its ability to flatten out geographical distance and difference. Although Indian sanitary habits might be dangerous to them, the notion of India as a world menace implies that Indians need to be civilized not simply for their *own* good but because their habits and practices represent a danger to the rest of the world.

This threat is made even more acute by the specter of Indian immigration to the United States. In painting Indians as carriers of dangerous contagions (both in the guise of diseases and of cultural practices), Mayo employs what Alan Kraut has dubbed "medicalized nativism": a pseudo-scientific discourse that redefines in the medical terms of contagious disease what nativists viewed as immigrants' racial or cultural unfitness for national membership.[30] She thereby codes the cultural contagion she sees in the Hindu craze as literally an issue of disease, relying upon contemporaneous sociological theories to characterize cultural transmission through metaphors of infection. As Priscilla Wald details in her 2008 book *Contagious,* the idea of "social contagion" pioneered by Robert E. Park expressed "the material of culture [as] transmissible and transformative."[31] While this could be a positive process of assimilation and social cohesion, it also "named the danger as well as the power of transformation" (134). By figuring cultural communication in terms of contagion, Mayo launches a plausible excuse for regulation; if culture is catching, then national boundaries need to be strictly policed. That she articulates this contagion around reproductive bodies and links it to an anti-imperial feminism, moreover, speaks to her race suicide concerns with dysgenic reproduction at home.

"When Asia Knocks at the Door"

Mayo establishes the connection between Indian and U.S. modernities in chapter 1, "The Argument," which opens with the statement: "Bombay is but three weeks' journey from New York" (11). If Western modernity is made vulnerable by its proximity to other (presumably contagious) cultures, then U.S. ties with India must be tightly controlled. This is why Mayo ultimately advocates an imperial strategy of containment that relies upon a two-pronged approach of rooting out dangerous practices abroad while also making sure they do not travel home. In part, Mayo is concerned with increased economic activity between the United States and India. As she explains in a 1928 article, India is "a large, potentially a huge, market for American goods. American and British ships are continually plying between Indian and American ports. Indians are increasingly coming amongst us."[32] The danger, as the rhetoric of this quotation suggests, is that economic ties between the countries will dissolve all distinctions between them. Mayo's description moves seamlessly from India as a "market for American goods" to "Indians . . . increasingly coming amongst us" to demonstrate the dangerous consequences of U.S. expansionist interests. Accordingly, Mayo most often describes U.S–Indian economic connections in terms of potentially dangerous and unfettered circulation, labeling Calcutta "wide-open to the traffic of the world and India, traffic of bullion, of jute, of cotton—of all that India and the world want out of each other's hands" (3). This equally suggests, however, that the United States is opening itself to all that the world does *not* want out of India's hands—that is, India's diseased bodies and perverse cultural practices. Precisely because Calcutta is so "wide-open," U.S. borders need to remain tightly shut.

Although, as both Sinha and Jha show, part of Mayo's explicit purpose in writing *Mother India* was to support U.S. commercial interests in India, I read in the preceding rhetoric a deep ambivalence about that agenda. At its base, Mayo's alarm at the situation in India reveals a fear of global markets. While the United States needs the "potentially huge" market that India represents, such a market also means potentially polluting "Indians . . . coming amongst us." This is one of the paradoxes of globalization and expansion—the need for a free exchange of goods and capital, but not of peoples, cultures, and potentially dangerous cultural practices. There are thus two consequences to Mayo's argument. The first is the predictably nativist view that the United States needs to tightly control all immigration. To this, however, she adds a decidedly imperialist twist. While classical theories of imperialism understand it as primarily serving the expansion, exportation, and penetration of capital, Mayo advocates imperialism as a mode of containment, as a way of solidifying imperial national boundaries.[33] Just as Cold War policies of containment were equally concerned with rooting out the communist threat overseas and at home, Mayo links immigration and imperialism to, in her reckoning, keep the Anglo-Saxon world safe. Unsurprisingly, for Mayo India represents the specifically gendered specter of dysgenic reproduction and miscegenation, a concern made all the more pressing by the possibility of closer ties (economic and otherwise) between the two countries.

Regulating citizenship is a crucial part of this containment strategy, and Mayo's argument in *Mother India* was intended to intervene in contemporaneous debates surrounding Indian eligibility for U.S. citizenship. In 1917, Asian Indians were barred from immigrating to the United States, and in 1923, the B. S. Thind case upheld the denaturalization of U.S. citizens of Indian origin on the basis of their not appearing recognizably white to the "common man." In 1926, the Hindu Citizenship Bill (otherwise known as the Copeland Bill for the senator who sponsored it) unsuccessfully attempted to challenge the Thind ruling by arguing that Indians, as Aryans, are racially Caucasian. In a slight of hand that erased the different religions and cultures within South Asia, the term *Hindu* in the bill's title was used to refer to all the immigrants from the subcontinent, even though most of the South Asian immigrants to the United States were Sikh and Muslim. Moreover, the Hindu Citizenship Bill proposed a "solution" to the problem of Indian citizenship that relied on the same racist logic as the Asian Exclusion Acts.[34] Such challenges to racist exclusion laws reinstated the metonymic relationship between "Hindu" and "India," a relationship that not only did damage to the other religious and ethnic groups of the subcontinent but also contributed to a racist politics in the United States.[35] Mayo was a staunch opponent of the Hindu Citizenship bill and reportedly wrote *Mother India* because of it. While she later denies this, there can be no doubt that she was steadfast critic of Indian immigration in general and the Hindu Citizenship Bill in particular.[36]

In fact, Mayo expressly promotes *Mother India* as a "unique opportunity to throw light on immigration problems that hitherto have received no public attention."[37] In a 1927 article entitled "When Asia Knocks at the Door," she points to domestic "racial and political unrest" and "movements of trade and emigration" as evidence that Asia and the United States are connected in surprising and disturbing ways. Asia is to Mayo an unwanted and uninvited houseguest: "The Far East even now knocks at our door, demanding full rights of American citizenship." She uses the language of the home to suggest a threat that strikes at the heart of the U.S. family, a family not only defined by citizenship but also constituted by race. She raises the specter of "the British East Indian" being "as eligible as the Swede or the Swiss or the Scotchman to a citizen's share in our government," and she warns of "entrust[ing]" him with co-guardianship" of "our own heritage." Citing "the safety of our homes . . . the preservation of our standards . . . [and] the unborn children of America, of India and of the world," Mayo describes an implicitly white U.S. family relinquishing control to an invader—a threat to the reproduction of the individual family understood as a threat to the nation as a whole.

As we would expect, Mayo disavows the overtly racist and nativist sentiments of "When Asia Knocks at the Door" by insisting her interest in India is only clinical; her concern is not race, culture, or religion—it is hygiene. Her inquiry into "what sort of American citizen . . . the British Indian [would] make" thus circulates around "social habits . . . in the sense of sanitation, respect for women and children and certain physical-moral laws." Though it is easy to see how the categories of race, culture, religion, and hygiene all bleed into each other here, Mayo asserts that these matters are not "abstractions" but of the "practical field." She makes similar claims in *Mother India,* stating that "John Smith of 23 Main Street may care little enough about the ancestry of Peter Jones, and still less about his religion, his philosophy, or his views on art. But if Peter cultivates a habit of living and ways of thinking that make him a physical menace not only to himself and his family, but to all the rest of the block, then practical John will want details" (14–15). Although it is clear from the rest of the book that Mayo believes "religion," "philosophy," and "views on art" dictate the "habits of living and ways of thinking" that she considers menacing, she rhetorically positions herself as arguing against U.S. fascination with such aspects of Hindu life. In fact, Mayo declares, such preoccupations are dangerous distractions from the issue at hand—the public health threat that Indians pose. As medical surveillance turns its gaze global, supposedly "private" practices come under scrutiny both abroad and at home. Peter Jones need not share John Smith's views of "religion," "philosophy," or "art," but he is to "cultivate a habit of living" that will not be harmful "to all the rest of the block." Just as the need to control immigration on the national level is about protecting the national body, Mayo takes this narrative global by marrying nativist concerns about immigration to imperialist concerns about native self-rule. Here, the imperial project gets rewritten not as one of conquest and riches, nor even the "white man's burden," but rather as one of protection from the global circulation of bodies.

Maternal Contagions

That Mayo focuses on the problematic of national reproduction is unsurprising given her larger concern with public health and hygiene in all its various guises. Even more important, however, the focus on re-production allows Mayo to adopt and pervert the terms of Indian na-tionalist debates, presenting the world with a vision of stillborn Indian nationalism that cannily perverts the maternal logic at its center. By refiguring Mother India as incapable of giving birth to a healthy child, let alone a nation, Mayo disrupts Indian nationalism's symbolic use of women to signify Indian cultural purity and distinctness. She sets up this ironic invocation of Mother India in the chapter titled "Slave Mentality," noting how "from every political platform" nationalists "stream flaming protests of devotion to the death to Mother India." Here she references the importance of the maternal ideal in Indian nationalism but distorts it by rewriting Mother India as a "sick—ignorant and helpless" mother (19). She points out what is to her the signal paradox of Indian nationalism: even as Indian nationalists say Mother India is an ideal worth dying for (as "flaming protests of devo-tion to the death" implies), Mayo claims that *actual* Indian mothers are dying (they are "sick," "ignorant, and helpless"). To this pathetic portrait of India's mothers, Mayo adds an unflattering commentary on India's sons. She describes them in the most unmanly terms, ar-guing that they "spend their time in quarrels together or else lie idly weeping over their own futility" (19). Mayo's direct contrast of India's mothers to India's sons in this passage sets up her depiction of Indian men as ineffectual and juvenile—"quarrel[ing]" and "weeping" like children. According to Mayo, with such men as protectors it is no wonder India has ever been "the flaccid subject of a foreign rule" (21). She thus represents all of India as the combination of a compromised masculinity and an uncomplaining and passive femininity. Instead of fighting the forces of "foreign rule," India is troped as a woman being repeatedly and uncomplainingly raped: "The ancient Hindu stock, softly absorbing each recurrent blow, quivered—and lay still" (21). In total, as Mayo puts it in one of her more excessive descriptions, Mother India is "shabby, threadbare, sick and poor . . . victim and slave of all recorded time" (288).

This easy metaphorization is troubled in the eponymous chapter, however, wherein Mother India comes to signify not only the "victim and slave of all recorded time" but also her torturer; the title of the chapter refers both to the Indian mother feebly reproducing the nation and the indigenous midwife, or *dai,* ineptly assisting her. Mayo's meta-phorical use of Mother India as the pathological body politic is disrupted by a metonymic movement wherein Mother India comes to represent a threat as well as a victim.[38] By splitting the sign Mother India to accommodate the *dai*, Mother India literally becomes "a bearer of multiple contagions" administering to the "sick and poor" mother (93). As Mayo describes her, the *dai* is a "Witch of Endor"-like figure, with "vermin-infested elf locks . . . hanging rags . . . dirty claws . . .[and] festered and almost sightless eyes" (94). Mayo writes that because the parturient woman is considered to be "ceremonially unclean . . . only those become *dhais* who are themselves of the unclean, 'untouchable' class, the class whose filthy habits will be adduced by the orthodox Hindu as his good and sufficient reason for barring them from contact with himself" (91). And yet the *dai* is the only sanctioned contact that the pregnant woman can have—and this contact turns the birthing chamber into a chamber of horrors:

> [The *dai*] kneads the patient with her fists; stands her against the wall and butts her with her head; props her upright on the bare ground, seizes her hands and shoves against her thighs with gruesome bare feet, until, so the doctors state, the patient's flesh is often torn to ribbons by the *dhai*'s long, ragged toe-nails. Or, she lays the woman flat and walks up and down her body, like one treading grapes. (95)

Utterly unrelated to the tasks a midwife is supposed to perform, the practices portrayed here read like a description of torture. Although the *dai* is an active agent, the birthing mother is an utterly passive puppet who does not seem to have even the ability to stand up or to lie down—rather the *dai* "props her upright" or "lays [her] flat." Instead of simply engendering sympathy for the Indian mother, the portrait of the *dai* presents an active threat. Because *both* of these figures are metonymically linked to the Mother India to which the chapter title refers, Mother India is at once the "ragged toe-nails" and the "flesh [being] torn."

The abject scene described in this chapter is one in which the mother is contaminated by the *dai*, as the sign Mother India splits to doubly signify the parturient mother and the polluting midwife.[39] By painting the Indian woman as the subaltern, Mayo does not simply ignore elite and educated women in her study, although that is part of her strategy here. Rather, Mayo suggests that underneath the Indian new woman's veneer of modernity there is always an atavistic, contagious, and not-quite-hidden abjectness. In other words, by defining Mother

India through India's most downtrodden, Mayo evokes *all* of India's
population as downtrodden, implying that all Indian women are the
polluted and polluting subaltern she so luridly describes.

In painting this portrait, Mayo ignores the fact that *dais* were
already being subjected to nationalist critiques from a variety of positions. For the most part, the movements to reform *dais* came from
middle-class, upper-caste positions: as Charu Gupta details in her
Sexuality, Obscenity, Community, "a critique of the dai was consonant
with the idea of all that was 'modern'—scientific, rational and new—
which were seen as the yardsticks of civilisation and prestige by the
Hindu middle classes."[40] As with other areas of reform, the point was
not simply to adopt "the western medical system and its rhetoric" but to
rather formulate new practices around childbirth that forwarded a version of indigenous identity that was uniquely modern.[41] Radical caste
reformers like Periyar in the south and Ambedkar in Maharashtra
also were involved in *dai* reform, but even here "the rhetoric of reform
often reworked and updated patriarchal norms and combined it with
a simultaneous assertion of homogenous identities and caste exclusivi-
ties."[42] Finally, in glossing over these nationalist movements for reform,
and in painting *all* Indian women as the polluted and polluting subaltern, Mayo paradoxically creates conditions through which a collective
subject of Indian womanhood is allowed to emerge. As Sinha argues in
Specters of Mother India, in the *Mother India* controversy "woman"
as a constituency needed to include subaltern women as well as elites
"to mobilize a construction of women as *both* the agents *and* the objects
of reform."[43]

By transforming Mother India from a nationalist symbol of rebirth
into a degraded symbol of pathological maternity, Mayo critiques
Indian nationalism by calling into question India's ability to reproduce
itself. She splits the sign Mother India into the dismembered and diseased maternal body and the "witch of Endor"–like figure of the *dai*
to signify maternity as something that needs to be protected precisely
because it simultaneously signifies such a threat. From this perspective, Mayo's argument for British imperialism is an attempt to police
national boundaries both globally and domestically. The real problem
is one of proximity between different cultures and bodies, and thus
Mayo's obsessive concern with Indian reproduction reveals her larger
anxieties about national reproductive processes in general. The problem of indigenous midwifery in India is not just a "family problem,"

so to speak. By engaging discourses concerning reproduction and the national body, Mayo turns Indian birthing practices into a concern for the "family of nations."

Seducing America's Mothers

Mayo's refiguration of Mother India as the pathological mother emanates not only from her interest in British imperial politics, then, but also from her concern about Indian penetration of the United States. I use the sexually charged language of penetration deliberately, because for Mayo India represents a sexual threat to which white, bourgeois U.S. women are peculiarly vulnerable. If eugenic feminism is always obsessed with claims to purity (or the lack thereof), then Mayo's race suicide argument remains within eugenic feminism's symbolic framework even if she is brandishing it for conservative gender politics. By arguing that feminism opens the way to national degeneration Mayo presents us with what at first glance looks like the reverse of Gilman's argument. Nonetheless, despite their different political positions both Gilman and Mayo share a fear of miscegenation, and both also see India as the site of a horrifying patriarchy.[44] A 1928 article titled "India" encapsulates the problem of Hinduism's sinister appeal. In it, Mayo describes attending a lecture by an unnamed "East Indian . . . a slim, handsome, graceful, well dressed young man, [who] spoke with an easy eloquence that seemed to exert upon his audience a sort of spell."[45] The main topic of this young man's speech "implied the spiritual, mental and moral inferiority of America and her need of guidance from the wisdom of the East."[46] Mayo paints a picture of an easy and seductive Eastern spirituality—one that is simply "well-dressed" surfaces but that nonetheless weaves a "sort of spell" on a stupefied audience—to argue that enthrallment with such superficial spiritually represents a symptom of a cultural crisis rather than its solution. Moreover, an interest in Hinduism inevitably raises the specter of miscegenation. Mayo's strongest warning in her article is thus directed at

Mrs. John J. Smith of Smithville, U.S.A. . . . . *Keep away, Mrs. John, from the swamis, the yogis, the traveling teaching men.* . . . In your innocence, in your good faith, in your eager-minded receptivity of high-sounding doctrine, in your hunger for color, romance, glamour, and dreams come true, you expose yourself, all unsuspecting, to things that, if you knew them, would kill you dead with unmerited shame.[47]

Mayo paints an evocative picture of "innocent" white women "exposing" themselves to a potentially lethal "shame." Yet even as she says that this exposure is "unsuspecting," there is also an element of reprimand. Though the main fault lies with "the swamis, the yogis, the traveling teaching men," the women have left themselves open to seduction: Mayo is putatively addressing a fascination with Hindu spirituality, but the phrase "hunger for color, romance, glamour, and dreams come true" seems to suggest that these women are seeking more than a spiritual awakening.

The picture of degraded Indian womanhood Mayo paints in *Mother India* gives weight to her warning in "India." Contrasting the "high-sounding doctrine" of "the traveling teaching men" with the reproductive practices she describes in her exposé, Mayo argues that U.S. women could, through their own carelessness and sexual hunger, be subjected to the same reproductive practices as their Indian counterparts. They too could become ciphers for an alternatively threatening and abject maternity, and in doing so betray their reproductive duty to their nation. In an essay titled "To the Women of Hindu India" Mayo explicitly addresses this concern. Attached to Mayo's collection of short stories, *Slaves of the Gods* (1929), the essay compares Indian and U.S. women in terms of their ability to reproduce the nation, not to "offer our Western performance as a model for [them] to copy," but rather to praise Indian women for their greater "discipline."[48] While U.S. women "have liberty . . . as great as [Indian women's] thralldom some neglect the privilege, and some selfishly, thoughtlessly and flagrantly abuse it."[49] Mayo criticizes new women who neglect their responsibilities to "loyally serve the family and the society of which they are a part" in favor of their own selfish desires.[50] Indian women are praiseworthy in their devotion to the maternal ideal (though, as Mayo strenuously argues throughout *Mother India* and her other writings, this ideal has been twisted), but U.S. women are in danger of abandoning it altogether. They thus represent opposite ends of the spectrum: Indian women have "discipline" but no "liberty"; U.S. women have "liberty" but lack "discipline." In both cases the results are potentially disastrous—by comparing the subjugated Indian woman to the selfish and thoughtless U.S. one, Mayo calls into question the ability of either nation to adequately reproduce itself.

Mayo further elaborates these concerns in a 1928 article for *Liberty* magazine titled "Companionate 'Marriage'—and Marriage: A Message to Girls." Though Mayo was herself unmarried (she spent most of her adult life living and traveling with Moyca Newell, an heiress who financed many of her research trips), she nonetheless felt both entitled and compelled to speak of proper conduct within marriage. In the article she attacks companionate marriage on the grounds that it twists the higher, procreative, purpose of marriage and debases women by reducing them to sexual objects. She opens by describing the marital woes of Roger and Anne. Roger, it seems, is having an affair, and all of Anne's friends and family urge her to leave him. To their surprise and dismay, she does nothing of the kind, insisting that when she married Roger "nothing was said about 'sickness and health' referring to the body only. If Roger had scarlet fever, would you expect me to desert him? My Roger is sick from another fever now, from which, in due course, he will quite recover."[51]

Here we have a familiar equation of sexual perversion and disease. Just as Mayo consistently links practices and morals to disease in *Mother India,* in "Companionate 'Marriage'" she deems Roger's infidelity a "fever" from which he will eventually recover. As the ending of the tale attests, this is exactly what happens; Roger and Anne "lived out a happy half century together, and Roger, in all human likelihood, never guessed that his wife knew [of his affair]."[52] This resolution implies that infidelity is a cause for little concern or comment—the thrust of Mayo's warning is aimed not at Roger but at women in Anne's position. Throughout the article Mayo equates women's desire for "self-expression" and "rights" with Roger's fever, saying just "because Roger caught a fever should [Anne] demand a 'right' to rush out and catch one too?"[53] While Roger seems to have contracted a fever through no fault of his own, if Anne were to seek the same infection (that is, if *she* were to go out and have an affair) the consequences would be very different.

Mayo's use of the fever metaphor is consistent with her focus on disease in her other works; in each case she deems deviant behavior contagious. In this particular instance, she uses the metaphor of fever to describe a drive toward self-fulfillment over good citizenship—the problem is placing one's own needs over the needs of society at large. Roger's affair selfishly interferes with his role as husband, but as long as Anne stays by his side this need not have fatal consequences. Relying on an ideology of separate spheres, Mayo argues that even if Roger has temporarily shirked his domestic duties, it doesn't matter because women are the guardians of the home and their marital behavior carries more weight. *As mothers* (or even as potential mothers) women must real-ize that they never are acting with only their own concerns in mind. Mayo defines motherhood loosely here, saying it is not "dependent on physical maternity" but is "the world expression of the woman soul from childhood to heaven's gate."[54] She contrasts women's and men's "souls," asserting that a man cannot help his fall from grace—at heart, every man is just a "boy whose needs are pathetically simple, whose spiritual loneliness is acute, and whose whole being cries out for the mother companion to comfort, stay and cure it, and to keep the helm straight."[55] In short, women are not just responsible for their own well-being, but for men's and by extension society's at large. This grave responsibility is more important than any individual woman's wants and desires. As Mayo warns U.S. women, "When you feel the phrase 'self-expression' forming in your minds, take warning as you would of the flagman's signal at a level crossing. For a death dealer is headed down your track."[56] Mayo's "message to girls" is for them to sublimate their needs in order to remain true to their real "gift"—"the Quality of Motherhood."[57] To ignore this gift is to strike a death blow not only to the individual girl but to the nation.

Mayo reminds her readers that "no nation . . . can rise higher than the level of its womankind."[58] Unsurprisingly, she turns to the Indian example to prove this point. While she again lauds Hindu society for "[perceiving] that motherhood is the meaning of womanhood," in the same breath she condemns it, arguing that it "has so debased and soiled and ruined the idea [of motherhood], taking the physical for master, that both men and women tend to become merely a function with a human frame behind it."[59] This emphasis on the "physical" unites Hindu marriage with companionate marriage, which Mayo similarly deems "a public blessing on the delivery of your body to sexual use for no nobler reason than the indulgence of your sexual craving."[60] In both companionate marriage in the United States and Hindu marriage in India, the sexual trumps the maternal to catastrophic ends. By plac-ing Indian and U.S. women on a continuum of motherhood, Mayo de-scribes it as a slippery slope down which the U.S. girl, "the mainspring of America's true progress," could easily fall.[61] If progress is so easily and thoughtlessly vulnerable to reversal, then here again is one of the dangers of the flow of bodies and practices between the United States and India. By framing the issue of U.S. marriage in the language of disease, and by once again mobilizing the plight of Indian women as an object lesson, Mayo reveals that her concern with Indian reproduction is also a means for policing U.S. womanhood.

Mayo's concerns are thus domestic in both senses of the word. In a logic that once again recalls Amy Kaplan's notion of "manifest domesticity," Mayo's focus on the private sphere of the home allows her to envision U.S. women as crusaders in the world at large.[62] As she declares, "The American girl is the most potential force for good on earth today."[63] The problem is that these "girls" are falling down on the job. Even as Mayo advocates imperialism, her descriptions of the United States and India as coeval reveal the real anxiety she feels about the United States' role on the global stage. These imperial anxieties find form and expression in Mayo's critique of U.S. women's sexual and cultural looseness. If they are so open, of course they could catch the fever Mayo describes. For her, the consequences of women embracing the ideals of companionate marriage and self-expression are dire: "Drop your standards, girls, and the national standard must trail in the mud. You are the keepers of the race. Our men are what you make them."[64] Understanding gender and nationalism as inextricably intertwined, Mayo compares female sexuality in India and the United States to promote gender containment in both sites. Mayo's model of imperial containment thus forms an interlocking strategy wherein ideas about proper U.S. gender roles are used to police Indian women, and representations of Indian female sexuality are used to police U.S. women. In this way, eugenic reproduction in each national site is articulated against the other, with both feminist and antifeminist consequences.

Sarojini Naidu's North American Tour

If U.S. and British imperialists celebrated *Mother India* as successfully exposing a degenerate culture, Indian nationalists were its most ferocious critics. As Gandhi memorably put it, *Mother India* was "a drain inspector's report,"[65] presenting a selective and interested portrayal of Indian social problems as a way of impugning Indian nationalism. Many books were published in response to *Mother India:* some (such as Lala Lajpat Rai's *Unhappy India* and Dhan Gopal Mukerji's *A Son of Mother India Answers*) refuted Mayo on the basis of facts, while others (*tu quoque* responses) employed her methods to expose U.S. evils.[66] Unsurprisingly, many of these took up the issues of gender roles and sexual practices that had formed the focal point of *Mother*

India. One of the most popular *tu quoque* responses, K. L. Gauba's colorfully titled *Uncle Sham: Tales of a Civilization Run Amok,* devotes no less than seven of eighteen chapters to sex problems in the United States, arguing that "if girls and boys go the way of fornication and adultery, if marriage becomes a fraud, then civilisation must go the way of Sodom and Gommorrah."[67] Despite his stated antagonism to Mayo, Gauba's assessment of companionate marriage is strikingly similar to hers. He likewise finds equal rights for women suspect, arguing that "equal rights [imply] equal [sexual] liberties."[68] While Mayo certainly would not agree with Gauba's picture of licentious and undisciplined U.S. women, the fact remains that their depictions of U.S. women are not as opposed as she would have liked; after all, Gauba based his assessment almost entirely on U.S. sources.

Such male nationalist *tu quoque* responses therefore kept the terms of the *Mother India* debate firmly in place. Even if improper reproductive practices are endemic to the United States instead of India, as Gauba contests, the problem of incorrect national reproduction remains central. In contradistinction from these direct attacks on Mayo's claims and methodology, other Indian nationalist critiques refuted her by returning to and valorizing the figure she takes up in her title. Indeed, Indian nationalist feminism had been laying claims to its inherent modernity through the very figure of Mother India that Mayo so reviled. Indian feminists and social reformers were prominent in the general nationalist outcry against *Mother India,* writing books in response (for instance, Chandravati Lakhanpal's *Mother India Ka Jawab [A Reply to Mother India],* Charulata Devi's *The Fair Sex of India: A Reply to "Mother India,"* and Padmabai Sanjeeva Rao's *Women's Views on Indian Problems*) and both participating in and organizing the many protests against *Mother India.*[69]

Sarojini Naidu launched one of the more prominent Indian feminist responses to *Mother India.* Naidu spoke out forcefully against Mayo's claims, sending a telegram to the famous September 1927 anti-Mayo Calcutta Town Hall meeting stating, "'The mouths of liars rot and perish with their own lies, but the glory of Indian womanhood shines pure and as the morning star.'"[70] This message exemplifies Naidu's approach to *Mother India:* rather than refute Mayo directly or censure U.S. womanhood in response, Naidu lets "the glory of Indian womanhood" speak for itself. Perhaps because of this high-minded approach as well as her prominence as a nationalist and feminist figure,

Gandhi dispatched Naidu on a 1928–29 publicity tour to the United States and Canada in the wake of Mayo's book; in this sense Indian nationalism's most effective response was not in print but through Naidu's very person. Not only did her visibility as a political figure contest Mayo's portrayal of the mass of Indian women as ignorant and abject victims of tradition (the fact that she was the former president of the Indian National Congress is repeatedly highlighted in the press coverage of her visit), her recognizably feminist politics rejected Mayo's claim that Indian women required colonialism to liberate and protect them. Naidu asserted instead that Indian women, like India itself, have always been feminist—the problem was Western colonialists and meddlers like Mayo. Presenting herself as the personification of modern Indian femininity, Naidu thus refuted Mayo's claims without ever directly mentioning her book. Declaring that "India has too beautiful [a] message to offer to the world for any Indian to be disturbed by the finding of a patch of dirt," she opposed *Mother India* by example rather than on its own terms.[71] When asked by a reporter in New York to comment on Mayo, she simply responded, "'Who is she?'"[72]

That Naidu refused to go on the offensive with Mayo is not surprising given her larger aim of increasing sympathy and understanding between the United States and India. Speaking as "the authentic and accredited voice of [her] nation," Naidu's travels were intended both to undo the damage done by Mayo's book and to engender further U.S. sympathy for the Indian nationalist cause.[73] Nonetheless, Naidu could not help but make veiled references to *Mother India* that dismiss it as trivial and sensationalistic, saying that "accounts of child-marriage in India . . . had been exaggerated in America; and some of the stories about India . . . were written by persons who had seen only 'a few gutters and a few drains.'"[74] Naidu's reference to "gutters" and "drains" undoubtedly recalls her mentor Gandhi's description of Mayo's book and likewise calls attention to Mayo's selective view of India. As such, Naidu suggests, Mayo's muckraking can be dismissed as an unimportant "stunt" that seeks only to divert a distractible U.S. public from the real issue at hand: India's freedom.

In order to bring India's lofty message to the U.S. public, Naidu forwards herself as an interpreter between cultures. As she recounts in her Presidential Address to the All-India Women's Conference (AIWC) in Bombay in January 1930:

It was as a woman of this ancient race with its millennia of experience that in my travels last year I looked at the lives of those child countries of Europe and those kindergarten countries of America. They expected me to fit into their notion of what an Indian woman should be a timid woman, a modest woman . . . who had come to learn from them. But Sarojini had come to them as a free woman who stood side by side with my comrade men. . . . Are you a typical Indian woman? Yes, I cried, I am she who carries the brass pot to the water, I am she who gave counsels to kings, I am she who showed forth all renunciation, I am she who went down to hell that her mighty country might rise, I am only the kind of the average Indian Woman. . . . We women hold the courageous *Savitri* as our ideal. We know how *Sita* defied those who entertained suspicion of her ability to keep chastity. We possess the creative energy to legislate for the morals of the world.[75]

Naidu positions India in relation to the United States and the countries of Europe as that of a parent to misguided children, willing to indulge them their fancies about "what an Indian woman should be" but quick to educate and correct them as well. Emphasizing the antiquity of India in order to paint it as the superior of a juvenile United States, Naidu militates against the equation of age with degeneracy that animates so much of Mayo's rhetoric. In Naidu's hands antiquity is linked to "millennia of experience" rather than the oppressive crush of years, thus reversing the idea that India has anything to "learn from" the United States or Europe. This is especially true when it comes to Indian feminism; against U.S. notions of Indian women as "timid" and "modest," Naidu is a "free woman" and "comrade" of Indian men. She uses the particularities of her own subject position to evoke the universal, drawing a direct line from Hindu goddesses Sita and Savitri to herself and referring to the Indian woman's importance within the home as well as in the public world of warfare and politics. Turning the "typical Indian woman" into a kind of superwoman, she both argues for Indian cultural distinctness and superiority and also proposes that this "typical" Indian woman represents a model that U.S. women would do well to follow.

Although Naidu understands the "average Indian woman" as an exemplar for the women of the world, the (mostly admiring) U.S. press coverage she receives emphasizes the cultural specificity of this figure, falling all too often into Orientalist commonplaces about India. Even though Naidu's strategy is to insist that she is simply "the average Indian woman," the U.S. press portrays her as the exception who proves the rule of native patriarchy. As the *New York Times* article announcing her arrival stresses, "Her coming to this country emphasizes the great strides which the women of India have made toward equality and social freedom."[76] The problem of feminism in India is couched in the usual language of "tradition," as is made clear in the subtitle of the article that announces "Sarojini Naidu Will Tell of the Changes That Are Coming over the Lives of Indian Women against the Most Ancient Traditions." The *Chicago Defender* similarly emphasizes "the oppression of custom and caste" and "moth-eaten tradition" that backs Naidu's message of the "new independence" of women.[77] Even though Naidu stresses that feminism *is* a "most ancient tradition" (as her references to Sita and Savitri attest), both articles portray tradition as an atavistic cultural excess, thus using Indian tradition as a foil against which to shore up U.S. national identity. Naidu may represent the modern Indian woman, but in this rendering she is only modern insofar as she is free of tradition, thus her out-of-caste marriage becomes simply one instance of the larger trend of "the breaking of traditions in India."[78] This framing ultimately remains within the terms set by Mayo, in which an (implicitly Hindu) Indian tradition is an antimodern force of degeneration. Although it is a conservative cultural argument in Mayo's hands, in this instance it is used to bolster U.S. feminism by allowing U.S. women to claim the grounds of feminist modernity. The *Defender* article thus ends with an injunction to "present-day women with every advantage and privilege on their side to come out for greater and more vigorous self-expression in the affairs of their communities and countries."[79]

The cultural distinctiveness that Naidu posits as the root of her feminism is here made to undermine it. Nevertheless, in Naidu's hands cultural distinctiveness does not mean that her message is inappropriate for U.S. women; instead she argues that U.S. women have much to learn from an Indian regenerative and eugenic feminism. She makes this clear in her public remarks in the United States, balancing her message of commonality between women with a sense of Indian cultural and feminist superiority. At a Brooklyn reception presided over by W. E. B. Du Bois, Naidu boldly states, "All over the world . . . women are becoming aware for the first time of their common sisterhood and their common destiny."[80] Even within this version of global sisterhood, however, Naidu retains a special place for Indian women, arguing that it is precisely the "spiritual quality within [the Indian] race" that will redeem a "material culture" of the West.[81] Thus Naidu envisions a trajectory of feminist development in which Indian women need to uplift their Western sisters rather than vice versa.

Not surprisingly, Mayo and her supporters were unimpressed by Naidu's visit. Labeling her a "sloppily garbed Negress," they tried to discredit her by accusing her of attempting to cover up the death of a U.S. engineer killed in Bombay during the riots attending the Prince of Wales's 1921 visit to the city.[82] Such claims did not find much ground, however, and Naidu's trip was largely a success, particularly with liberal feminist groups in the United States. Of course, such groups were exactly those targeted by Mayo in essays such as "India," "Companionate 'Marriage,'" and "To The Women of Hindu India," in which she links the allures of India to a dangerous U.S. feminism that distracts women from their more proper reproductive roles within the (white) U.S. home. In making alliances with U.S. feminists, Naidu sidesteps the terms set by Mayo by positing Indian women as role models for their U.S. counterparts. According to her reckoning, U.S. feminists have much to gain, not lose, through their association with India.

Introducing India to the United States is only half her work; Naidu is equally invested in interpreting U.S. culture to an Indian audience. During her time in North America she writes long letters to Gandhi describing her journey, which he in turn publishes in his newspaper, *Young India*. Because Naidu wants to enlist the United States as an ally in the freedom struggle, her view of the country is largely positive, though in general it can be characterized as the attitude of a mother to a clever, if occasionally misguided, child. Commenting that the United States "express[es] the challenge and dream of youth in all its unspent and invincible courage, ambition, power and insolent pride," Naidu balances praise with caution. Even if, as she goes on to say, "it is the birthright and destiny of youth to send up just such a challenge to the old," she nevertheless meets that challenge with both an appreciation of the United States and with a strong sense of what India can teach it.[83] That is, she issues her *own* challenge to the United States to support India's "*self*-deliverance from *every* kind of personal and national, economic, social, intellectual, political and spiritual bondage."[84] Insisting that India needs allies rather than saviors, Naidu once again contests Mayo's portrayal of a helpless India unworthy of self-rule by stressing that India's deliverance will be one of "self-deliverance," just as the United States' was.

Indeed, Naidu exploits the analogy between the American Revolution and India's quest for independence throughout her time in the United States. In a November 1928 New York speech titled "Better Understanding between India of the Old World and America of the New," for example, Naidu announced, "'Like the founders of your Republic . . . the Young India of today has proclaimed to the world a Declaration of Independence."[85] Aligning the United States and India through their struggles against foreign rule, she attempts to disrupt Mayo's appeal to an Anglo-American racial solidarity that would make the United States and Britain imperial partners rather than former colony and colonized.[86] As is typical in such moments, however, Naidu does not simply leave the analogy as such, but instead asserts Indian cultural difference and superiority. Arguing that India's "Declaration of Independence" will be achieved by "evoking its ancient *dharma* of renunciation and *ahimsa*," she suggests that Indian independence will be gained in a uniquely Indian way.[87] Contesting a trajectory in which India's path to independence will simply repeat the one laid out by the United States, she highlights what the "New" can learn from the "Old."

Despite these calls to U.S.–Indian solidarity, Naidu does not cast a blind eye to U.S. inequalities. In her letters to Gandhi she remarks on the plight of both African Americans and Native Americans as dispossessed peoples, suggesting their kinship with colonized Indians. Perhaps because of this message of antiracist and anti-imperialist solidarity, she was well received by the African American press, and in general part of her mission in the United States was to strengthen ties with African American as well as Anglo-American supporters. The affiliations she claims when talking about African Americans, however, reveal that she falls short of truly making common cause with minority groups in the United States. In a letter she writes Gandhi from Cincinnati, Naidu first mentions African Americans within the context of praise for Harriet Beecher Stowe. Calling Stowe "a very noble woman who dedicated her genius to the deliverance of the Negroes from their pitiful bondage," Naidu places all agency into the hands of the white woman liberating those who are helpless to free themselves.[88] Saying "Mine was, like Harriet Beecher Stowe's, also a message of deliverance from bondage" (1), Naidu both compares herself to Stowe and turns the history of African American struggle in the United States into a metaphor for the Indian nationalist movement. This not only obscures their very different histories, it also disrupts a more proper analogy between African Americans and oppressed groups in India. Furthermore, while Naidu's comparison of the struggle for U.S. racial equality and Indian nationalism would seemingly put her in opposition to the United States, her positioning vis-à-vis Stowe aligns her with white reformers. Such an impression is reinforced, moreover, by the contrast she draws between African American "deliverance" and Indian "*self*-deliverance."[89] The context within which she talks of self-deliverance more properly references the American Revolution than it does African American emancipation. Thus, as Anupama Arora argues in a recent article on Naidu's North American travels, "while [Naidu] is an active resisting subject who denounces British oppression and colonialism at every opportunity, she strangely refuses to afford a similar agency to African Americans."[90]

Though sympathetic, Naidu's discussion of Native Americans similarly denies their agency. Whereas in referencing African Americans she aligns herself with Stowe even while metaphorically equating the plight of African Americans and Indians, her stance toward Native Americans is reminiscent of how she views subaltern subjects in India. Native Americans, like Indian subalterns, are atavistic throwbacks to a time in the process of being eclipsed by the onward march of modernity. Naidu's descriptions of Native Americans thereby participate in the same kind of developmentalist nostalgia I discuss in chapter 2, wherein people and practices being rendered obsolete by the project of national development are celebrated for that very obsolescence. Indulging in Romantic portrayals of Native Americans as noble savages, Naidu's nostalgia toward Native Americans reveals a eugenic impulse that contends they have no place in the modernizing nation but must belong to the past.

Naidu's developmental imaginary is apparent in her description of the physical and temporal landscapes Native Americans inhabit. Describing her train trip through the midwestern and western United States, she depicts "the wheat, copper, oil, cattle and cotton countries, [as] a vast area that bears testimony to the triumph of man over nature, of his courage, enterprise, endurance, resource, industry and vision that could coax or compel such rich results in such a short period."[91] This encomium to development stresses the rapid transformation of nature into products to fuel a robust national economy. Naidu's Romantic nostalgia reveals this "triumph" as tenuous, however, as in the next sentence she describes how "the power of man becomes no more than a feather or a ball of thistle puff in the presence of Nature in the Grand Canyon."[92] It is here, at the edges of this developed land where "Nature" threatens to undo the power of "man," that she describes meeting "Red Indian tribes."[93] Assuming a stance of evolutionary superiority in relation to Native Americans and calling them "picturesque and primitive," she uses the trope of the vanishing Indian to suggest, despite her assertion that "Nature" will trump "the power of man," that both Native Americans and "Nature" are passing away.[94]

Once again Naidu charts a complex set of affiliations and disaffiliations with Native Americans, initially stressing a common heritage and saying Native Americans "are more akin to [Indians] than to the foreign Western peoples who have taken away [their] heritage."[95] Here, she would seem to shift into an adversarial position in relation to a United States defined as "foreign Western peoples" robbing an indigenous people's heritage. In the end, however, she uses Native American dispossession as a warning, not as a call to common cause. She quotes "a proud young representative of an Indian tribe" who states, "This country once belonged to me and my people. We are dying out, but *they may kill us, they can never conquer us.*"[96] Agreeing with this statement and affirming, "Who can conquer their spirit?," Naidu seemingly resolves the problem of Native American dispossession by placing it in the past and romanticizing it rather than understanding it as a contemporaneous struggle for sovereignty. Moreover, given the connections she draws between Indians and Native Americans, the implication is that the absence of sovereignty would eventually render Indians moribund as well. Thus the vanishing Indian is mobilized as proof of the urgency of Indian national sovereignty.

Naidu reserves her greatest sympathy, however, for South Asian immigrants, citing how they had moved to the United States to farm, but because of the changes in land and citizenship laws were not allowed to own land or become citizens. She describes the hardships of diasporic South Asians, detailing their "hunger" and "nostalgia" for their homeland.[97] But just as she does with Native Americans and African Americans, she ultimately metaphorizes this suffering as the suffering of the Indian nation, saying, "I have come to the conclusion after all my visits to Africa and America that the status of Indian settlers can *never* be satisfactory anywhere till the status of India is definitely assured among the free nations of the world."[98] The problem is not just that Indian settlers cannot obtain U.S. citizenship, but rather that they cannot be citizens of a sovereign Indian nation. Moreover, U.S. citizenship laws present a barrier to these diasporics' return to India. Musing "I do not suppose that many of them originally came with the intention of making a permanent home in California," Naidu describes how citizenship and land laws have deprived Indian immigrants of the money needed "to return to their own village homes in India."[99] Nonetheless, that India is their "home," no matter how many years these immigrants have been in residence in the United States, is clear to Naidu. She lauds them for their "profound and passionate devotion to their country" (India, not the United States) and offers suggestions to help them maintain a "living link" with "the beating heart of India."[100] In these ways she seems to reject a notion of diasporic affiliations, privileging instead homeland connections.

At the same time, despite her appreciation of these Indian immigrants' devotion to their homeland, Naidu chides these settlers for not settling. Because they always planned on returning to India, she writes, "They drifted on, never bothered about establishing a social tradition or educational record similar to the activities of other immigrant races who became in the real sense *American,* and therefore an integral and acceptable unit of the new nation in the new world."[101] Their diasporic attachment to the homeland renders them unfit for U.S. citizenship—rather than the problem being U.S. citizenship laws, the problem is that they did not attempt to assimilate. For Naidu this is counter to the Aryan roots that South Asian immigrants proclaim in their arguments for citizenship rights—for her to be Aryan means to represent a syncretic culture that can adapt to and assimilate other cultures. Crucially, the inability to "[become] in the real sense *American*" is coded for Naidu as a reproductive lack. She notes, "There are . . . a few Sikh families with darling babies and growing sons and daughters, but all too few, all too few among a community numbering over five thousand people."[102] The cultural sterility of being in exile without adapting to their new environment leads to an inability to adequately reproduce the community. While Naidu forwards reproduction as the means of India's regeneration and ultimate liberation, here the "unfitness" of Indian immigrants to their new environment problematizes reproduction, thus creating a vanishing Indian of another sort. Naidu's reproductive nationalism thereby serves as a model for immigrant communities in the United States, suggesting its fitness within the diaspora. Naidu's diagnosis of cultural and reproductive degeneration resonates with Mayo's even if articulated in sympathy rather than disgust. While for Mayo dysgenic national reproductive practices render a people ineligible for nationhood, for Naidu the lack of national sovereignty leads to the inability to properly reproduce.

Just as Mayo's indictment of Indian reproductive practices travels to reflect back upon the United States, Naidu's eugenic feminism is operative even in the diaspora. Ultimately, both women focus on national reproduction to trouble commonplaces about gender roles; for Mayo this becomes a culturally conservative argument that maintains that if the United States is to continue to advance in a new era of international circulation of goods and bodies, then it must tighten its borders. So too must U.S. women strengthen their moral resolve to withstand the seductions of Indian spirituality on the one hand, and the ideology of the "new woman" on the other. Mayo thus recasts the problem of global markets in terms of sexual contamination in order to argue for an imperial policy of containment both at home and abroad. For Naidu, however, the focus on national reproduction rewrites Indian women as the originators of a nationalist and feminist modernity. In Naidu's response to Mayo in her North American tour she presents herself as *the* model of Indian womanhood—a woman who is both traditional and modern, and who is so inherently feminist that she does not even need to refer to herself as such. In doing so she forms complex affiliations and disaffiliations with U.S. nationalism, nationalist feminism, and minority groups of different kinds. In attempting to align the Indian nationalist struggle with the struggle of oppressed groups within the U.S., however, she ultimately shows a eugenic impulse toward those groups, formulating a kind of reproductive *trans*nationalism that makes reproductively clear, connective affiliations in the diaspora.

In reading the *Mother India* controversy in its U.S. as well as Indian contexts, I suggest that Mayo advocates a strong arm overseas as a means of policing the boundaries of the nation at home. Not only do unfit Indian reproductive practices make them unworthy for nationhood, so too could cultural and sexual promiscuity in the United States undo the U.S. national project. Finally, I focus on Mayo's specific solution to the problem of U.S. imperialism to propose that the relationship she draws among national reproduction, public health, and imperial containment is recapitulated in various forms in the discourse of postwar development. Even though Mayo is concerned with perverse reproductive practices rendering the population moribund (that is, the problem is barrenness rather than fecundity), the threat posed by so-called overpopulation is similarly understood in terms of its ability to derail national development. Thus, I argue, we can trace in *Mother India* a view of the world and of the need for containment that will be rearticulated, albeit differently, in the Cold War strategies of development and population control I turn to in the next chapter.

4 THE VANISHING PEASANT MOTHER

Reimagining Mother India for the 1950s

> It has been a truism to state that in the early decades of planning
> in independent India . . . women were only looked at as components
> of social welfare programmes and not of development. . . . Why was
> this so and how was it that after women's very visible presence and
> participation in the national struggle for freedom . . . women as
> women were so ignored?
>
> —Nirmala Buch, "State Welfare Policy and Women, 1950–1975"

> To many the years after Independence seemed the site of a severe
> setback for feminists. . . . In the fifties and sixties, therefore, there
> was a lull in feminist campaigning.
>
> —Radha Kumar, *The History of Doing*

DESPITE THE FORMAL EQUALITY granted to women by the
Indian Constitution and the continued visibility of elite nationalist
feminists in politics, the decades following Indian independence have
been labeled the "'silent period' of the women's movement."[1] The
mainstream women's organizations (such as the All-India Women's
Conference) became institutionalized into primarily welfarist bureau-
cracies in the service of the Congress government, while more radical
feminists turned their energies to other organizations and causes.[2] This
"lull" is variously attributed to the traumatic aftermath of partition,
disappointment at the dilution of the Hindu Civil Code, and faith in
the new nation to right the wrongs of gender inequality.[3] Given the
somewhat diffuse nature of feminism in the 1950s and 1960s, accounts
of Indian feminism typically pass over these decades, moving swiftly
from independence to the next flashpoint—the 1974 Committee on the

Status of Women in India's groundbreaking report, *Towards Equality*. I return to feminism and figurations of women in 1950s India, however, to suggest that understanding how women figure in Indian modernity in the post-independence era is crucial to the story of eugenic feminism I am telling. If eugenic feminism is partially enacted through a rhetorical logic whereby all women are measured against an ideal eugenic woman and deemed fit or unfit, then the 1950s are vital because it is in this decade that new national mythologies are being forged and new symbolic roles for women imagined. While up to this point I have focused on an elite Indian feminism (as, for instance, embodied in the figure of Sarojini Naidu), in this chapter I argue that in place of the liberated "new woman" at the forefront of feminist modernity the peasant mother suddenly takes center stage as the symbol of the nation. This is not to suggest that the peasant mother is the new figure for nationalist feminism; my point instead is that in the years after independence nationalist feminist energies get co-opted by the state, and thus a new eugenic woman (who is concertedly *not* feminist) is forwarded as the national ideal. Like the subaltern figures in Naidu's poetry, moreover, the peasant mother comes into focus precisely because she is a figure in the process of vanishing away.

In order to tell the story of the post-independence eugenic woman I turn to a variety of seemingly divergent sources. Although the cultural works I survey in the second part of this chapter—Kamala Markandaya's 1954 novel *Nectar in a Sieve* and Mehboob Khan's 1957 film *Mother India*—prominently feature and celebrate peasant mothers working the land, they do so against the backdrop of an Indian developmental modernity that is attempting to render women's agricultural labor obsolete. This connection is not accidental, as these works abet developmental policies by narrating women's removal from the land as part of the heroic march of a masculine national modernity. That is, both *Nectar* and *Mother India* describe women's agricultural labor as belonging to a feudal past that the modernizing nation will destroy. To chart the means by which this eugenic logic works, therefore, I turn to several development planning documents in addition to the cultural texts. The first is a little-known (and almost immediately forgotten) report of the National Planning Committee, *Women's Role in Planned Economy* (WRPE).[4] Written in 1938 by a subcommittee of prominent Indian feminists (including Sarojini Naidu), it stands as the lone feminist planning document of its time. Nonetheless, it contains a eugenic feminist impulse in the way it figures the subaltern women of the nation to be developed. By bifurcating the "Women" of the title into subjects to be developed and those to do the developing, it charts a new relationship between the elites and the masses in the independent nation. Although the radical recommendations of the committee are ignored, this bifurcation of women persists into the first two five-year plans (spanning 1951–61). Looking at how women appear (or, more accurately, do not appear) in the plans, I argue that they predictably reinforce a separate spheres ideology in which women are most visible in their domestic roles within the home.

Next, I turn to the report of the Sub-committee on Population (similarly commissioned by the National Planning Committee in 1938) in order to analyze how both it and the WRPE explicitly promote a eugenic agenda.[5] Although these reports of the National Planning Committee follow an essentially modernization theory view of the relationship between reproduction and economic growth, believing that birth rates would naturally fall as the nation modernizes, they nonetheless recommend eugenic measures to weed the unfit from the national polity. In the first two five-year plans, this agenda is translated into the somewhat more neutral idiom of family planning, in which the family itself becomes an area of development crucial (as opposed to incidental) to development. In each case, the documents focus on national reproduction to the exclusion of women's productive labor, eliding women's agricultural work in particular. Looking at the nexus of agricultural and reproductive policies (two sectors understood to be locked in a "Malthusian race"), I argue that attention to national reproduction is linked to policies that insist women's agricultural labor is a thing of the past: in order to modernize both agriculture and the family, women must move out of the fields and into the home.

Against this policy background, I analyze Kamala Markandaya's novel *Nectar in a Sieve* and Mehboob Khan's film *Mother India*—two popular, contemporaneous representations of peasant mothers—to argue that their romantic celebrations of women working the land are part and parcel of women's invisibility in agricultural policy. If modernizing agriculture requires modernizing women off of the land, then these works narrate that tale as part of the heroic forward movement of national progress. Both texts, moreover, mobilize the constancy of the all-suffering peasant mother to negotiate the competing claims of modernity and tradition on the developing nation, utilizing a discourse of nostalgia and memorialization to conceive of a national future continuous with the past. In doing so they celebrate the very figure that development would destroy: the peasant mother who is represented in these works as a product of feudalism and colonialism. In that sense, the nostalgia of these cultural works is of a piece with the disappearance of women in agriculture in the planning documents. However, both *Mother India* and *Nectar in a Sieve* also assert the continued importance of such peasant women as national reproducers, as each text surely and decisively moves peasant women off of the land and into their domestic and reproductive roles in the home. By showing women's agricultural labor as part of a passing feudal order, they obscure what is in fact a violent outcome of development policy. They also, I suggest, strike a chord in the U.S. developmental imaginary precisely to the extent that they disarm the potentially destabilizing problem of "third world" development by offering India as a vision of the U.S. past.

Nationalist Feminism in the Era of Development

I turn to the story of national development because after the end of World War II and the beginning of formal decolonization Indian nationalism finds its particular form and expression in the developmental state. Despite Gandhi's well-known critique of industrial capitalism, Nehru's faith in industrialization as the most effective way to alleviate Indian poverty and usher in Indian modernity ultimately prevailed as national policy.[6] After independence Nehru's vision was expressed through the adoption of the Five-Year Plan series, beginning with the First Five-Year Plan in 1951. The keystone of the first two plans was rapid industrialization, with agriculture playing a supporting if crucial role.[7] The hope was that land reform would naturally improve food outputs by incentivizing farmers to greater production, thereby turning subsistence farmers into capitalists. Concerns regarding population were also written into both plans, not only giving India the dubious distinction of being the first country to explicitly set out a policy of population limitation, but also pitting population against agriculture in a Malthusian contest. The nationalist logic of the five-year plans divided the nation into a series of problems to be fixed: productivities to be maximized, national subjects to be reformed, populations to be managed.

This "mixed" model of centralized state planning for capitalist development was the economic expression of India's nonaligned political stance. Although India's pursuit of rapid industrialization explicitly naturalized the process of development in the West (and, indeed, modernization theory as an economic policy was developed and advocated by the United States), India received substantial development aid from both the United States and the Soviet Union, and its plan for development combined elements of capitalism and socialism alike. I focus on policies surrounding agriculture and population, however, to highlight the specific influence of the United States on Indian national development. In the first place, the links between Indian and U.S. agriculture are long-standing, initially through agricultural extension programs funded by the U.S. government and modeled after programs pioneered in the United States in the first part of the twentieth century, and then through the so-called Green Revolution.[8] While the Green Revolution proper does not begin until the Third Five-Year Plan (1961–66), the agricultural extension programs begin with the first plan and lay the groundwork for the Green Revolution to come. In the second place, the need to increase agricultural production was dictated, in part, by concerns over India's growing population. As such, post-independence population policies (and aid) were largely derived from a U.S.-led population control regime that was linked to U.S. eugenics movements both ideologically and institutionally.

Against this backdrop, what happens to Indian nationalist feminism in the age of development? I have already noted feminism's "disappearance" in the 1950s, and in charting the ideological stakes of the early years of development in India, I suggest that one of the reasons for this disappearance is the highly gendered nature of development itself. As María Josefina Saldaña-Portillo stresses in her discussion of development as a regime of subjection, development is "masculinist, whether the agent/object of a development strategy is a man or a woman, an adult or a child."[9] Nonetheless, development does not merely render women invisible but instead interpellates them in particular ways, advancing Western gender norms as crucial to becoming modern, and both reinforcing existing structures of patriarchy and superseding traditional practices in which women may have had more rights.

Beginning with Ester Boserup's landmark 1970 *Women's Role in Economic Development*, Women in Development (WID) approaches revealed that gender-blind development had actually worsened women's economic and social positions in developing nations.[10] This deterioration is particularly striking when we turn to the issue of women in agriculture. Despite the fact that during the 1950s and 1960s more than 80 percent of working women in India were laboring on the land in some form, in terms of developmental policy these women were, in Carolyn Sachs's memorable phrase, "invisible farmers."[11] In part, women's deteriorating position in agricultural was due to gender-biased land reform programs undertaken after independence.[12] The newly independent government reinforced colonial practices that overwrote women's rights to land, even in contravention of traditional practices. It wasn't until the Fourth Five-Year Plan (1969–74) that women's agricultural labor was taken into account at all. By this point, however, twenty years of development had done their damage and the position of women in agriculture had worsened, with more women working as agricultural laborers and fewer as cultivators—a shift that reveals that women agricultural laborers were disenfranchised and impoverished by the early decades of development.[13]

At the same time as women's productive labor was rendered virtually invisible by the discourse of development, women's biological reproductive labor was made into an issue of national importance. In the early years of development women figure primarily in their roles as mothers, under the auspices of either programs for population limitation or programs for maternal and infant health. Understanding the burgeoning population as an impediment to national development, the First Five-Year Plan articulated the need to bring the population in line with the requirements of the national economy. The first two five-year plans emphasized providing information and contraception to those who requested it (assuming birth control was only an issue of access), and changing attitudes and behavior through outreach and education. As neither of these approaches proved successful in lowering fertility rates, however, by the middle of the second plan government officials introduced the use of incentives and disincentives and target-oriented sterilization camps. The use of such coercive methods reached its apex during the state of emergency declared by Indira Gandhi in 1975 when, as historian Michael Latham quotes an Indian analyst as saying, "Even the façade of voluntarism was ripped off."[14]

The consequences of women's invisibility in agriculture and hypervisibility in reproductive labor are threefold. First, because women are primarily seen in their reproductive roles they become problems to be managed rather than productivities to be utilized. Second, even when women's agricultural labor *is* visible (as it is in the cultural works I turn to at the end of this chapter), it is pathologized: the story of modernizing agriculture is the story of removing women from the land and installing them within the home. Women's agricultural labor is therefore understood as an exploitative "traditional" practice that the developing nation will happily relegate to the past. Finally, by insisting that women's "modern" place is in the home, it argues for state intervention in the domestic sphere as a means of controlling reproduction for the nation. The symbolic eugenics evident in Naidu's pronouncements become translated into a policy for action.

"Her Own Best Enemy": Women as Subjects and Objects of Development

If feminism disappears in the 1950s in part because of the masculinist project of development, then this problem is compounded by the fact that many mainstream feminists put their faith in development's modernizing project, trusting that the benefits of development would naturally "trickle down" to all national subjects regardless of gender. Believing in a developmental discourse that unproblematically relegates gender problems to the inner sphere of traditional culture, nationalist feminists thought that gender inequalities were relics that would naturally pass away in the onward march of modernity. Although accepting development's regime of subjection would seem to contradict the viewpoint expressed by Naidu's explicit rejection of modernization theory's mimetic model (that is, she argues traditional Indian culture is more modern and feminist than that of the West), this contradiction is resolved through a division between the subjects to be developed and the subjects doing the developing. Whereas Naidu's regenerative eugenic feminism focused on elite reproduction to argue that such nationalist women were the embodiment of Vedic womanhood, subaltern women represent the degeneration of those enlightened ideals in the present. Therefore development turns its gaze to subaltern subjects who must be developed in the name of national progress. The consequence of this shift in focus is that even as bourgeois rights for women are written into the Indian Constitution, working-class women are almost entirely forgotten as productive subjects, targeted instead under the purview of education, maternal and child health, and family planning.

In order to chart the history of how this bifurcation of the subject of women comes into place post-independence, I turn to a pre-independence feminist planning document: the report of the National Planning Committee's Sub-committee on Women, *Women's Role in Planned Economy*. This report was one of twenty-nine commissioned by the National Planning Committee, which was set up in 1938 by then-Congress President Subash Chandra Bose with Jawaharlal Nehru as its chairman. With independence on the horizon (even if nearly a decade away), Bose and Nehru set out to chart the path that India's future development would take. Toward this end, subcommittees took up topics ranging from agriculture to industry to such "human factors" as labor and population.[15] The subcommittees began their work in 1938, but because they were interrupted by World War II their findings were not published until July 1947. The insights from many of these documents (both in terms of facts and figures and in general schemes of planning) would end up in the First Five-Year Plan, but the findings of the Sub-committee on Women were completely ignored.

I look to this singular vision of feminist planning for two reasons. First, it presents us with a different understanding of the relationship between women and the economy than the welfarist view of women that ultimately prevails in the first two five-year plans, which I also briefly survey here. Even though the WRPE reflects a late 1930s moment of feminist possibilities foreclosed after independence, it remains a unique example of what feminist planning would look like. Second, and more important, the WRPE is essential to the story of eugenic feminism I am telling in that it models the relationship between different kinds of female subjects in the incipient nation. The educated, bourgeois "new woman" who was the focus of the nationalist feminist rhetoric I surveyed in my second chapter recedes into the background as the nation casts its modernizing eye on her "underdeveloped" sisters. Although women like Naidu (who, indeed, was one of the drafters of the WRPE) remain at the vanguard of feminist modernity, the implication of her rhetoric—that the subaltern must be developed in service of the nation—now becomes the focus of the nationalist feminist project. The WRPE's radical focus on women as economic subjects dissolves when this document is disregarded, but the interpellation of poor women as subjects of development to be reformed by the nation remains in its wake.[16]

Even though I focus on the ways in which the WRPE parses out the roles of elite and subaltern women within the nation, I do not want to underestimate its revolutionary aspects. In viewing women as economic subjects with vital contributions to make to the national economy, the WRPE is markedly different from the planning documents that would follow. Split into three sections ("Individual Status," "Social Status," and a final section consisting of summary and recommendations), the WRPE attempts to survey the totality of women's lives from their "economic" and "property rights" to "marriage and its problems" and "family life."[17] The WRPE's groundbreaking recommendations bespeak its radical nature. It insists that women be viewed as individual workers rather than solely as members of families, and maintains that economic freedom is essential for women's overall emancipation. It advocates remunerating women for their household work by giving them access to state services such as medical care and crèches, and also proposes that women should have absolute control over a portion of the household income. Last, the report is prescient in the relationship it charts between women and development. While its reliance on modernization theory means that it looks to industrialization and the withering away of traditional culture to solve the problems of gender inequality, by figuring women as economic subjects vital to the national economy it anticipates the efficiency arguments of the Women in Development approaches of the 1970s and beyond. Instead of speaking of women as victims in need of reform or welfare, the WRPE considers women as productive subjects with vital roles to play in the national economy.

Perhaps because of the boldness of its claims, the findings of the report went almost entirely unheeded. Even though Nehru commissioned it and was clearly aware of its contents, none of the insights of the WRPE make it into the First Five-Year Plan. In fact, the WRPE vanished so completely that the otherwise exhaustive 1974 Committee on the Status of Women in India's report, *Towards Equality,* makes no mention of it. The WRPE does not resurface until 1995, when Maitreyi Krishnaraj reprinted the recommendations of the subcommittee in her *Remaking Society for Women: Visions from the Past and Present.*[18] Since then, several scholars have analyzed the WRPE, though for the most part it remains a footnote in the history of women and development.[19] In turning to the WRPE I suggest that the report in some ways contains its own undoing. By trusting that modernization would naturally do away with gender inequality, it subordinates its call for real redistributive measures to the nation's modernizing project. The more radical measures it proposes (like compensating women for their labor in the home) are understood to be logical outcomes of a new social order that will arrive once the nation is fully modernized. In endorsing industrial modernization, moreover, the WRPE ends up making one of the mistakes that would be repeated in WID approaches to follow some thirty-odd years later: its essentially liberal feminist assessment of women's roles leads to a prescription for equality that elides the differential positioning of women in the nation.

At issue here is that even as the WRPE tries to imagine a fundamentally new social order, the focus throughout is on the individual to be developed. Development becomes a matter of individual conversion wherein the subject chooses to free herself from stultifying tradition and step into full-fledged modernity. In keeping with this telos, the final chapter of the report, titled "Propaganda," argues, "We have to create an environment where the will to change can develop. To that end [propaganda] has to build character and a new outlook on life amongst men and women" (194). The report maintains that "superstitions," "customs," and "old traditions" "hamper the advance of women" (194); changing such things, however, requires not just a new "environment," but a change in consciousness ("a new outlook on life").

While this passage focuses on destroying deleterious customs and developing a new consciousness, it also assigns distinct subject positions for these tasks. This too is an essential part of development's regime of subjection, which depends upon a vanguard leadership making the masses ready for development. As suggested by the *we* in the penultimate sentence ("We have to create an environment"), the document is clearly divided between the enlightened, liberated women writing the report (women who are aligned with the state project of planned development) and the subaltern masses to be modernized. This divide is likewise apparent in the introduction of the WRPE, which argues:

> The consciousness of her rights—or rather of her wrongs—has dawned upon women in India in quite recent years. And then, too, it is confined to a microscopic minority who scarcely raise an echo in the national heart when they plead for the Rights of Sex. Woman is herself ignorant, superstitious, hidebound in the chains of superstition mis-called Religion. . . . She is, therefore, still her own best enemy in any campaign against usage that denies her freedom or equality or opportunity to realize the purpose of her being. (19)

The subject of "woman" proliferates here. At once she is abject victim and perpetrator ("her own best enemy"). Curiously, men's part in women's oppression vanishes, displaced onto a "superstition mis-called

Religion" that "ignorant" women believe. At the same time, woman is also the "microscopic minority" conscious of her "rights" and "wrongs." The "microscopic minority" are the drafters of the document, who in addition to Sarojini Naidu include other prominent women of the day (Lakshmibai Rajwade, Vijyalakshmi Pandit, Rameshwari Nehru, and Saraladevi Chaudhuri, to name just a few). Although these Indian feminists—who would be the primary beneficiaries of gender equity measures in post-independence India—were the drafters of this document they were not necessarily the subjects interpellated by it. Instead the "woman" of the title more accurately refers to the masses in need of development by the state.

While most of the findings of the WRPE do not make it into policy, the first two five-year plans similarly reinforce this split between the women doing the developing and those to be developed: between subjects and subalterns.[20] This cleavage is partially enacted through the plans' selective mention of women; in the first plan, women only appear in the sections on education, health, and family planning, and though the second plan does consider women workers, even there it emphasizes welfare measures. In these ways, the plans reinforce an ideology of separate spheres that forwards middle- and upper-class norms as the model for all, primarily viewing women in their roles as mothers.[21] In insisting on seeing women only in their maternal roles, the plans reinforce what Nirmala Buch calls a "middle class bias": in the plans "women were essentially home-makers and sometimes the unfortunate victims who had specific problems which needed help."[22] Development planning therefore does not simply ignore women so much as seek to make over "undeveloped" women in the image of their middle-class sisters. A crucial aspect of this uplift project is teaching rural women a more "modern" relationship to reproduction—instead of having many children to supply necessary labor and provide social security, families should have fewer children and train them to enter the wage labor market. As such, the transformation in the mode of production is linked to the transformation of families, both through what Maria Mies has famously theorized as "housewivification" and through population demography that understands lowering birth rates as essential to economic development.[23] Demographic transition theory may have argued that birth rates would naturally fall as a society modernizes, but by the early 1950s population demographers had decided the reverse logic also pertained: lower birth rates and modernity would follow. As such, it is not that the desire to treat women as abstract workers is betrayed by a retreat into conservative portrayals of women as mothers, but that the reproductive—in terms of producing value, in terms of reproducing the means of production, and in terms of reproducing bodies—is inextricably linked to production.[24]

The Malthusian Race: Population and Agriculture in Indian Planning

Eugenics are an explicit concern in the WRPE and *Population:* both advocate "the control of population," arguing that "from the eugenic point of view the Indian stock is definitely deteriorating for want of proper selection as well as due to poverty, malnutrition, etc. factors which are detrimental to the nation's health."[25] The report at once asserts the primacy of "proper selection" and figures human reproduction as manipulatable as the economy and food supply, implying that all can be resolved through proper government planning. In the five-year plans, however, the overtly eugenic language of the WRPE and *Population* is translated into family planning, with the primary emphasis on family size. Thus the focus on eugenics—which is largely about quality rather than quantity—turns into a numbers game that nonetheless retains the notion of the fitness of some and the unfitness of others for national reproduction. This numbers game, moreover, is intimately linked to agricultural development through a twofold logic: not only are agricultural production and population pitted against each other in a Malthusian race, but modernizing reproductive practices and gender roles are understood to be crucial to modernizing agriculture.

Population takes a view of population as expansive as the one the WRPE takes of women, with five chapters that survey "The Trends of Population," "Planned Food Policy," "Social Reform and Legislature," "Unemployment and Industries," and "Social Welfare and Eugenics." Because most of the general points about eugenics made in the WRPE are simply restatements of the Sub-committee on Population's report (and, indeed, the subcommittees shared members such as Vijayalakshmi Pandit and Rameshwari Nehru), I focus on *Population*'s discussion of eugenics, arguing that even though it utilizes a Malthusian calculus in which an unfit population presents an "excess burden to a society handicapped by food shortage," in general it believes that modernization will prevail.[26] The report thus pits population against agricultural production, attempting to plot a food policy that dictates cultivating more land, improving methods of cultivation, and reforming the laws governing the distribution of farming land. Taking an essentially biopolitical view of the population as an entity requiring regulation, it argues that human population is as available to scientific control and management as farming, contrasting the "plentiful crop of abnormal and anti-social individuals" with the specter of "food shortage[s]" to argue for government intervention in human reproduction and agricultural methods alike.[27]

Population proposes typical eugenic measures to deal with the "plentiful crop" of unfit national subjects, advocating "a programme of *compulsory* segregation and sterilization of the feeble-minded, insane, deformed or other markedly defective person."[28] As this list suggests, the category of "unfit" is rather flexible; what, after all, defines a "markedly defective person"? Not surprisingly, *Population* uses such labels as alibis for other social problems and as a means for asserting gender norms, attesting, for instance, that feeble-minded women have illegitimate children and thus should be sterilized: "The majority of illegitimate children in India are born of mentally deficient mothers; while the greater proportion of prostitutes are mentally inferior and many are definitely feeble-minded."[29] By claiming that only "mentally deficient mothers" would give birth to illegitimate children and/or engage in prostitution, the report utilizes an easily reversible logic—if a woman has an illegitimate child or is involved in prostitution she is feeble minded and should be sterilized.[30]

The label "unfit" applies not just to individuals but to whole swaths of the population: the authors of *Population* evoke the specter of "defective families," saying, "Crime, murder, pauperism, prostitution and illegitimacy is generally the characteristic of the history of the defective families."[31] Although these categories encompass antisocial types of various sorts and attribute their deviancy to a genetic predisposition after the fact, more disturbing is the salutary effect the report attributes to the caste system, where deviancy is seemingly predetermined: "Caste has created the outcastes and contributes to make the problems of eradication of the defective types probably easier than in the West."[32] Because they are already marked as such, "outcastes" can be "eradicated" through a program of "selectively sterilizing the entire group of hereditary defectives."[33] Rather than waiting for "defective" behaviors to express themselves in subsequent generations, caste-based group sterilizations can eliminate "unfit" sectors of the population in the name of the nation's future health. *Population* therefore evokes cultural particularity (as signified by the caste system) as granting India an advantage over the West when it comes to singling out populations for eugenic measures.

Alongside the focus on removing dysgenic sections of the population the report brandishes "race-suicide" rhetoric: the upper classes aren't reproducing enough. Thus *Population* laments, "Throughout India the backward sections are more progressive demologically than the rest of the population," noting that "the general increase of population is more in evidence among the more fertile but less intellectual strata of society."[34] To remedy this problem, *Population* advocates removing barriers to inter/upper-caste marriages, allowing widow remarriage, and eliminating dowry.[35] Using the language of degenerate enervation familiar from Charlotte Perkins Gilman and Katherine Mayo, the report also chides the upper castes for disdaining agricultural labor, saying, "The long accustomed aversion of the upper-caste Hindus to manual labour and their dwindling strength have become serious handicaps."[36] This is not just a neurasthenic argument; because the "lower agricultural castes" are both more skillful in cultivating the land and are having more children (due, in part, to upper-caste adoption of birth control), their "very numbers will in future add to their economic and political advantage."[37] In time, this will lead to "a gradual predominance of the inferior social strata." One is left to wonder, though: if farmers of the "inferior social strata" are better at cultivating the land, then why is their "gradual predominance" a "dysgenic" trend?[38]

One answer to this question is contained within the agricultural reforms proposed by *Population*. In the report the rationalization of farming and reproduction are linked, as both are inevitable outcomes of the thoroughgoing change in life that will be brought about through the process of development. Integrating peasant farmers into developmental modernity therefore follows an essentially economistic logic— give them the means to produce for the market and they will behave like rational economic subjects. *Population* defines the problem:

> At present agriculture is not a business but only a method of living. . . . The hope of improving the standard of earning in industry and agriculture will alone strengthen the movement for a rational life of which population planning would be a part. Though it is true that an agrarian revolution, an industrial revolution, and a regulated population are mutually interconnected

phenomena, it seems that the complete modernization of agriculture and of the outlook of the agriculturist are essential preliminaries to any large scale improvement in the situation regarding population and employment.[39]

Narrated here is the agricultural worker's arrival into full-fledged capitalist modernity. Contrary to the report's argument that agriculture must become a "business" instead of a "method of life," what is being described *is* a new way of life, even if one guided by the exigencies of the market. As such, "the complete modernization of agriculture and of the outlook of the agriculturalist" are equally important. Once farmers become integrated into the capitalist mode of production they will experience a transformation in consciousness and begin to live "rational [lives]." Once they begin to think like rational economic actors they will be able to "regulate" their families and replace uncontrolled, animalistic fecundity with a family matched to available resources (this, then, is one of the ways of reversing the "dysgenic" trend identified earlier). The causal link among these steps is remarkably clear, as modernizing agriculture and agricultural workers "are essential preliminaries" to the problem of population with which the report is explicitly concerned. *Population* thereby utilizes a demographic transition model wherein population growth will naturally be solved through the process of modernization—it may be necessary to rid the nation of the "unfit," but the problem of overpopulation will be solved through the process of development itself.

Although the agriculturalist is not overtly gendered, the previously quoted passage comes from a section on "Rural Unemployment" that is calculated based only on the male population.[40] Agricultural development, therefore, is for men. Even the WRPE, which is devoted to surveying women's productive labor in all of its various manifestations, pays only cursory attention to the agricultural sector. In a section titled "Heavy Industry," the report declares that the problems of women in agriculture "will soon become matters of decreasing importance as the future planned order comes into being."[41] Here, the logic is that because women's agricultural labor is subsumed within reproductive labor in the household and rendered invisible, moving women out of the informal agricultural sector and into wage labor is the key to women's economic independence. Despite the different ideologies that motivate the erasure of women in agriculture in the two reports (in *Population* it is an oversight while the WRPE believes women's economic empowerment will come through their entrance into the wage labor force) the end result is the same: by insisting that women should not be working in agriculture it ignores that one very real way to improve women's lot would be to give them access to land.[42]

I read the eugenic measures proposed by *Population* (measures echoed in a truncated form in the WRPE) against the view of agriculture, and women in agriculture specifically, to point to a crucial difference between these pre-independence reports and what will follow. In the reports the essential concern is with modernization—subscribing to the basic tenets of demographic transition theory, the WRPE and *Population* are optimistic that with modernization birth rates will fall. Following this, the focus of both reports is on differential fertility—the problem is the quality of people rather than the quantity. If population growth overall were the issue, then why would the reports recommend measures to increase reproduction among the upper castes? Just as the WRPE bifurcates the subject of woman between subject and subaltern, the eugenic policies outlined in the WRPE and *Population* aim to increase fertility among the "fit" and curb it among the "unfit," thereby reforming the subaltern reproductive subject. Furthermore, the documents' faith that agriculture will win the Malthusian race rests on a logic in which modernizing agriculture is an "essential preliminary" to rationalizing reproduction.

The explicitly eugenic language of both the WRPE and *Population* is missing in the First Five-Year Plan, replaced instead by allegedly more neutral concerns with family planning and population. In one sense the reason for this is obvious: after the horrors of Nazi eugenics policies come to light, eugenics falls out of fashion. But the concerns about population underlying eugenics do not disappear so much as they are funneled into the neo-Malthusianism of population control. Echoing the consensus created by the 1950 study of the Rockefeller Foundation, *Public Health and Demography in the Far East,* the relation between national demographics and modernization is flipped in the five-year plans. Whereas the late 1930s reports believed population would naturally fall with modernization, the first two five-year plans viewed population as a separate area of development that must be brought under control in order for modernization to succeed. Rather than view population as a positive force—as, for instance, a healthy labor pool—population becomes a detriment, a drain on capital: "While lowering the birth rate may occur as a result of improvements in the standard of living, such improvements are not likely to materialize if there is a concurrent increase of population."[43]

The program for family planning in the First Five-Year Plan is articulated in the chapter titled "Health," where we find the somewhat more emphatic statement that "population control can be achieved only by the reduction of the birth-rate to the extent necessary to stabilize the population at a level consistent with the requirements of national economy."[44] At this point what population control would mean remains inchoate; while it may have been bold to introduce population policies into planning, in general the recommendations of the first plan were fairly cautious. Only 6.5 million rupees were allocated to family planning programs (of which a mere 1.5 million were spent), and in general the emphasis was on education and research.[45] Such principles motivated the world's first population control experiment: the Khanna Study, which ran from 1953 to 1956.[46]

After the caution of the first plan and the failure of the Khanna Study (birth rates in the test villages rose during the course of the study), the Second Five-Year Plan pumped up the resources and rhetoric of population control. It doubled the stated objectives of family planning from four to eight, and while it continued the focus on education and research, its main thrust was setting up family planning clinics.[47] To this end, it established the Central Family Planning Board, increased the number of clinics to 549 in urban and 1,100 in rural areas, and began a publicity campaign of family planning posters and radio ads in different local languages.[48] The second plan also increased family planning funding to 50 million rupees, an almost fivefold rise in the monies spent in the first plan.[49] Despite the creation of a central administrative organization and the increase in funds and outreach, the clinics were understaffed, the personnel were undertrained, and contraceptive supplies were limited. Moreover, although both plans were optimistic that national reproductive subjects would be easily amenable to reform, the fact remained that the economic and cultural value of having a large family was unshaken. In frustration, government officials began turning to sterilization as a more permanent means of population reduction. As Matthew Connelly reports, in 1958 the chief secretary of Madras, R. A. Gopalaswami, introduced an incentive program by paying people 30 rupees for being sterilized, with another 15 rupees for each additional person they convinced to undergo the operation. Inspired by Gopalaswami's innovation, the Central Family Planning Board began to encourage sterilizations by compensating their patients for travel expenses and lost wages, and the age of population control incentives was born.[50]

Population planning may have been growing in importance over the course of the first two plans, but their primary emphasis (particularly of the second plan) was rapid industrialization and large-scale development projects like big dams for water and electricity. Even while Nehru deemed the agricultural sector "the keystone of our planning," the majority of funds went to heavy industry in the public sector.[51] While this priority was pronounced in the first plan it was intensified in the second, with the monies allocated to agriculture declining from 34.6 percent to 17.5 percent.[52] The approach to agriculture in the plans largely centered on restructuring the fabric of rural agricultural life through land and tenancy reform and through agricultural extension programs such as the Community Development Programme (CDP). Instead of technical and scientific inputs into agriculture, "the Community Development Projects became the 'focal centers' of the agricultural strategy."[53]

Featured in the section on community development in the first plan and launched by the Indian government in 1952, the CDP was funded in part by the U.S. government and modeled after U.S. extension programs from the first part of the twentieth century. The CDP took a holistic approach to the problem of agricultural development, at once targeting agricultural practices and trying to improve the health, education, and local governance systems of rural communities. The goal was to revolutionize agricultural practice, thereby increasing productivity and reforming rural peasant farmers. While this appears similar to the approach preached in *Population,* the difference is that instead of merely assuming that modernizing agriculture would modernize the family, the family becomes a direct area of development under the CDP; agricultural reform now involves the bourgeoisification of the family, with its corresponding assumption of a sexual division of labor according to separate spheres.

As Kim Berry argues in "Lakshmi and the Scientific Housewife," the CDP promoted Western gender norms as a crucial component of "progressive" (as opposed to "traditional") agricultural practices. Importantly, these norms had been put in place by the very agricultural extension models the United States was now exporting to India; before their implementation U.S. women had worked as farmers alongside men just like their Indian counterparts. Providing training in capital intensive farming for men and instruction in scientific housewifery for women, the point of such programs was to shift agriculture from a subsistence activity to an enterprise geared toward the market. They focused on turning women from farmers into housewives, arguing that once women were devoted to the scientific management of their homes they would develop a taste for consumer goods and catapult the rural family into capitalist modernity: "If women could be educated to desire a higher material level of living, then they would encourage 'progressive' agricultural practices and simultaneously expand markets for numerous commodities."[54] This model was successful in the United States, and the U.S. and Indian governments hoped it would work in India as well. Although the nuclear family (with its concomitant gendered division of labor) was mainly alien to rural communities in which multigenerational joint family households were more often the norm, turning women into "Lakshmi[s] of the household" was nevertheless appealing.[55] As the evocation of Lakshmi (the Hindu goddess of prosperity and beauty) suggests, moreover, in its Indian incarnation the extension program emphasized Hindu and urban middle-class Indian values, thereby resonating both with Western gender roles and with patriarchal Hindu nationalist recastings of women's role in the nation.

Part of turning rural Indian women into housewives involved charging them with proper reproduction for the nation. Though family planning was a responsibility supposedly shared by men and women alike, the sexual division of labor dictated by the CDP in fact made it one of women's primary tasks. Indeed, the family planning emphasis in training for women distinguished the CDP from its U.S. predecessor. As Berry explains, "The U.S.-based home economics curriculum . . . [was] altered to fit Indian homemaking contexts. Programmes for improved mud-brick stoves ('chullas') replaced programmes for electric and gas ranges . . . [and] more attention was paid to immunisation campaigns and to family planning."[56] As housewives, moreover, the CDP attempted to shape rural women into the purveyors (as a 1959 Government of India report states) "of national priorities in the direction of: more food production, more family planning, more small savings."[57] In her biological and cultural reproductive roles, the rural peasant woman was charged with inculcating the aims of the nation within her family, a role we will see narrated on the level of national myth making in the cultural works to which I now turn.

Nostalgia and the Vanishing Peasant Mother

In accordance with its "Janus-faced" nature, national temporality vac-illates between utopia and nostalgia. If the planning documents repre-sent the nation's utopian temporality by imagining a future in which the problems of the present will be resolved, then the works I consider next—Kamala Markandaya's *Nectar in a Sieve* and Mehboob Khan's *Mother India*—operate primarily in a nostalgic mode. They do so in the name of the future, however, by proposing a new Mother India forged for the now independent nation: the peasant mother. In place of the liberated Vedic woman who formed a response to colonial percep-tions of Indian women as oppressed or downtrodden, this new Mother India is the symbol for a traditional past at once being preserved and superseded. While Sarojini Naidu's feminism reversed the typical gen-dering of national temporality by figuring women as progressive agents struggling against male atavism, in this post-independence moment women are once again made to "[embody] nationalism's conservative principle of continuity."[58] Nonetheless, the figure of the peasant mother that now comes into focus is not merely static; even as she represents a "conservative principle of continuity," she is not so much unchanging as in the process of passing away. Using the concept of developmental-ist nostalgia I elaborated in relation to Naidu's poetry in chapter 2, I suggest that national development memorializes what it destroys, cre-ating a long-suffering peasant Mother India whose very travails attest to the necessity of a masculinist developmental modernity. In this, the past-ness of the peasant mother makes her the necessary midwife of the developing nation's future.

Mehboob Khan's wildly popular 1957 film, *Mother India,* firmly es-tablishes the peasant mother as a figure for nation. The peasant mother is also the central character of Markandaya's 1954 novel, *Nectar in a Sieve,* which was not nearly as influential in India as was *Mother India* but became the definitive version of India consumed in the United States in the 1950s. Although these works share several key narrative elements, *Mother India* was not based on *Nectar,* deriving inspiration instead from two Pearl Buck novels—*The Good Earth* and *The Mother.* Regardless, the similarities between the two works are striking: both feature strong women struggling against man and nature to feed their families, both contain romantic depictions of the land, and both critique money-lending and tenant farming practices. In con-

sidering why the valorized peasant mother captures the popular imagination both at home and abroad, I suggest that each work's ambivalent
endorsement of modernity—in *Nectar* in the realm of Western medicine and in *Mother India* in the realm of industrialized agriculture—
allows for the transformation of the peasant mother from a drudge
laboring in the fields to a "Lakshmi of the household." This transformation, moreover, abets the policy documents' erasure of women in
agriculture by narrating women's agricultural labor as part of a feudal
past to be overcome. That is, each work ascribes to a modernization
theory view of the transformation of the mode of production and the
family; in contrast to the five-year plans, which take up the family as a
separate area of development, these works narrate the process of demographic transition as entirely inevitable. To cite just one example, the
mothers in both give birth to multiple children (four in one case, seven
in the other), but in each case only one son remains at the end, and he is
the appropriate, masculinist, subject of development. The implication
is that even if the body of the narrative is the mother's story, the son's
will constitute the next chapter.

Nectar tells the tale of Rukmani, a woman married to a tenant farmer,
Nathan, at the age of twelve. Although this marriage is beneath her (she
is educated and comes from a somewhat more prosperous family), it is
a happy one, and the novel tells of their joys and hardships. It charts
their struggles against the forces of nature (flood, drought, and failed
crops), Rukmani's difficulty conceiving sons, the changes wrought upon
the village by the coming of a tannery, Rukmani and Nathan's removal
from their land and journey to the city, where Nathan dies, and finally,
Rukmani's return to the village. One of the central relationships in the
novel is between Rukmani and an English doctor named Kensington
(Kenny). Markandaya uses their relationship to juxtapose "Eastern"
and "Western" worldviews, with Kenny protesting Rukmani's placid
acceptance of her plight and Rukmani pitying Kenny's disconnection
from his family and culture. Despite the novel's critique of industrialization and modernization, as launched through Rukmani's views
of the tannery and the changes it brings to village life, however, the
novel ultimately sanctions modernity through the relationship between
Kenny and Rukmani. In particular, it authorizes the regimes of modern
medicine and hygiene that Kenny represents.

Like *Nectar*, Mehboob Khan's self-proclaimed "unforgettable epic
of our country," *Mother India* tells the story of a heroic, all-suffering

mother. It begins with Radha's marriage to Shamu, a marriage Shamu's mother pays for by mortgaging land to the usurious money lender Sukhilala. This loan initiates a cycle of poverty from which the family cannot escape. The film recounts Radha's various travails: the birth of their four sons, Shamu's injury and desertion of his family, a flood that devastates the village and kills her two youngest sons, Sukhilala's proposition of Radha and her refusal to submit to his advances. It culminates in Radha shooting her favorite son, Birju, after he kills Sukhilala and attempts to abduct Sukhilala's daughter, Rupa, on her wedding day; Radha makes the ultimate sacrifice in order to uphold the larger social order.[59] The changing nature of agricultural labor is one of the central themes of *Mother India;* though it, like *Nectar,* revels in scenes of peasant farming, it ultimately endorses modernity, though here in the form of Nehruvian development.

If *Nectar* was somewhat ambivalently received by Indian critics, *Mother India's* success is unequivocal. *Mother India* was so popular, in fact, that "it was in continuous circulation for over three decades [from its release in 1957 to the mid-1990s]—not only in India but all across the globe."[60] Part of the spectacular success of Mehboob Khan's film derives from the rich symbolic tradition of "Mother India" upon which it builds; in fact, it was in part an attempt to transpose Mayo's use of the Mother India icon into a more seemly nationalist idiom. Because Mayo's *Mother India* still loomed large in the public imagination, the Ministry of Foreign Affairs requested to review the film's script, concerned that it was somehow related to Mayo's 1927 book. Mehboob Khan put such fears to rest, stating, "Not only are the two incompatible but totally different and indeed opposite. . . . We have intentionally called our film 'Mother India,' as a challenge to this book, in an attempt to evict from the minds of the people the scurrilous work that is Miss Mayo's book."[61] His success is clear; Mayo's book is largely forgotten in the popular imagination, replaced by the iconic image of Nargis as Mother India. In effect, as Mrinalini Sinha argues, "The controversy [surrounding Mayo's *Mother India*] was now enfolded within a nationalist narrative that affirmed a seemingly unbroken tradition of Mother India: the identification of the Indian woman as mother with the nation at large."[62]

Although I agree with Sinha's assessment that Mehboob Khan's film attempted to "[affirm] a seemingly unbroken tradition," I focus upon the discontinuities between nationalist representations of Mother

India in the colonial period and post-independence. If in colonial times Mother India was represented as the victim of foreign rule, she is now beset by the problems of a moribund social order that the modernizing nation is in the process of obliterating. But where the struggle against colonialism required a revolutionary figure—such as Shanti in Chatterjee's *Anandamath*—in her postcolonial guise Mother India is necessarily conservative. She may be aligned with the modernizing state, but her purpose is to endow it with the authority of tradition. In *Mother India* Radha's son Birju is the revolutionary—he kills Sukhilala and burns his records, thus obliterating all of the villagers' debts. Rather than endorse this heroic if lawless act, however, the movie condemns it by coupling it with a gendered act of brutality. After killing Sukhilala, Birju attempts to abduct his daughter Rupa. This abduction links transgressions against the law with transgressions against women. In order to defend "the honor of the whole village," Radha shoots Birju as a necessary sacrifice to the larger order of the postcolonial state, in which individuals cannot take the law into their own hands. Moreover she does this in the name of women's honor—even though Birju is attempting to redeem Radha's honor by doing to Rupa what Sukhilala attempted to do to Radha, such lawless acts are not to be sanctioned. By ending the cycle of violence, however, Radha becomes an obsolescent figure for feudal suffering that has passed.

The obsolescence of the peasant mother is reinforced by the nostalgic structuring of each work. Both *Nectar* and *Mother India* are told as flashbacks: the hardships and joys described in the bodies of the narratives are temporally separated from a present tense marked by triumphant modernity. In the opening lines of *Nectar* nostalgia is expressed as Rukmani's longing for her dead husband, Nathan: "Sometimes at night I think that my husband is with me again, coming gently through the mists. . . . Then morning comes . . . and he softly departs."[63] In this wavering vision of her former life, the dream lover cannot be uncoupled from the farmer-husband; in embodying Rukmani's past, Nathan necessarily represents a way of life and a mode of production that has vanished and is only visible "through the mists" of time.

There follows a series of displacements as the present comes into focus. Rukmani continues, "In the distance when it is a fine day and my sight is not too dim, I can see the building where my son works. He and Kenny, the young and the old. A large building, spruce and white; not only money has built it but men's hope and pity, as I know who have seen it grow brick by brick and year by year" (3). Nathan has been replaced by Kenny, the English doctor, who serves as the benevolent symbol of Western modernity. Instead of farming, Kenny and Selvam (Rukmani's son) build the "spruce and white" hospital that "grow[s] brick by brick and year by year" in the place of crops. Certainly, the novel registers ambivalence toward the processes of industrialization and modernization; indeed, at some level it adheres to a Romantic nostalgic belief that industrialization has ruined a more graceful way of life, as suggested by the title's reference to the Coleridge poem "Work without Hope" ("work without hope draws nectar in a sieve, and hope without an object cannot live").[64] Nevertheless, the first way in which we encounter Western modernity is through the positive association of the hospital and the healing power of medicine. Moreover, despite the nostalgia that infuses Rukmani's remembrance of Nathan and their past, it is firmly past, as is Rukmani herself, as the dimness of her vision in the present implies. From this moment onward the novel cycles backward and describes the various travails of Rukmani and Nathan, but I call attention to this framing not only to point out that it endorses modernity in the form of the hospital, but also to say that it destabilizes and contains the threat contained by the premodern moments.

Mother India similarly unfolds through a series of flashbacks. The opening shot of actress Nargis as Radha—"Mother India"—shows her as an old woman holding a lump of earth to her face, which is the same color as the clay. Lest we miss the symbolism of Radha as Mother Earth, the background music sings, "All our life Mother-Earth we will sing in your praise. And each time we are born, we will be born into your lap."[65] As the shot pans out we see the field being plowed by a tractor colored the same faded red as Radha's sari. The red tractor also echoes one of the most iconic images of the film: Radha in her red sari pulling a plow. The opening sequence continues in a documentary style, lovingly showing images of high-tension wires, automobiles, large-scale farming equipment, a bridge and a dam: the equipment of national development. This opening section is separate from the rest of the film not just in time but in style, as it mimics documentary and newsreel footage. As Vijay Mishra argues in his 2001 *Bollywood Cinema: Temples of Desire,* the opening of the film is therefore "meant to direct the spectators' view to the profilmic India of 1957, ten years after independence. In this respect some degree of documentary (and even ethnographic) framing of the film is part of its conscious design."[66] This opening sequence is a paean to large development projects, particularly in the repeated and loving shots of the bridge and dam. The irony here is that while the first two plans emphasized infrastructural projects such as the construction of large dams (specifically the Bhakra Nangal, Damodar Valley, and Hirakud dams), relatively fewer resources were spent on technical and scientific inputs into farming. Thus the mechanization of farming that the film depicts is more on the level of wish fulfillment than of achieved reality.

The next scene shows Radha being approached by the men of the village, clad in Gandhi caps that identify them with the National Congress Party. They ask her to inaugurate a canal that has reached the village. Though she demurs, they insist and finally convince her by saying, "You are our mother, mother to the entire village! If you don't agree we will not start anything!" In the following scene, the men try to garland her at the inauguration. After her initial protests she relents, and in smelling the garland she is transported backward through time to her wedding day; the movie then unfolds from this point. Thus the beginning of the film shows the title character in an important symbolic role at the same time that the labor she does throughout the movie (that is, farming with her bare hands and body) has been taken over by machines. She is still important—as the men say, she must inaugurate the canal—but her status derives from her cultural reproductive role as "mother of the whole village."

Both of these works, then, initially figure the peasant mother in terms of a nostalgic evocation of a way of life that has passed. It is important to note, however, that although *Nectar* and *Mother India* are nostalgic—in each case the protagonist actively longs for the past—neither romanticizes that past. Indeed, it is marked by various forms of suffering: hunger, illness, suffering against the ravages of nature, suffering against the depredations of usurious money lenders and exploitative tenant farming practices. Nonetheless, as the national past it is to be lovingly remembered and memorialized not just for the joys but also for the travails that make the modern present more meaningful. The very survival of the nation depends upon the preservation of an abjected past in the present in the form of cultural memory.

I turn again to the concept of a developmentalist nostalgia that I developed in chapter 2 to suggest that the past being destroyed must be preserved on the level of national myth making. Given her mobility and deep resonances with the cultural nationalism of the colonial period,

Mother India is the perfect figure to signify national distinctiveness in the face of national change. But I do not mean to suggest that the post-independence Mother India serves as a simple reinstantiation of the divide between the inner and outer spheres of nationalism that Partha Chatterjee famously proposed. Instead I argue that the very structure of nostalgia in which this figure is embedded means that she is not constant but fading away. In this she has much in common with what Marilyn Ivy has termed in the context of modern Japan the "vanishing": "something passing away, gone but not quite, suspended between presence and absence, located at a point that both is and is not here in the repetitive process of *absenting*. . . . Practices and discourses now situated on the edge of presence (yet continuously repositioned at the core of the national-cultural imaginary) live out partial destinies of spectacular recovery."[67] The "vanishing" thus evokes an ambivalent longing for an authentic past that is nonetheless never a desire to make that past return. As such, in both texts the peasant mothers are celebrated precisely because the way of life they represent has become obsolete—hence their introduction within a framing narrative that assures readers and viewers that the struggles contained in the body of the narrative are those of the "bad old days" and are only relevant to the present day insofar as they present a point of contrast. And who better to represent continuity through change than the ever-mobile figure of Mother India, who in this latest incarnation is a symbol for the difficulties the nation has overcome?

Although the nostalgia I've identified in *Mother India* and *Nectar in a Sieve* does not erase past suffering (indeed, bygone misery is a necessary counterpoint to the nationalist present), what *is* erased is the violence of developmental modernity. After all, the process by which women were displaced from the land, even if portrayed heroically in *Mother India,* was far from innocent. As Brigette Schulze argues in "The Cinematic 'Discovery of India': Mehboob's Re-Invention of the Nation in *Mother India*," the film "is neither in touch with the reality of the largely economic, social and political exploitation of Indian women, nor does it sympathize in any way with the real plights of peasants. On the contrary, *Mother India* serves to obscure real lives, and that is exactly how modern national myths work."[68] Similarly, while modern medicine is understood to be wholly benevolent in *Nectar,* the story, as we've already seen, is far more complicated. In fact, one of the crucial ways in which Western medicine is shown to be positive in the novel—

the mysterious reproductive technology that allows Rukmani to bear six sons—is a revisionist take on Western intervention into Indian reproduction. After all, when the international population establishment turned its attention to India in the 1950s it emphasized population control over all else, a fact that angered many in the target population. As Connelly reports, during the Khanna study "some [villagers] grew deeply resentful, noting that those who found it hard to conceive children received no help with *their* family planning."[69]

Modernizing Reproduction

If one of the stories that *Nectar in a Sieve* and *Mother India* tell is that of female peasant farmers becoming "Lakshmis of the household," then the protagonists are ultimately prized for the cultural and biological reproductive work they perform; they are at once important as symbolic "mothers of the village" and for the sons they bear and turn into proper national subjects. Nonetheless, biological reproduction and maternity is incredibly fraught in each work. In *Nectar,* Rukmani requires Western medicine to cure her infertility, while in *Mother India,* Radha is most properly "mother of the village" when she kills her wayward son.

I turn first to *Nectar,* because its treatment of reproduction is one of its more puzzling aspects. Though Rukmani has a daughter, Irawaddy, early on in her marriage to Nathan, six long years pass when she is unable to conceive. But then she meets Kenny, who attends her mother as she is dying, and he offers to treat her infertility. Rukmani initially refuses his help: "I slunk away, frightened of I know not what. I placed even more faith in the charm my mother had given me. . . . Nothing happened. At last I went again to him, begging him to do what he could. He did not even remind me of the past" (20). Her religious "faith," aligned here with the "past," is an ineffective strategy for future reproduction; instead she requires the intervention of Western medicine. The nature of the reproductive technology Kenny employs is not explained, but it succeeds and Rukmani is soon pregnant with the first of six sons. Although Kenny understands the sheer number of sons she bears to be an abuse of his help (he refers to them as her "excesses"), without this technology she would not have had Selvam, the modern masculine national subject we are left with at the end of the novel (32). Importantly, however, even such "excesses" are understood to belong to a prior era in which the very harshness of life means that although

Rukmani gives birth to seven children, only two remain at the end: her daughter Ira and her son Selvam. Thus in some ways *Nectar* narrates the changing values around reproduction. Rukmani may have needed to give birth to six sons in order to be left with one (two of the others die and three leave in search of economic opportunity elsewhere), but the implication is that in the future such excessive reproduction would be unnecessary because the conditions that require it would be ameliorated.

Moreover, Rukmani's need for Kenny's help is complicated by its representation throughout the novel as a betrayal on the level of adultery. When Kenny meets Nathan for the first time Rukmani worries that her secret will be revealed, thinking, "My heart quailed . . . for fear [Kenny] should betray me, yet no betrayal, since how could he guess my husband did not know I had gone to him for treatment? Why had I, stupidest of women, not told him?" (33). The secrecy surrounding her infertility treatments suggests at once her shame and Nathan's potential disapproval, implying that Kenny's intervention into the reproductive sphere is somehow inappropriate and scandalous. This is supported by the fact that the rest of the village suspects the relationship between Kenny and Rukmani is illicit. Ironically, this rumor is spread by Rukmani's neighbor and rival, Kunthi, who has had two sons by Nathan unbeknownst to Rukmani. Rukmani forgives Nathan's adultery, but she never tells him of going to Kenny for treatment, saying, "Because I have deceived you and cannot deny all [Kunthi] proclaims, you may believe the more" (82). The adulterous implication of Rukmani's use of Western reproductive technology suggests that the national man of the future (as represented by Selvam) is in some ways the hybrid subject of miscegenation. Returning to the series of displacements at the beginning of *Nectar,* if Kenny replaces Nathan, then Kenny is Selvam's surrogate father. Thus the inference of a sexual liaison between Kenny and Rukmani is the somewhat vulgar expression of the fact that Kenny is, in a sense, the progenitor of her sons.

The ambivalent implications of Western medical incursions into the procreative sphere come to fruition in the case of her daughter Ira, whose husband abandons her because she is infertile. Rukmani once more turns to Kenny, hoping that if he can resolve Ira's infertility her husband will take her back. Again she keeps Kenny's assistance a secret from Nathan, remarking that she is "sure Nathan would not like his daughter going to a white man, a foreigner" (59). Ira's husband does not take her back, and the sad result of Kenny's help is the birth of an albino child conceived when Ira turns to prostitution to feed the family. Here, the fruit of medical technology gone wrong is the pathologically white child who signifies the consequences of dysgenic reproduction. Resonating with the statements from *Population* I quoted earlier about illegitimate children and feeble-minded mothers, despite the fact that we, the readers, understand that Ira was forced into prostitution to help her family out of starvation (originally she turns to prostitution to buy food for her younger brother, Kuti, who nonetheless dies of starvation), her albino child Sacrabani seems a form of retribution for her acts, a visible expression of the dysgenic means of his conception. The causes for her fall are threefold: the first is Kenny's help; the second is the drought and the widespread starvation it causes; the third is the tannery, because without it Ira would not have any customers. Although the novel does not particularly moralize about Ira's choice, painting her instead as a victim, the fact of Sacrabani's being born an albino is confounding to say the least. It's at once a critique of industrialization (through the father's association with the tannery), colonialism (Sacrabani's white skin could not be a more direct metaphor), and Ira's loss of virtue. It is never, however, a critique of Kenny and the help that he offers. That is why in the end the novel's Romantic nostalgia does not extend to the realm of Western medicine and hygiene. Rukmani may long for the past, but she nonetheless watches with pride and hope as the hospital replaces the crops.

In *Mother India* Radha easily bears four sons without medical intervention, but in the end only her eldest son, Ramu, remains. Like Selvam, Ramu becomes a model of the new man for the new era; he is one of the Gandhi-capped men who approach Radha at the beginning of the film. Responsible and sober, he is married and with a son of his own. Once again, in *Mother India* reproductive loss is understood to respond to the changing exigencies of the times; at the beginning of the film Shamu tells Radha he wants four sons, one for each corner of the plow. She obliges, but two of her sons (the last born after Shamu deserts her) die in the flood, and when Birju transgresses the very law and order for which Ramu stands, Radha must kill him. Still, her remaining son more than adequately meets the needs of the present and the future. After all, instead of four sons pulling a plow we have the tractors of the opening sequence, and instead of floods or droughts, we have the dam and the irrigation canals controlling the unruly forces of nature.

In contrast to their portrayals of these modern sons, both works represent the husbands as ineffectual and emasculated. This is most obvious in the case of Shamu in *Mother India*. Frustrated by Sukhilala's usury and unable to pay off the principal of the original loan (because Sukhilala takes three-fourths of the crop as interest on the loan, nothing remains to pay against the principal of 500 rupees), he and Radha try to break some fallow land on the idea that Sukhilala will have no rights to any produce from it. As they struggle to rid the land of debris they come across a large boulder; in the process of moving it first one of the oxen dies, and then Shamu slips and crushes his arms, which need to be amputated. Frustrated and unmanned, he leaves the family rather than be a burden to them. Significantly, he leaves but is not killed; in this way Radha retains the potent status of wife and mother rather than being reduced to an inauspicious widow. Shamu's emasculation, however, signifies doubly: at once referencing the emasculation of colonialism, in which Indians are separated from their land, and critiquing a feudal and usurious money lending system as signified by Sukhilala, both of which must be overthrown by the nation's forward march.

Similarly, Nathan in *Nectar* is portrayed as a good farmer—"In all these matters he had no master" (63)—but this skill is no longer relevant. While he "[looked] forward to the day when [his sons] would join him in working the land" (52), none of them does. Three of the sons argue that because Nathan does not own the land, to work it is to keep in place an exploitative relationship, and Selvam abandons farming to become Kenny's assistant, declaring, "The land has no liking for me and I have no time for it" (109). Finally, when the land Nathan and Rukmani have farmed their whole lives is sold to the tannery and they go to the city to search for one of their sons, Nathan fails to help them survive. Not only is he sickly, but he lacks Rukmani's toughness and cannot fight for food: "Many a time my husband stood aside unable to face the fray: if I had not reproached him his distaste of the whole procedure would have led him to starvation" (165). Thus Nathan, like Shamu, is unfit to struggle for his own survival and the survival of his family; as emasculated men they have no place in a future India. As we have seen, this is a popular nationalist trope. But whereas in a work like *Anandamath* women are responsible for remasculinizing effeminate and degenerate men not simply through their presence but also through their actions, here remasculinization is not possible. The only way to reinvigorate the nation is through birthing sons who will be the nation's future leaders. Rukmani and Radha may be the foci of their respective narratives, both of which nostalgically evoke a difficult past, but *Mother India*'s sons are the true guardians of the present and future. Thus Selvam in *Nectar*, the one son who remains, is aligned with a modernizing regime of medicine just as the Gandhi-capped Ramu of *Mother India* is aligned with the modernizing nation.

The difficult past that each text evokes is one in which women are deeply connected to the land both through the labor they perform and through their symbolic association with "Mother Earth," as established in the opening shot of *Mother India,* and as reinforced throughout *Nectar* by Rukmani's natural instinct for, and love of, the land. Although both works figure the relationship to the land as a reproductive one, in both cases it requires modern intervention. Rukmani needs Western reproductive technology, and Radha is most properly mother earth when the work of tilling the soil and growing crops is taken over by modern machinery. That these crops are nourished by the very blood of her failed maternity suggests the sacrifices she must make as "earth mother"—after she shoots Birju the screen dissolves into the present moment of the canal's inauguration. As the sluicegate opens, the water flows red to mirror Birju's blood. It then turns clear as it flows out to the fields, and the film's final moments are loving long shots of productive, nourished fields. Improper reproduction (as signified by Birju's attempted abduction of Rupa) must be thwarted in order to assure the continued productivity of the nation, even if that strangely means a *negation* of maternity itself, as it does at the end of the film.

Therefore, even as *Mother India* is Radha's story, she remains the handmaiden of development rather than its subject. Through the framing narrative that contrasts the travails of Radha with an optimistic era suitably shorn of colonial and feudal oppression (in place of the *panchayat* who side with Sukhilala because they are afraid of bringing the police to the village we have the men in the Gandhi caps—the new patriarchs of the village are firmly aligned with the national government), the film neatly sidesteps many of the realities of 1950s India. Most tellingly, the film's endorsement of big development projects outlined in the first two five-year plans ignores the ways in which the harsh conditions of peasant life were not ameliorated by independence. At the same time, the valorization of the obsolescent peasant mother obscured the fact that despite the promises of the constitution the social status of women had not improved.[70]

The film's celebration of big dams also attests to the selective nature of its vision. Its opening sequences visually affirm Nehru's famous statement, made in 1954 at the inauguration of the Bhakra-Nangal, that "dams are the temples of modern India."[71] At the same time, the film disavows the real victims of development that Nehru referenced six years earlier when speaking to villagers displaced by the Hirakud Dam: "If you are to suffer, you should suffer in the interest of the country."[72] "Suffering for the country" in the film is translated into a personal, familial drama safely contained by the past. Past sufferers, moreover, are now the recipients of the largesse of development; there is no trace of those displaced by the dam. Nargis herself supported this salutary view of the nation's modernizing drive; in a 1980 parliamentary debate as a member of the Upper House of Indian Parliament (the *Rayja Sabha*) she criticized Bengali filmmaker Satyajit Ray's films for propagating a negative image of India abroad by depicting Indian poverty rather than Indian modernity. When asked in an interview to define modern India she replied simply, "Dams."[73] For Nargis, modern India and poverty are mutually exclusive, a view that ignores the reality of poverty and hardship created by the mechanisms of modern development, as the ongoing struggle over the Sardar Sarovar Dam in the Narmada River Valley attests.

Domesticating India in the U.S. Developmental Imaginary

While Mehboob Khan's film erased Mayo's *Mother India* from the Indian landscape, Markandaya's novel forged a new vision of India in the United States; no longer a "world menace" to be quarantined, India now appears infinitely available to domestication through technologies of modernization. Mehboob Khan's and Marakandaya's (by turns romantic and harrowing) visions of village India strike a chord in the U.S. developmental imaginary precisely to the extent that they disarm the potentially destabilizing problem of "third world" development by offering India as a vision of the United States' past. Both works therefore entail a reimagining of strategies of containment; in place of Mayo's prescription for protecting national and cultural boundaries through immigration restriction on the one hand and a conservative gender politics on the other, development becomes a means of containing communism by positioning the United States as both the model for, and benefactor of, postcolonial development. If, as a *New York Times* review of *Nectar* submits, the novel poses the problem of "ignorance, ignorance of everything that might have helped . . . birth control, hygiene, modern agriculture," then these are problems the United States is uniquely poised to resolve.[74]

As Michael Latham argues in his 2011 history of U.S.-led modernization projects in the postcolonial world, *The Right Kind of Revolution,* the United States turned to development in the postwar period for several crucial reasons. First, development promised to transform societies from traditional to modern, and in doing so contain communism by promoting democracy (that U.S. interventions in postcolonial countries often resulted in the installation of brutal dictatorships is a point that Latham explores in depth). Second, as attested to by President Harry Truman's 1949 inaugural address, known as the "Point Four" speech and widely viewed as inaugurating the age of development, development in this early moment emphasized "making the benefits of [U.S.] scientific advances and industrial progress available for the improvement and growth of underdeveloped areas."[75] In this early articulation (which, notably, came from a U.S. president), development was conceived as the transfer of technical knowledge from the developed to the underdeveloped world, with the linked goals of promoting democracy, creating markets, and "stir[ring] the peoples of the world into triumphant action, not only against their human oppressor, but also against their ancient enemies—hungry, misery, and despair."[76] Aligning the struggle against the "human oppressor[s]" of imperialism and communism with the more "ancient enemies" of deprivation, the United States suggested that both could be resolved through the technology and democracy the United States had on offer. Perhaps even more significantly, as Gilbert Rist notes in his 1996 *The History of Development,* the Point Four speech uses the appellation *underdeveloped* for the first time to identify vast swathes of the world. In doing so, it creates the world as a continuum—instead of being viewed in terms of opposites, the world was now organized in stages, some underdeveloped, some developed, but at base fundamentally the same.

If development was a vital U.S. Cold War strategy in general, then India's geographic location, growing population, and status as the world's largest democracy rendered it particularly important to what historian Andrew Rotter calls the "new great game" between the United States and

Soviet Union.[77] As Senator John F. Kennedy declared, "No thoughtful citizen can fail to see our stake in the survival of the free government of India. . . . India . . . stands as the only effective competitor to China for the faith and following of the millions of uncommitted and restless people."[78] India's nonalignment presented a problem, however; though from Nehru's point of view nonalignment was just that—a refusal to become a pawn in U.S.–Soviet Cold War politics—to the United States it looked like veiled support for communism. Thus the United States hoped that modernization and development would "channel the non-aligned and nationalist aspirations in [India, Egypt and Ghana] in more clearly pro-Western directions."[79]

Despite a commitment to modernization, Nehru (like Gamal Abdel Nasser and Kwame Nkrumah) was steadfast in his nonaligned stance. At stake was the vision of modernity itself; although U.S. proponents of development defined modernity as synonymous with Americanization, this view did not prevail in the postcolonial world. Both in terms of methodology and ideology, postcolonial nations wanted to chart their own paths. Nonaligned leaders skipped stages on the road to modernization, and (more troubling from the U.S. perspective) turned to the Soviet Union for development aid and as a model for accelerating modernization. Because of India's continued commitment to nonalignment, the United States used development aid to India as one arm of a two-part strategy in South Asia, with military bases in Pakistan and economic development in India intended to stabilize the region. For these reasons, despite the humanitarian rhetoric of the Point Four speech, "economic assistance to India was more a matter of national security than national sentiment."[80]

Even so, Markandaya's widely popular *Nectar in a Sieve* (and, to a lesser extent, *Mother India*) rewrote the discourse of modernization in the language of sentiment, thus ameliorating the lingering impact of Mayo's *Mother India* and charting a new context for the relationship between the United States and India. Despite the thirty years that had elapsed since the publication of Mayo's text, its sensational account of India still held sway in the United States, as Harold Isaacs reports in his 1958 study of U.S. opinions on India and China, *Scratches on the Mind*. In contrast to Mayo's portrayal of India as the abject and threatening other, Markandaya and Mehboob Khan helped to humanize Indian strife through their sympathetic portrayals of Indian peasant life. In this, Pearl Buck's *The Good Earth* is an important antecedent. Upon reading Markandaya's novel, John Day Company editor Richard Walsh (who also happened to be Pearl Buck's husband) remarked that "we feel strongly enough about this novel of peasant life in India to think it possible that it may arouse in America something of interest in the ordinary people of India that *The Good Earth* did for China."[81] As Walsh implies, the appeal of *Nectar* (like *The Good Earth*) derives from its ability to present "ordinary" Indian peasant life in a way that the U.S. public could embrace. Thus Colleen Lye's insight regarding *The Good Earth* holds true for *Nectar* as well; it was "valued by its contemporary reader for both its putative empirical fidelity and the universal truths it purportedly revealed."[82] As Chris Vials further suggests, this claim to universalism comes at the cost of erasing meaningful cultural differences.[83] Although this erasure made *Nectar* so successful, the retention of meaningful cultural difference (specifically in terms of its formal characteristics and in the guise of its explicit nationalism) may explain why *Mother India* was not a commercial success in the United States. Although *Mother India* was also based on both Buck's novel and the 1937 MGM film version of *The Good Earth*, it failed to resonate in the U.S. imagination in the same way it did in India and in other parts of the colonial and postcolonial world.

If part of *Nectar*'s appeal was its "putative empirical fidelity," then it is not surprising that U.S. readers judged it on the basis of its authenticity. In fact, the contemporary reviews stress that Markandaya's book was "acquired by strenuous investigation" over the course of six years, which yielded her the "intimate knowledge of peasant life" that she so ably translates to her U.S. readers.[84] Such reviews move from statements of Markandaya's authority to point out a dissonance in her own subject position—she is not Rukmani, but a "Brahmin" woman, living in London and writing under a pseudonym. It is only through Markandaya's artistry that we can know the India she describes; as one reviewer puts it, "That Rukmani could write her story so well, with such limpid beauty and such touching understatement, is not to be believed." Markandaya's blend of authority and artistry, however, "makes Rukmani intelligible to our alien minds."[85] In India, however, *Nectar* was contested precisely on the terms of "authority," with many critics cataloguing what they saw as inaccuracies in Markandaya's portrayal of rural India.[86] In both the United States and India, then, the book's success rested on its ability to seamlessly represent Indian peasant life, making the stakes more ethnographic than literary. In contrast to this focus on cultural specificity, Markandaya herself stressed the humanist reading, arguing, "Your peasant is Everyman. . . . The fundamental mistake is to think that a peasant thinks differently from you."[87] In her own estimation, the story is less about India than it is about the human spirit. Reinforcing her humanist reading is the lack of specificity she assigns to her village—she provides few linguistic or caste markers.

Nonetheless, Markandaya's novel was celebrated in the United States for its humanizing portrayal of the hitherto unknown "reality" of Indian peasant life. As one *New York Times* reviewer asserted, "The absolute poverty in which most Indian villagers are condemned to live is a grim and pathetic statistical fact to most Americans. In 'Nectar in a Sieve' that poverty is dramatized with such skill and restrained power that its cruel reality becomes for a brief time part of one's own experience."[88] Perhaps because of this pedagogical ability to turn "statistical fact" into "one's own experience," *Nectar in a Sieve* was named a 1955 Notable Book by the American Library Association and was also a dual selection of the Book of the Month club that same year. In contrast, *Mother India* was not as popularly received in the United States. Although it was nominated for an Academy Award for Best Foreign Language Film in 1958, and lost to Fellini's *The Nights of Cabiria* by only one vote, it failed at the box office when Columbia Pictures released it in July 1959.[89] Condensed to ninety-two minutes and retitled *A Handful of Grain,* it was for the most part received as too foreign to appeal; as Irene Thirer wrote in the *New York Post, Mother India* "might be difficult for average movie fans to appreciate completely."[90] In contrast to *Nectar*'s middlebrow attraction for "most Americans," *Mother India* eludes the "average movie fan."

Christina Klein's concept of "Cold War Orientalism" offers one explanation for why *Nectar* held so much more appeal for U.S. audiences than *Mother India.* Although in Said's classic formulation Orientalism, as a way of managing and controlling the Orient, was concerned with establishing a hierarchy based on the absolute differences between the East and West, for Klein U.S. cultural texts of the Cold War period partake in an Orientalism of a different sort—one that stresses affiliation over difference. Looking at middlebrow sentimental texts like Rodgers and Hammerstein's *The King and I,* Klein demonstrates how such works serve a crucial pedagogical function for U.S. imaginings of Asia, suggesting that "middlebrow intellectuals and Washington policymakers produced a sentimental discourse of integration that imagined the forging of bonds between Asians and Americans both at home and abroad."[91] This new form of Orientalism arose due to the novel nature of a U.S. neoimperialism that claimed to be predicated on a belief in the fundamental similarities between peoples despite differences in culture—that is, within the developmental imaginary some may be "developed" and some "underdeveloped," but they are essentially the same. Although Klein does not explicitly discuss *Nectar in a Sieve* (and in general India is subordinated to the Far East in this study), it is fruitful to take up *Nectar* in this context, particularly given its middlebrow credentials as a Book of the Month club selection. In this, the very humanism of *Nectar* makes it amenable to what Klein calls a "literature of commitment"—instead of stressing the differences between the Indian characters and the American readers, the characters' reality becomes "for a brief time part of one's own experience," as noted by the *New York Times* reviewer cited earlier.[92]

In contrast, the U.S. reception of *Mother India* (in its guise as *A Handful of Grain*) repeatedly calls attention to its foreignness. The somewhat baffled *New York Times* review of *A Handful of Grain* critiques the film on this basis, calling it an "unorthodox import—rather typical for the home country, we understand."[93] What makes it both unorthodox and typical is its very otherness: unorthodox for the U.S. context and typical for its own. While acknowledging the film's various appeals (noting Nargis's masterful performance and describing the musical sequences as "rang[ing] from charming to spectacular"), the review concludes that *A Handful of Grain* is "different, to say the least." Unable to ground himself in the world of the film (or, to put it another way, to make the world of the film "part of [his] own experience"), the reviewer gamely tries to place it in the U.S. context. He compares the rural setting of movie to the U.S. frontier, saying that *A Handful of Grain* contained "enough violence to flatten Buffalo Bill, horse included."[94] Transplanting the movie to the U.S. frontier and comparing it to a Western, the review unsuccessfully attempts to domesticate it, suggesting that the violence of subcontinental Indians metaphorically "flattens" the spectacle of U.S. frontier masculinity as represented by Buffalo Bill. Unlike the humanism of *Nectar,* such comparisons ultimately point to the distance between cultures.

In thinking through the different ways in which these works were received in the United States, I submit that at stake is the very reality of the India being represented—one that is amenable to U.S.-led modernization, or one that insists on retaining its national difference. While both texts present a rural past that might resonate with U.S. audiences, viewers must also contend with the future each imagines. Returning to Nargis's critique of Satyajit Ray in the interview I discussed earlier, the thrust of her protest is that "films like *Pather Panchali* became so popular abroad . . . because people there want to see India in an abject condition. That is the image they have of our country and a film that confirms that image *seems to them authentic.*"[95] Although Ray's films conform to preexisting Western expectations and thus "seem authentic," Nargis claims that Ray's films do "not represent poverty in its true form."[96] Here, Nargis's criticisms align with those of an Indian government official who suggested Ray rewrite the ending of *Pather Panchali* "to represent what would be the shape of the Village Community in the present age with the provision of land reforms, of the Community Development Projects, the National Extension Schemes."[97] For both Nargis and this government official, the "true form" of poverty is one amenable to resolution by government intervention. This "true" representation is ultimately a nationalist one, not only placing faith in the nation to right the ills of poverty but also concerning itself with the image of India in the international realm. Projecting the nation as modern means viewing the present through the promise of the future—"to represent what would be the shape of the Village Community," as the government official puts it. Nargis complains that the image of poverty Ray depicts is untrue because it represents India as underdeveloped rather than proving that India possesses the ways and means of development: or, in her formulation, "dams."

The contested ground, then, is the very version of modernity each work projects. I bring up the Nargis–Ray debate in relation to my discussion of *Nectar in a Sieve* and *Mother India* because it reveals the importance of projections of national modernity on the international stage. Both *Nectar* and *Mother India* may narrate the transition from a feudal agricultural past to modernity, but whereas *Nectar*'s more ambivalent embrace of modernity through the guise of Western medicine does not present a threat (indeed, it is a modernity bestowed via Kenny, and little mention is made of Indian nationalism), the Indian nationalist context of Mehboob Khan's "unforgettable epic of our country" is startling insofar as it presents a modernity that retains the very cultural difference that modernization theory would wish to destroy.

Thus the explicitly nationalist text of *Mother India* is overwritten by more than just the change in title to A *Handful of Grain*. Although the original title both draws upon the rich cultural and nationalist symbolization of Mother India and wrests it from Mayo's perversion, *A Handful of Grain* neither challenges Mayo's conception of Mother India nor the idea of Indian poverty.[98] In reclaiming the image of Mother India for India, it reveals how the figure of the "goddess in the household," a Victorian ideal transplanted to rural U.S. families and exported to India, is made over into a specifically Indian nationalist figure. As such, the humanism of *Nectar* makes it suitable for U.S. audiences, while *Mother India* had a greater appeal in the colonial and postcolonial world because of its retention of a nationalist version of modernity registered as inspirational.

In thus charting the story of Indian women as represented in the 1950s I have confronted the standard narrative that "little happens in Indian feminism" in that decade to suggest that instead there occur a series of displacements and replacements that begin with the utopian vision of the WRPE. By bifurcating the feminist subject between the elite and the subaltern and empowering one with the role of developing the other out of existence, the WRPE creates the conditions for the visibility and eventual disappearance of the subaltern mother. Therefore, while the revaluation of the peasant mother I take up in these works would seem to recuperate the figure of the subaltern lost in Sarojini Naidu's feminism, the opposite is true. The peasant mother is once again revered for her obsolescence: she comes sharply into view only because she is to disappear.

5 SEVERED LIMBS, SEVERED LEGACIES

Indira Gandhi's Emergency and the Problem
of Subalternity

ON AUGUST 15, 1975, just a little less than two months after her declaration of a state of Emergency, Indira Gandhi gave an Independence Day address at the Red Fort in Delhi. In it, she outlined a new vision for democracy and independence for the postcolonial nation, arguing, "Independence does not merely mean a Government by Indians. It means that the Government should be capable of taking independent decisions courageously."[1] Her assertion of governmental independence at once resonates with the event (after all, she is speaking on the twenty-eighth anniversary of Indian independence) and describes a model of government curiously divorced from the people it claims to represent. Insofar as Gandhi references the relationship between the government and the people, it is as a paternalistic (or, as we will see, a *maternal*istic) one, claiming that "independence . . . offers us an opportunity to do our duty."[2] This duty is defined as "lift[ing] the people who had remained oppressed for centuries" in an effort to uplift the nation as a whole.[3] In making this assertion Gandhi claims to be speaking and acting for the people in the same moment as she is disavowing democracy, a stance implied in the ambiguity of the sentence "Independence does not merely mean a government by Indians." This sentence, aside from establishing the division between the people and the government, claims the government is acting in the people's best interests—interests the people themselves may not be trusted to know.[4]

What for Indira Gandhi is an issue of representing the "people who had remained oppressed for centuries" (even while suspending the basic rights of democracy) is for her cousin, author Nayantara Sahgal, a specifically literary problem of representing subaltern agency and suffering. In her 1993 essay, "Some Thoughts on the Puzzle of Identity,"

Sahgal poses the conundrum of national representation, asking, "But who, really, are 'we'? At one end of the spectrum is a majority who still cannot write and have yet to write their experience. So present writing may well be an elite rehearsal for the more representative performance yet to come once these Indians—which means most Indians—can express themselves directly."[5] In recognizing that much Indian writing is simply an "elite rehearsal" in which a privileged few speak their own experiences at the expense of an underprivileged majority, Sahgal addresses the very issue of representation that Indira Gandhi would seem to eschew. Her confidence that there will come a time for a more "representative performance" when "most Indians" "can express themselves directly," however, thrusts us squarely into debates about the possibilities and impossibilities of subaltern speech acts.

Leaving behind the heady decade of nation building I surveyed in the previous chapter, in this final chapter I turn to the moment of that nationalism's unraveling: Indira Gandhi's period of Emergency rule (1975–77). In doing so I focus on the problem of subalternity that has implicitly animated *Eugenic Feminism*. Each chapter of this book has taken up different moments in U.S. and Indian nationalism, focusing at once on U.S. imperial anxieties about (and developmental management of) Indian others at home and abroad, and on Indian articulations of its own nationalist modernity in relation to its others. Throughout, I have concentrated on the imbrication of feminism and nationalism, suggesting that the concomitant management of reproduction and gender is central to these nationalist, and nationalist imperialist, projects. Underwriting all of this has been a concern for the ways in which subaltern subjects have been rendered dysgenic and thus unfit for national futurity. In taking up the Emergency in this final chapter, I examine how subalternity is mobilized as a critique of the nation-state in a postnational moment, looking first to Indira Gandhi's populist rhetoric and self-positioning as Mother India, and next to Nayantara Sahgal's critique of the Emergency in her 1985 novel, *Rich Like Us*.

I ended the previous chapter with a discussion of the circulation of the Indian peasant mother in the United States, suggesting that this reimagined Mother India was a figure of the moment both at home and abroad because she had been transformed by the imperatives of development. By revolutionizing agricultural practices through modernizing gender relations, developmental modernity renders the peasant mother iconic precisely as an obsolescent subject of development. In this sense, what the policy documents and cultural texts I surveyed in chapter 4 demonstrate is the narration of the subaltern protagonist from under-developed to developed. Perhaps most significantly, this movement is less a question of individual development than it is about replacing the peasant mother with her modern son (thus the displacement of Rukmani by Selvam and Radha by Ramu). Following the logic of these cultural texts and development documents, with proper national management and resources feminized subaltern suffering would simply cease to exist. Therefore while chapter 4 identified how the split between subjects to be developed and those to do the developing created the new visibility of the obsolescent subaltern subject, in this final chapter I consider how the persistence of subaltern subjects is used to critique a nation gone wrong. That is, the continued existence of dysgenic subalterns becomes emblematic of the failures of the postcolonial nation-state.

In exploring this problem I first consider the theoretical implications of speaking the subaltern as a means of critiquing the state. I then look to how Indira Gandhi becomes a new Mother India for a new era. Detailing her rise to power and the history of the Emergency, I examine the contradictions inherent in her repressive population policies and self-fashioning as the nation mother. In harnessing a populist politics that allows her to position herself as both representative and savior of the nation's poor, Gandhi uses the symbolic resonances of Mother India to disavow the very abuses she perpetuates in Mother India's name. I turn next to Nayantara Sahgal's critique of the Emergency in her 1985 novel, *Rich Like Us*. Contesting the claims to progress and modernity that Gandhi espouses, Sahgal argues that Gandhi represents an anti-modern return to feudalism. By way of corrective Sahgal forwards the liberated feminist subject as national redeemer, in a move reminiscent of Sarojini Naidu's feminism that I discussed in chapter 2. What is at stake, therefore, for both politician and writer is the very nature of national modernity and the place (or the absence) of the subaltern within it.

Speaking the Subaltern

Throughout *Eugenic Feminism* I have used the term *subaltern* in the sense it was originally conceived by the Subaltern Studies Group: that is, as an identity constructed in distinction from variously construed "elites."[6] In taking up the problem of subalternity and the Emergency, however, I turn to Gayatri Spivak's theorization of subalternity as an illegible space altogether outside of representation in her paradigm-shifting 1983 essay, "Can the Subaltern Speak?" I do so first to consider the representational politics involved in Indira Gandhi's violent appropriation of subaltern subjects (subjects, it must be noted, who bore the brunt of her repressive policies during the Emergency). Second, I take up Sahgal's critique of Gandhi to suggest the ways in which her admirable project nonetheless remains within the representational bind of instrumentalizing the subaltern. Let me be clear; in thinking through the ways in which representations of subaltern subjects are troubled by both Indira Gandhi and Nayantara Sahgal I do not mean to suggest that they are in any way equivalent. I do argue, however, that tracing the problematics of representation in each is necessary to avoid instrumentalizing the subaltern, no matter to what political end that instrumentalization occurs.

In "Can the Subaltern Speak?," Spivak's critique of the intellectual's desire to speak the subaltern proceeds on two counts. She first takes up a conversation between Gilles Deleuze and Michel Foucault, arguing that in their desire to render subaltern speech transparent, they represent subalterns as "undeceived" and thus capable of self-representation. In doing so, moreover, Spivak argues that despite their "much-publicized critique of the sovereign subject" they "actually [inaugurate] a Subject."[7] Second, she intervenes into the work of the South Asian Subaltern Studies Group to argue that their much more careful conceptualization of the subaltern nevertheless reveals a positivistic desire for subaltern agency. She does not wholly reject this project, but she does introduce the problem of gender, arguing, "If, in the contest of colonial production, the subaltern has no history and cannot speak, the subaltern as female is even more deeply in shadow."[8]

In her discussion of the conversation between Deleuze and Foucault, Spivak elaborates the distinction, via Marx, between representation as political representation *(vertreten)* and representation as re-presentation *(darstellen)*—the difference between "proxy" and "portrait."[9] In making this distinction Spivak takes up Foucault's assertion that "'the masses know perfectly well, clearly . . . they know far better than [the intellectual] and they certainly say it very well'" to argue that this portrayal of the masses as the "unduped" reveals a slippage between representation as *vertreten* and as *darstellen*.[10] This slippage presents us with two problems. The first is that by saying subalterns can represent themselves, the intellectual is abdicating the responsibility of representation. The second is that such celebrations of an accessible subaltern consciousness elide the manner in which subaltern voices and bodies are instrumentalized by the intellectual—as Spivak puts it, "The ventriloquism of the speaking subaltern is the left intellectual's stock-in-trade."[11] Furthermore, through this ventriloquism the "left intellectual" positions himself as the sovereign subject who can transparently represent the subaltern. In the name of "speaking-for" *(vertreten),* he ignores the way in which his re-presentation is actually "speaking as" *(darstellen);* thus the intellectual disappears in the face of the reality the subaltern supposedly represents.

The project of the Subaltern Studies historians is rather different, particularly in its recognition that, as an "identity-in-differential" there is not an actual subaltern to retrieve and then make speak. As Spivak puts it, "There is no unrepresentable subaltern subject that can know and speak itself" (40). Where the Subaltern Studies Group accords with Foucault and Deleuze, however, is in the belief that there is a "pure form of [subaltern] consciousness" (40), whether retrievable or not. The further problem, however, is that "within the effaced itinerary of the subaltern subject, the track of sexual difference is doubly effaced" (41). That is, even if it were possible to discern the traces of male subaltern agency and or subjectivity (and that these are distinct is one of the important critiques Spivak makes in the essay), there is no place for the gendered subaltern within such a conceptual framework.

One of the reasons I use Spivak's formulation of the problem of subaltern representation in relation to Indira Gandhi's political speeches and Nayantara Sahgal's fictional critique of Gandhi is to chart the different kinds of slippages apparent in their differently configured claims to represent the subaltern. In the first place, how is Gandhi's prerogative to "speak for" the people complicated and enabled by her tropological reliance on the figure of Mother India to "speak as" the people? In the second place, how does Sahgal's "empty" portrayal of subalterns (as we will see, the reader is never given access to the interiorities of the subaltern subjects that populate her text, which I read as an attempt to *not* "speak as" the subaltern) result in an abdication of "speaking for"?

"Indira Is India, India Is Indira"

If the previous chapter surveyed the refiguration of Mother India from Katherine Mayo's abject and pathologically reproductive mother to the peasant mother continuous with the fertile land she represents, then in this chapter Mother India is made to live once again in the person of

Indira Gandhi. Although Gandhi herself borrowed from the vocabulary established by Mehboob Khan's film—a linkage made all the more powerful by her self-positioning through her populist politics as a champion of the nation's rural poor—in her critic's eyes she was the castrating, annihilating mother (this, for instance, is Salman Rushdie's famous rendering of the Widow in his 1981 *Midnight's Children*).[12] I argue it is important to read Indira Gandhi against the longer history of Mother India for what these different iterations of Mother India tell us about the durability and mobility of the links between nation and reproduction in both the feminist and antifeminist nationalist imaginaries.

As Jawaharlal Nehru's daughter Indira Gandhi had been involved in politics her whole life, but she narrated her formal entrance into politics as a somewhat reluctant one, saying she "didn't think that [she] was cut out for that type of work."[13] Nonetheless, she was appointed to the Congress Working Committee in 1955, was active in the 1957 general election, and was elected president of the Congress Party in 1959. She also served as her father's hostess during his tenure as prime minster (from 1947 to 1964), a job she disliked, saying she "was simply terrified of the so-called social duties . . . 'socializing' and small talk and that sort of thing."[14] When Nehru died in 1964, and Lal Bahadur Shastri became the prime minister, he appointed Indira Gandhi minister of information and broadcasting. With Shastri's death only two years later, the Congress Party machinery supported her in a contest against Morarji Desai for prime minister, largely because they thought she would be more tractable. She led the Congress to victory in the 1967 general election, though with fewer votes and seats than the party had ever garnered before. There followed, in 1969, a split in the Congress, and Indira Gandhi dissolved the parliament, thus delinking parliamentary elections from local ones. Her party was expected to lose the popular vote in 1971, but she won, largely because of her populist campaign.[15]

As Akhil Gupta explains in *Postcolonial Developments,* the typical narrative of Indira Gandhi's turn to populism locates it as a response to the food crisis of 1966–67, a crisis "precipitated by two disastrous monsoons, a war with Pakistan, and an unsuccessful devaluation" of the rupee.[16] The year 1967 also marked the beginning of the Green Revolution, which raised agricultural output but also increased inequalities.[17] Nevertheless, the focus on agriculture boosted the impression that Indira Gandhi was taking rural concerns seriously and fighting for the rural poor against an urban elite. Gandhi's political style also fostered this image; in the 1971 campaign Gandhi broke the tradition of having the party locals canvass for her and took her message of fighting "on behalf of the poor against vested interests" directly to the people.[18] This, combined with her surprisingly popular 1969 nationalization of the country's largest banks, led to her victory in 1971 behind her slogan *"Giribi hatao"* ("Abolish poverty"). By brandishing populist politics, Gandhi turned the failure of the nation-state to improve the lives of the rural poor into a rallying cry, appointing herself the poor's representative and champion. Although, as Gupta argues, Indira Gandhi's populism has most often been viewed as a cynical rhetorical ploy, its consequences were much farther reaching, in fact laying the groundwork for a different orientation to development. In place of the assumption that growth would naturally lead to equity, Gandhi instituted welfare as a separate strategy operating alongside growth. At the same time, as Vijay Prashad argues in *The Darker Nations,* Gandhi's policies in this era were the first step toward ending Nehruvian state socialism and beginning the process of economic liberalization; in place of real redistributive justice along socialist lines Gandhi turned to welfarist handouts.[19] I explore this process in more depth in the epilogue.

Despite Indira Gandhi's initial popularity, allegations of corruption and unease with her autocratic style led to increasing dissent. At the same time, the global oil crisis and the depletion of resources due to the 1971 war against Pakistan (India interceded on the side of East Pakistan in the struggle that ultimately led to the establishment of Bangladesh) led to growing food insecurity and unrest. With the high court ruling that invalidated the 1971 election results because of various irregularities, protests from opposition parties increased. To silence them Indira Gandhi declared a state of Emergency on June 26, 1975. The Emergency suspended the constitution and allowed Gandhi to rule by decree, imprison opposition leaders, and censor the press. It would remain in place until January 1977 when Gandhi surprised onlookers by calling for new elections; her government was ousted from power by the coalition Janata Party led by Morarji Desai. The Emergency formally ended on March 23, 1977.

The official discourse of the Emergency, as Emma Tarlo parses it in her powerful ethnography of the impact of the Emergency on a "resettlement colony" in Delhi, painted it as a necessary measure to keep the country safe from foreign and domestic enemies who would stunt the nation's progress.[20] Indeed, developmental progress was both the justification for and the modus operandi of the Emergency, as spelled out in Gandhi's Twenty-Point Programme and her son Sanjay Gandhi's Five-Point Programme. As Vijay Prashad points out in *The Darker Nations,* the economic policies outlined in Gandhi's Twenty-Point Programme matched point by point recommendations issued by the World Bank.[21] Furthermore, as is well known both through exposés after the Emergency and through fictional accounts such as Rushdie's *Midnight's Children* and Rohinton Mistry's *A Fine Balance,* the emphasis on population control (one of Sanjay Gandhi's five points) and city beautification led to violent slum clearance and forced sterilizations policies.

If the slogan "Indira is India, India is Indira" was meant to cover over these excesses by naturalizing Indira Gandhi as continuous with the nation (the slogan was coined during the Emergency by Dev Kant Barooah, who was the Indian president at the time), the groundwork of the identification of Indira Gandhi with Mother India had already been established.[22] As Sumathi Ramaswamy demonstrates in *The Goddess and the Nation,* her fascinating history of Indian pictorial and cartographic imaginations of Mother India throughout the twentieth century, while in her early years in politics Indira Gandhi was normally rendered in a photorealist style, her successful conduct of the 1971 war transformed her into the Hindu goddess Durga in artists' imaginations and canvases. The image of Indira Gandhi as Durga is repeated in the controversial triptych created at the onset of the Emergency by prominent modernist painter M. F. Husain, with "Indira as India in Danger and Indira as the Savior-of-the-Nation."[23] In the second panel of the triptych Indira Gandhi's body is made to represent the map of India, in this case as a depiction of "Mother India in distress."[24] As Ramaswamy demonstrates throughout *The Goddess and the Nation,* Husain is borrowing on the long tradition of connecting nationalist figures with the map of India. At the same time, "in associating Indira with India and the map of India Husain was not alone, as we know from verbal rhetoric as well as from other contemporary images" that also portrayed Gandhi in relation to or as the map of India.[25] What is significant about the cartographic Indira Gandhi, however, particularly in contrast to the ways in which nationalist men had been rendered in relationships to maps, is that "as a woman [Gandhi] could pass for Mother India in a manner that they obviously could not, hence the potency of her occupation of Indian cartographic space."[26]

In "passing for Mother India" Gandhi not only evokes the long-standing nationalist symbol, she also calls up Nargis's specific portrayal of Mother India in Mehboob Khan's film. Not coincidentally, Husain based his portrait of Indira Gandhi on Nargis in her iconic Mother India role.[27] Sunil Dutt (the actor who played Birju and married Nargis shortly after they completed shooting *Mother India*) also drew upon this association in his 1985 election poster. In it Indira Gandhi's figure fills the map of India, with the words "Mother India Needs You" in bold white letters above it. Hers is the dominant image, with a much smaller picture of Dutt in the lower right-hand corner of the poster above the words "Vote Sunil Dutt Congress (I) Candidate."[28] Part of the poignancy of the image derives from Indira Gandhi's assassination just one year earlier in 1984 and Nargis's death from pancreatic cancer in 1981; with death the transformation of Indira Gandhi into an icon is complete.

The link between Indira Gandhi and Mehboob Khan's specific rendering of Mother India is crucial, moreover, because of the particular model for female agency and leadership that Nargis as Radha represents. As Rajeswari Sunder Rajan argues in her discussion of Gandhi in *Real and Imagined Women,* this model asserts that

> the acceptable face of leadership is service; it denies power, stresses sacrifice, and positions the hierarchy of public duty and private affections to give primacy to the first. There was no need for Indira Gandhi to draw conscious attention to the parallels—the mythic resources of such symbolic transformation already existed. Subaltern peasant and elite leader are united by class-transcendent patriotism and motherhood.[29]

In pointing to this union between "subaltern peasant and elite leader," Sunder Rajan highlights the problem of speaking for the people with which I began this chapter, suggesting that if Indira Gandhi and the subaltern peasant are one, then she automatically knows and is acting in their best interests.

Even if, as Sunder Rajan notes, such conscious attention was not needed, Gandhi consistently drew upon these resonances in her own political self-fashioning. As early as 1967 she was presenting herself as Mother India, declaring to a village audience, "Your burdens are relatively light because your families are limited and viable. But my burden is manifold because crores of my family members are poverty-stricken and I have to look after them."[30] Gandhi simultaneously evokes the responsibilities of motherhood and the problem of overpopulation, contrasting "limited and viable" families with "manifold" poor that require "look[ing] after." This maternalistic attitude of being burdened by her responsibilities but nonetheless acting out of the best interests of her family members is even more pronounced in her declarations around the Emergency. Speaking in a radio broadcast titled "Rights, Duties, and Tasks" on November 11, 1975, just three months after declaring a state of Emergency, Gandhi compares India to a sick and stubborn child. "The country had developed a disease," she pronounced, insisting that "if [the nation] is to be cured soon, it has to be given a dose of medicine, even if it is a bitter dose. However dear a child may be, if the doctor has prescribed bitter pills for him, they have to be administered for his cure."[31] Within this analogy Gandhi paints herself as a stern but loving mother suffering alongside her reluctant child, saying, "When a child suffers, the mother suffers too. Thus, we were not very pleased to take this step. . . . But we saw that it worked just as the dose of the doctor works."[32] Here, Gandhi capitalizes on the language of the nation as a child not only to cement her symbolic relationship to the nation as Mother India, but also to naturalize a biopolitical narrative of national progress. Modernization and progress must be attained at all costs; thus the violence of the Emergency is justified through eugenicist notions of the nation as child to be managed, perfected, and disciplined. This was the "dose" the people would have to accept.

The "Bitter Pill" of Population Control

Although the zeal with which Sanjay Gandhi pursued population policies during the Emergency became, in the words of one congressman, "something like the greased cartridge of 1857," the increased focus on population policies during Indira Gandhi's premiership preceded the Emergency.[33] Picking up the story of population control from where I left it in chapter 4, the emphasis on population policies in the Second Five-Year Plan was intensified from the Third Five-Year Plan onward and became something of a personal cause for Gandhi. As Connelly notes in *Fatal Misconception,* as the minister of information Gandhi pushed for the dissemination of family planning information throughout the country and advocated paying women for IUD insertion. Further proving her commitment to family planning, on her first full day in office as prime minister in 1966 she renamed the Ministry of Health the Ministry of Health and Family Planning.[34]

With the increased visibility of family planning, the use of incentives begun at the end of the second plan became an increasingly important strategy. To this was added the innovation of targets, with Gandhi setting a 1966 target of "6 million IUD insertions and 1.23 million sterilizations."[35] The use of incentives and disincentives was not confined to the domestic population alone, but also characterized relations between the United States and India in this period. In Indira Gandhi's first meeting with U.S. ambassador to India Chester Bowles, he told her that continued good relations with the United States depended on three things: no more wars with Pakistan, true neutrality in Cold War politics, and practical economic and family planning policies.[36] On this last point, at least, Gandhi was only too willing to oblige. In case she needed any more convincing, however, President Lyndon Johnson linked food aid to India to the Indian government's enforcement of family planning policies, saying to one of his advisors, "I'm not going to piss away foreign aid in nations where they refuse to deal with their own population problems."[37] When Gandhi and Johnson met in Washington, D.C., on March 28, 1966, Johnson must have been satisfied by Gandhi's commitment to family planning because he approved the food aid for India. The situation was made all the more poignant by the famine of 1966–67; in such conditions even meager monetary incentives for vasectomy or IUD insertion could make a drastic difference to the lives of those who received them. Although, as Connelly notes, "at no point did anyone state as a matter of policy that poor people would starve if they did not accept IUDs or sterilization," that was all too often the upshot of such policies on both the national and international levels.[38]

This last point highlights that family planning incentives were implicitly coercive, but explicitly coercive disincentive policies were introduced as well. These disincentives ranged from denying benefits (Connelly reports that in 1966 both Kerala and Mysore stopped granting maternity leave to government employees with more than three children) to threatening the livelihood of government employees.[39] According to a 1977 newspaper report, "In Bihar the salaries of 50,000 government employees were withheld for three months, while 600 or more lost their jobs because they had failed to bring in 'volunteers' for sterilization."[40] During the Emergency such policies were strengthened and enacted on an even larger scale, with "the denial of public food rations to families with more than three children, the delivery of irrigation water at subsidized rates only to villages that met sterilization quotas, and legislation requiring that teachers be sterilized or forfeit a month's pay."[41] The worst victims of population control abuses during the Emergency, however, were the nation's poor. They were targeted for sterilization (often forcible), and the urban poor were additionally victimized by slum clearance programs.[42] As Emma Tarlo reports, "Speculation even arose as to whether Sanjay Gandhi's resettlement and family planning measures were not part of a systematic plot to obliterate the poor."[43] Despite these clear abuses, Indira Gandhi received the United Nations Population Award in 1983, proving that to the international community the ends were more important than the means.[44]

Indira Gandhi's use of populist rhetoric and maternal metaphors would seem to sit uneasily with such policies. After all, how could such violence be done to Mother India's children in her very name? Nevertheless, Gandhi consistently framed family planning policies in such terms. At a 1968 speech at the Sixth All-India Conference on Family Planning (hosted by the Family Planning Association and led by Dhanvanthi Rama Rau), she claimed once again not just to be speaking in the best interests of the nation's mothers but in their very voice. Claiming that population control should appeal to the nation's masses she asserted, "You will find the women of our country to be very responsive to any programme of action which ensures the health and future of their children."[45] Aligning her own position as Mother India with the nation's mothers, she attempts to co-opt them in her struggle in the name of the future of their children and by extension the nation. Family planning is at once about the health of the nation-child and actual children, and Gandhi interpellates the nation's women as mothers who must (like her) do the difficult job of tending them, even if this means not having children at all.

Despite being couched in quantitative concerns about overall population numbers, the issue inevitably turns into a qualitative problem of differential fertility. As Gandhi explains it, "The success [of family planning] has been limited to . . . the most affluent sections of our populations and perhaps those groups which are driven by the desire to improve their standard of living, namely the urban middle class and the skilled industrial workers."[46] These sectors contain the good mothers referenced by Gandhi, those she believed to be "responsive" to family planning. Paradoxically, however, those in the "greatest need"[47] (such as people living in "very backward and highly populated areas") are the most resistant and therefore need to be incentivized in various ways.[48] Citing the "lassitude of the people," Gandhi claims that family planning could not be left to "individual motivation" on the part of those who already have access to modernity (defined here as "a certain level of literacy or economic betterment"), but rather required active outreach by governmental and voluntary agencies.[49]

Although in this 1968 speech Gandhi points to the problems of voluntary population control, in a December 1976 speech at the diamond jubilee celebrations of the Shreemati Nathibai Damodar Thackersey (S.N.D.T) Women's University in Pune she justifies the use of more coercive methods. Outlining the rationalizations for the use of incentives and disincentives she once again turns to the metaphor of disease, but this time gives it a feminist emphasis:

> Family planning is vital to us for two reasons. If the growth of population is not slowed down, the progress of the nation will be slowed down. Doctors tell us that when there is fever, every degree's rise in the temperature means faster using up of the body's resources. Similarly, a high rate of population means faster using up of the body's resources. . . . But the family planning movement is also a major measure of social reform. It redresses the imbalance between the sexes. . . . Personally, I have emphasized the voluntary aspect of this movement. But those who oppose any element of pressure ought to remember that conservative groups once argued that forcing them to send their girls to school was a violation of their rights![50]

Pitting population against resources (and likening the country's economic state to a "fever"), Gandhi once again appeals to maternal instinct to enlist the support of her listeners in curing the nation-child. At the same time, she yokes this maternal language to a feminist one, arguing that family planning (even if coerced) is necessary for women's equality. Any resistance to family planning is linked to a backwardness akin to believing women's education is a violation of their rights. Of course the links between educating women and lowering population growth have long been established; while not suggesting that access to birth control and better reproductive care is only a tool for social control, I am saying that Gandhi reverses the causal relationship between equality and reproduction in a logic that mirrors the reversal of demographic transition theory. Just as there lowering population growth is automatically meant to lead to modernity, here family planning is automatically meant to "redress the imbalance between the sexes." It goes without saying that Gandhi ignores the contradiction between coercive incentives and the discourse of rights she is espousing.

Moreover, although in the context of the S.N.D.T. Women's University's speech Indira Gandhi frames family planning in the language of feminism, in general she disavowed the label. In an echo of Sarojini Naidu's famous 1930 "I am not a feminist" speech, Gandhi ambivalently rejects the term in a 1980 address inaugurating the new conference complex of the All-India Women's Conference in New Delhi (a complex named, not coincidentally, after Naidu). In the speech, "The True Liberation of Women," Gandhi rejects feminism because of its Western taint, saying, "In the West, women's so-called freedom is often equated with imitation of man. Frankly, I feel that is merely an exchange of one kind of bondage for another."[51] In contrast to this, Gandhi forwards a cultural feminism that resembles Naidu's, saying that "Indian women are traditionally conservative but they also have the genius of synthesis, to adapt and to absorb. That is what gives them resilience to face suffering and to meet upheavals with a degree of calm, to change constantly and yet remain changeless, which is the quality of India herself." Here, Gandhi presents the familiar equation of gender and national identity in which the cultural core is located and reproduced through the nation's women. Where Gandhi parts company from Naidu, however, is in her portrayal of Indian women (and women in general) as an oppressed mass. She contends, "I have often said that I am not a feminist. Yet, in my concern for the underprivileged, how can I ignore women who, since the beginning of history, have been dominated over and discriminated against in social customs and in laws?" It is curious that as a female prime minister Gandhi conceives of women as simply a subset of the underprivileged, thus using the language of the nation mother seemingly to set herself against a liberal feminism that would speak in an idiom of equality and rights. She does so, however, to once again forward the mother as the site of cultural reproduction, which paradoxically is ensured by curbing and controlling biological reproduction.

The success of Indira Gandhi's self-fashioning is evident in one of the surprising twists in the story of her rise and fall: the fact that her fall was so temporary. She was roundly defeated in the 1977 elections (a loss often attributed to her repressive population policies during the Emergency), but she returned to power in 1980 and served as prime minister until her assassination in 1984.[52] As Emma Tarlo remarks with some surprise, Indira Gandhi was remembered with fondness and longing even by those who had been the targets of her policies. Speaking of the inhabitants of the resettlement colony in Delhi that form the subjects of her ethnography, Tarlo notes that "all spoke of the Emergency as a time of fear and were highly critical of the way the sterilization campaign had been carried out. Yet none associated their suffering with Indira Gandhi, whose image remained above recrimination, beyond the realm of doubt."[53] Similarly, in his ethnography of agricultural development in a small village in Western Uttar Pradesh, Akhil Gupta reports that the lower-caste villagers attributed an improvement in literacy and working conditions to Indira Gandhi. I cite these examples of the enduring popularity of Gandhi to speak to the success of her use of maternal metaphors—by aligning herself with the poor through her very representation of them as their nation Mother, Gandhi insists she has their best interests at heart. The blame for the excesses during the Emergency is thus placed on overzealous intermediaries who had perverted her meritorious aims.

In surveying how Gandhi's self-fashioning as Mother India injects a maternal discourse into the language of national progress in general and family planning in particular, I suggest that she locates a reproductive, eugenic model as the means of national futurity. The nation's future will be assured by good mothers properly reproducing the nation and in doing so usher in modernity. Gandhi thus understands her work in the Emergency as fighting against the atavistic forces (either in the guise of her political enemies or in the overproductive wombs of the nation's underprivileged) that threaten to overwhelm and stall India's progress. She does so, moreover, through her claims to represent the very subaltern subjects she is abjecting—"Indira is India" indeed. Returning to the discussion of Spivak with which I began, my point here is that it is precisely Gandhi's re-presentation of herself as Mother India (representation as *darstellen*) that authorizes her abuse of the subaltern subjects she claims to be politically representing.[54]

In place of Gandhi's pathological Mother India, Nayantara Sahgal's 1985 novel, *Rich Like Us,* forwards the agency of the liberal feminist subject. A searing critique of Gandhi, Sahgal's novel investigates not only the abuses of the Emergency but also the continuous state of emergency inhabited by the nation's least privileged citizens. In moving from Gandhi's speeches to Sahgal's novel, I argue that Sahgal rewrites the eugenic reproductive model of national futurity that Gandhi attempts to enact. Instead of the era of progress Gandhi believes she is inaugurating, Sahgal views the Emergency as an archaic return to feudalism, a degeneration that endangers Indian national progress.

Even as she views Indira Gandhi's Emergency as a perversion of national progress, however, Sahgal's investment in the nation remains. As Pranav Jani argues in his recent examination of post-independence Indian fiction, *Decentering Rushdie,* Gandhi's despotism during the Emergency signaled to many writers the end of the promise of anticolonial nationalism and a turn to cosmopolitanism (Rushdie's *Midnight's Children* is paradigmatic here). As Jani describes it, "It is only after the Emergency and the crackdown on democracy and popular struggle conducted by Nehru's daughter, under the aegis of 'secularism' and 'socialism' no less, that we see English-novelists look away from the nation as a potential site for fulfilling the promises of decolonization."[55] In other words, the Emergency ushers in the Indian cosmopolitan "postnational." Occupying precisely this postnational moment of disillusionment with the nation-state, *Rich Like Us* focuses on the way the state oppresses and excludes subaltern subjects. At the same time, however, for most of the novel it refuses to abandon Indian nationalism altogether. Indeed, nationalism is reborn in the figure of Sahgal's feminist protagonist, Sonali, where it becomes a program of feminist self-improvement designed to save the nation from itself.

Sahgal's Anti-Developmental Nationalism

Rich Like Us mines two potent moments in Indian history: the period leading up to Indian independence in 1947 and the Emergency. To move between these two moments, the novel shifts between two different narrative voices: the third-person narrative of Rose, a British woman married to a Hindu man, Ram, and the first-person narrative of Sonali, an Indian civil servant. Rose's narrative describes the years before Indian independence: it tells of her courtship with Ram in London; her adjustment to her new life in Lahore with Ram, his first wife, Mona, and his son Dev; and finally of the family's move from Lahore to Delhi at partition. Sonali's narrative defines the present tense of the novel: the period of the Emergency. Sonali is a civil servant who loses her post after refusing to approve the establishment of a Happyola Drink factory. This frivolous business venture has been sanctioned by Indira Gandhi's government and thus stands as a symbol of that government's corruption. Rose's stepson, Dev, is hired to build and run the factory. Like the government, he is corrupt; he has swindled the money to finance the deal by forging his comatose father's signature. When Rose realizes what is happening and confronts Dev, he arranges to have her killed by members of the "youth wing" of the governing party. Through these two narrative and temporal perspectives, the novel is centrally concerned with the betrayal of Indian nationalism, its falling off from the promise of the Independence movement to what Sahgal labels as Gandhi's "feudalism." In contrast to Gandhi's self-representation in terms of the forces of progress (a progress that would necessarily resolve the problem of poverty, even if through eradicating the poor), Sahgal insists that Gandhi's rule is a throwback to a pre-independence era.

Despite her investment in the nationalist ideals of India's founding, Sahgal critiques a developmental view of nationalism that understands it as moving through necessary, linear stages. In a 1995 essay entitled "The Myth Reincarnated," she explicitly refuses a modernization theory paradigm that views tradition (here parodied as "ignorance and monstrous superstition") as a barrier to development. Instead she rightly sees modernization theory as a continuation of imperial relations:

> The reigning reality divided the map into rulers and the lesser breeds they ruled. . . . Embedded and implicit in this scheme of things was a master civilization, Hellenic in origin; a master religion called Christianity . . . ; a master philosophy which started from the Greeks, and from which all legitimate philosophical enquiry and scientific investigation must proceed, since progress, both as an idea and as a development, was an achievement of the West. . . . All this fragmentation, compartmentalization, and irreconcilability, was enthroned as knowledge, and any other view of life was ignorance and monstrous superstition.[56]

Sahgal rejects the authorized, "master" knowledges that claim that "progress . . . as an idea and as a development . . . of the West" must obliterate tradition in the march of modernity. Instead, she posits a specifically Indian modernity, not one that simply parrots the West. Arguing against a developmental logic that "[takes] as its starting-point the proposition that inside of every human breast there was an American struggling to come out,"[57] Sahgal insists that "inside of me there was an Indian, buried for centuries, struggling to come out."[58] Importantly, even as the idea of an identity "buried for centuries" would imply a retreat to an ossified identity of the past, a traditional identity that remains untouched and unchanged by time, Sahgal professes an identity that is "rootedly Indian, yet modern in its twentieth-century legacy."[59] This twentieth-century legacy, moreover, is the political one of the struggle against colonialism.

The very title of the novel, *Rich Like Us,* ironizes modernization theory. The novel opens at a dinner party hosted by Dev for Mr. Neuman, a European businessman charged with setting up the Happyola factory. From the point of view of Mr. Neuman, who after this opening scene disappears for the rest of the novel, the reader is presented with the excesses of the Indian "clique at the top"—the fine whiskey, the lavish house, the "vast amounts of food" (12). The opulence of the dinner party is immediately contrasted to the abjectness of a beggar Mr. Neuman sees outside his car window on his way home. His encounter with the beggar prompts the observation from which the novel takes its title: "If they do like we do," Neuman speculates, "they'd be rich like us." The statement sounds, he muses, "the way his host's cheeks looked, fat, sleek, and unbelievable in the monstrous heat."[60] The world this representative of imperial Europe encounters in a city "eleven thousand miles distant" would seem to indicate that India is following the developmental logic forged by the West. But the appearance of the subaltern (personified throughout the novel by this armless beggar) pulls the semiotic rug out from under this claim. The regular appearance of the beggar reveals the limits of modernization—what Ranajit Guha describes as the *"historic failure of the nation to come into its own."*[61] An Indian nation formed according to the Western model seems "fat, sleek, and unbelievable" in the face of the economic reality and "heat" of the subcontinent, itself a form of "monstrous" excess. It is significant that the line is uttered by Mr. Neuman, a model of the "new man" who abandons his interest in ancient history and archeology, "once his great fascination," because they "did not contribute to the financial basis of his happiness" (8). By putting the title line in the mouth of this Western businessman, Sahgal confronts the developmental narrative that says that if India follows the West's example it will eventually be "rich like us." She also challenges the ideology of richness itself. Material wealth has sapped away human shape and reality, making the Indian elite "fat, sleek, and unbelievable."

At the same time, the beggar seems less than human, simply another part of the "monstrous" landscape. Before seeing the beggar Mr. Neuman notices a Turkish tomb "decaying peacefully under the summer sun, sweating out the monsoon with a peculiarly human resignation" (13). Just as this monument belongs to the past, the beggar equally conveys a sense of obsolescence. Indeed, the monument is more "human" than the man:

Only the face was still a face, tilted sideways at the car, on a neck no thicker than a stalk. Where the stumps, once arms, joined the body, were archways of bone. Altogether a great bone arch, more insect than animal, inching diagonally across the road on its knees. A monster ant, but for the eyes gleaming with intelligence. . . . Obviously not a candidate for a job when construction labourers' shanties sprouted. (13–14)

Here is someone who can never be incorporated in the developmentalist vision of the nation—his body disqualifies him from that. Instead he represents a species anomaly—as implied in the phrase "more insect than animal," the beggar questions the very boundaries of the human. At the same time, he suggests both the inhuman workings of precapitalist structures of exploitation and the inability of capitalism to make him, or the nation, whole.

The beggar (who is never named) used to be a farmer. After he defies his landlord by trying to harvest his fair share of the crop, the landlord cuts off his arms "as an example" to the other farmers. A year earlier, his wife and the other village women were raped by police and then forced to work in the brick kilns along the Ganges, "where now, not in centuries B.C., women labourers disappeared into the kilns where they worked and the pigholes where they lived . . . used by the kiln masters and their men when they finished carrying brickloads for the day" (68). In both cases the horrors the beggar and his wife have experienced are mobilized to point out the hypocrisy of the Indian elite, the Indian government, and the lie of modernization. Indeed, the beggar's story functions throughout the novel as a critique, interpolated into the text to demonstrate what the modern nation has done and yet cannot acknowledge. Rose tells a room of dinner party guests about the brick kilns when they complain that their servants will be too scandalized by kissing scenes to see Western movies. Rose retorts, "They're used to rape, aren't they, so a bit of love-making on the screen can't be very 'ard for them to get used to" (216–17). Similarly, when the beggar tells Sonali about having his arms cut off for attempting to claim the products of his labor, she realizes the lie at the center of the national ideology: "When [had] the saga of peaceful change I had been serving from behind my desk become a saga of another kind, with citizens broken on the wheel for remembering their rights?" (227). In both of these instances the critique could not be more clear; the beggar's story reveals as false the promises of the modern nation.

It is significant, I believe, that the novel does not allow the unnamed beggar to tell his own story; we receive the narrative of the brick kiln through Rose and the narrative of his mutilation through Sonali. The beggar's eyes may be described as "gleaming with intelligence," but we are never allowed access to what that intelligence might reveal. Sahgal thus dramatizes the impossibility of subaltern speech acts. Instead of endowing this figure with interiority, which would imply the problem of ventriloquizing of the subaltern I discussed in relation to Spivak, she keeps him as a spectral figure whose (largely mute) appearance testifies to the inhumanity of a government that "now, not in centuries B.C.," does nothing to prevent the atrocities that have befallen him and those like him (and indeed the government perpetrates them—the police bring the women to the kilns, after all). Sahgal thus critiques the ways that different groups impute desires onto mute subaltern bodies. At the same time, however, she similarly makes the beggar into a symbol of the failures of the nation. He is insistently paired with the tomb—the monument—in which he finds shelter. Both the tomb and the beggar are understood as anachronisms within the novel, but whereas the tomb represents a bygone Mughal past, the beggar signifies the existence of other temporalities within the modern nation—temporalities that point to the nation's failure. While the tomb represents the lost splendor of the Mughal Empire, the beggar represents the failure of national ideology. As such, he is a symbolic embodiment of the *material* costs of that ideology.

Sahgal thus resists making the beggar into a figure whose reality renders him more authentic than the other characters—indeed, in this realist novel the beggar appears to be an almost fantastical figure. At the same time, she makes him into a monument to the concrete price the national subject has to pay. Even as Sahgal rejects modernization theory's assumption that there is one path to national development, she recapitulates modernization theory's assertion that the problem is tradition. The beggar was unable to assert his rights as citizen because traditional feudal land relations still endure.

"Indianizing India": *Sati* and the Eugenic Feminist Subject

If the story of the beggar represents the nation's failures in the past and their continuance in the present, then Sonali represents the nation's future salvation. As a civil servant who spends her life in rebellion against what she sees as traditional gender roles, Sonali represents the new Indian woman. Her father, also a civil servant and ardent nationalist, says to her, "Sonali, people like you, especially women like you, are going to Indianize India" (24). Here, Sonali embodies the professional Indian woman whose "liberated" status is to be a positive reflection on the nation as a whole. This statement also reflects a larger eugenic feminist ideology; if the nation is to be made by women like Sonali, what role is there for a woman like the beggar's wife? Sadly, the novel tells us exactly what such a woman's role is within the nation— she is sent to the brick kilns. Sahgal thus critiques eugenic feminist ideology by exposing the dissonance between the symbolic glorification of women as Mother India and the actual treatment of many women within the nation. As Sonali puts it in relationship to her own disillusionment with nationalism, "[She] had been obsessed with symbols" (31). Sahgal thus comments on the way in which the symbols of Indian nationalism fail to correspond to reality—specifically the reality of Indira Gandhi's government. There is a certain irony here, of course, because Gandhi is, like Sonali, a liberated woman and member of an educated elite devoted to Indian nationalism. In having Sonali become disillusioned with the symbols of nationalism, however, Sahgal sidesteps the whole issue of why it is "especially" up to *women* like Sonali to Indianize India.

The stubborn fact remains that one of the stories of *Rich Like Us* is an account of women's development, as Sahgal contrasts a recursive narrative of women's oppression with a progressive narrative of nationalist development. She performs this contradictory movement through the figure of *sati*. The novel presents us with two *satis*—that of Sonali's great-grandmother and that of Rose. Sonali stumbles across her grandfather's account of his mother's *sati* while going through her father's papers. The novel reproduces the grandfather's manuscript in full, allowing it to occupy the next eighteen pages. Located in the exact middle of the novel, a placement that suggests its central importance, this interpolated narrative transforms Sonali's great-grandmother into a silent symbol of oppression. The manuscript that relates her story is narrated by Sonali's grandfather and contained within the larger narrative of the text, placing it at one remove from the present moment of the novel. In this way, the reader is deliberately removed from the immediacy of Sonali's great-grandmother's experience or voice. This distancing both invests the narrative with a symbolic weight that exceeds that of the other incidents in the novel and dramatizes the silence of Sonali's great-grandmother. Like the beggar, her voice is embedded within multiple discourses, and once again, I read Sahgal's careful representation of the *sati* as multiply mediated as a comment on the inaccessibility of the subjectivity of the *sati*/subaltern. In other words, Sahgal's portrait resonates with Spivak's assessment of the impossibility of subaltern speech.[62]

The manuscript goes to some lengths to describe Sonali's great-grandfather's reformist ideals, his adamant objection to *sati,* and his critique of British laxity and lack of moral fervor in enforcing the ban on *sati.* In the midst of these reminiscences are two nineteenth-century newspaper accounts of *sati,* one labeled voluntary and one involuntary. Through these accounts Sahgal grounds her literary gloss on the issue of *sati* within history, thus figuring an exceptional incident as actually quite commonplace.[63] These newspaper accounts furthermore bleed into the action of the novel when Sonali's great-grandfather dies unexpectedly and his wife becomes a *sati.* Sonali's grandfather attempts to stop her, but he arrives on the scene too late to prevent her death. His conservative uncle says that her act was a voluntary one, done to ensure her son's inheritance and education abroad. But Sonali's grandfather cannot believe this to be true, "for how could she have imagined [he] would begin a new life in a new world with [the] knowledge [of her sacrifice]"? (135). Instead, he remains convinced that his mother is killed by his father's family, not only because of his father's financial resources but also because "she who had embraced my father's world and his ideas was too offensive a reminder of them" (135).

This notion of Sonali's great-grandmother as "too offensive a reminder" of her husband's "world and ideas" is a useful launching point for looking at how Sonali's great-grandmother is made to stand in as a symbol of Indian womanhood writ large. Sonali's grandfather describes his mother not only as selfless and devout but also as uniquely modern. In contrast to his father, who had "the support of his family and society in getting an education, making a career," he remembers his mother as mysteriously "grow[ing] from one era into another, to span centuries of progress in her lifetime" (129). Despite this capacity to "develop," she remains faithful to traditional values: "Her pieties had meaning, for in striving to keep up with the world she found herself in, she gave up nothing precious of the world she had known. The candles of her private shrines stayed lit" (129). The "centuries of progress" that she spans calls to mind Partha Chatterjee's formulation of the new woman who is neither too Westernized nor too traditional. It also resonates with claims that the progress of women symbolizes the relative progress of a nation in the international arena, or, to put it another way, the centrality of the modern Indian woman to the project of "Indianizing India." Regardless of whether Sonali's great-grandmother decided to sacrifice herself for her son or was murdered, in the context of the novel her death poses a problem of Indian nationalism. As Sonali's grandfather writes, "We have been promised political reforms. I believe in a gradual progress towards self-government. But underneath there will be the subterranean layers of ourselves we cannot escape" (135). The idea of "subterranean layers" turns the problem of nationalism into the problem of tradition versus modernity.

Located at both the literal and symbolic center of the novel, *sati* does not disappear with the narrative shift to the modern period but is explicitly linked to Rose's death at the end of the novel. When Rose struggles with her stepson Dev over control of her husband Ram's estate, she is suffocated by an unnamed man and her body is thrown in a well. The official explanation for her death is that she stumbled into the well while drunk. It is clear to Sonali (as it is to the reader, who is presented with the scene of Rose's suffocation) that Dev hired a man to kill Rose in order to prevent her from interfering with his plans. As the relentless truth teller throughout the novel, Rose threatens Dev's manipulation of the national machinery in his setting up of the Happyola factory. Rose, like Sonali's great-grandmother, is "too offensive a reminder." Thus the economic and symbolic reasons for Rose's death link her to Sonali's great-grandmother. The text makes this link explicit as well. While Sonali sorts through Rose's belongings after her death, she suddenly reflects on her great-grandmother. Immediately her mind connects these two women's deaths, noting that "within minutes of my arrival fables had arisen and become eternal verities. My murdered great-grandmother's relatives had said she had sacrificed herself . . . on the altar of sati. . . . I was in a rage as I got down to sorting Rose's possessions, dark tides of blood around me ending in monuments and shrines" (222). Here the three different temporalities and narrative voices in the novel—Sonali's, Rose's, and Sonali's grandfather's—come together to speak in one voice against a culture that would enshrine acts of murder. In making this statement Sonali refers to an actual shrine built on the site of her great-grandmother's *sati* and fears Rose's death being similarly monumentalized.

Sonali's rage aside, however, she too makes the materiality of Rose's death into a different kind of monument—an invisible monument to the failure of a nationalist promise: "It was plain [Rose] had been killed and plainer still that Rose's killers would never be brought to justice. They would live out their comfortable lives and die patriotic citizens" (223). The point that Sahgal brings out here—that violence against, indeed murder of, women is easily assimilable to the role of a "patriotic citizen"—is a powerful one. It must nevertheless be said that in making this point Sahgal repeats a different kind of epistemic violence—that of monumentalizing these two women's deaths in order to critique national failure: "Fables had arisen and become eternal verities." Even as she storms against the ways in which the "dark tides of blood" shed by her great-grandmother and Rose end in "monuments and shrines," by connecting these two deaths she erases the specificities of each, turning them into mere "fables" that testify to the "eternal" problems of nationalism. Even as she dramatizes how certain kinds of subjects are instrumentalized and silenced by the state, she repeats this violence— once again subalterns are instrumentalized in her critique.

Thus the link between the *sati* in the colonial moment and Rose's death during Emergency is there to point to the betrayal of nationalism by the endurance of tradition. Indeed, in an interview Sahgal calls Rose "a modern-day sati," arguing that in each instance of *sati* in *Rich Like Us* women are "sacrificed . . . for the greed and ambitions of men." In making this point, Sahgal suggests "that times haven't changed very much . . . and nor have women."[64] Sahgal thus ends up mobilizing a recursive view of national time as a way of critiquing the failures of Indian nationalism; in other words, Sahgal links these two deaths to say, "The more things change the more they stay the same." She does this, however, through a static vision of women's oppression in India—this is what stays the same. Even as she explicitly rejects a view of development that says that modernity needs to obliterate tradition, Sahgal repeatedly shows that tradition is what stands in the way of the modernizing nation. As such, real change cannot be initiated by male nationalism but must come in the figure of Sonali, who can rescue India from itself with the historical knowledge she has gained through the beggar and through Rose.

The ways in which Sonali is going to rescue the nation, however, are more reminiscent of what Jani terms "cosmopolitan postnationalism" than of the nationalism Sahgal herself professes. The novel ends with Sonali beginning a new career researching mid-seventeenth- to mid-eighteenth-century Indian art. She is hired by an English woman named Marcella (Ram's ex-mistress) and Marcella's husband Brian to help them set up an exhibition for Brian's London gallery. Immersing herself in the history of the Mughal Empire, Sonali discovers an Indian history that predates the nationalist one with which she'd been obsessed. She turns to one of her old school textbooks where she reads the following account of India's past:

> India presented an impressive picture to the world and created the modern legend of wealth and power which lasted well into the nineteenth century. . . . For the first time since classical days India was open to detailed and skilled European observations. She ceased to be a legend about which tales could be spun with little relation to the facts. . . . India had become real to Europe. (234)

Here Sahgal is sketching the longer relationship between India and the rest of the world; she is tracing circuits of global commerce that precede the nationalist moments that occupy the bulk of the novel. At the same time, by unearthing this history whereby "India had become real to Europe," she is arguing for some timeless essence of Indian culture that can be distilled and perpetuated through the ages. By having Sonali look to India's past, Sahgal can dismiss the Emergency as merely an anomaly in India's longer "legend of wealth and power." She can also reject the regime that Mr. Neuman, the businessman we meet at the beginning of the novel, embraces—after all, he sacrifices his love of ancient history and archeology because they are not properly capitalist ventures (or, as he puts it, do "not contribute to the financial basis of his happiness" [8]). Thus the last moment of the novel seeks to look beyond the nation, to a history that is global rather than national, and to a community that is not based on any essentialist categories.

In sketching this new community, both in this final moment and throughout the novel, it is laudable that Sahgal does not simply polarize her British and Indian characters into villains and heroes, and in fact the novel is dedicated "to the Indo-British Experience and what its sharers have learned from each other." By turning Rose into the symbol of universal sympathy (and arguably suffering) in the novel Sahgal nevertheless reinforces an idea of what Chandra Mohanty calls "third world difference"—"that stable, ahistorical something that apparently oppresses most if not all the women in these countries."[65] Rather than race or nationality, something like "culture" is the thing that oppresses

Indian women, regardless of race, nationality, or historical positioning. As such, as Jani notes, despite its value, Sonali's "entry into the privatized world of the academic study . . . lends itself to a reading of Sonali's academic work as a kind of escapism, as it drops by the wayside the novel's earlier insights about the emergencies that would continue to exist—at the expense of those at the bottom of hierarchies of power."[66] Sonali's rejection of the state in return for India's glorious past is available to her, but what of the beggar? At the end of the novel she fits him with hands so he can engage in work, but even so, is he suddenly beyond the nation? Sonali has made him just human enough to reenter an exploitative work force. Indeed, only Sonali escapes from "third world difference," and she does so, moreover, by turning away from the nation and toward a form of cosmopolitanism. The last paragraph of the novel reads, "Immersed in the past, I was preparing all the while for the future. . . . Though it was really Rose's legacy again, the paths that had crossed hers now crossing mine, reminding me I was young and alive, with my own century stretched out before me, waiting to be lived" (234). In reminding herself of her past (that is, India's past), she can remake her future, using Rose's cosmopolitanism as a model.

By resolving the problems Sonali grapples with throughout the novel in this way, Sahgal attempts to gesture beyond the nation to different communities of feminist belonging. But even so she cannot get away from the nation and from global commodifications of national culture. Though Sonali's turn to cosmopolitanism need not be a rejection of the nation, it is, as Jani puts it, "a kind of escapism."[67] Moreover, even as subaltern figures are central to her critical assessment of the nation-state, they are conspicuously absent from the feminist community Sonali creates. Instead, Sonali's partnership with Marcella is framed in eugenic terms, with Sonali describing Marcella as possessing "a translucence . . . that belied her strength. So was the civilization that had produced her, matchless in the Western world for its unbroken continuity" (233). Although Sonali views the Emergency as disturbing India's continuity perhaps even more than British colonialism, in turning to the past she seeks to recover an Indian continuity that has the same "translucence and strength" she finds in Marcella's Britishness. She does so, however, as part of a neoimperialist project of commodifying India and Indian art to market to a British audience. Even as she attempts to think beyond the nation in terms of community she nonetheless must remake the nation in order to do so. In a move reminiscent of Sarojini Naidu's eugenic, developmentalist nostalgia, Sonali ends up embracing a eugenic feminism that excises the subaltern from the national narrative. The modern legend to which she turns is one that erases the problems of subaltern subjects in the past and the present in exchange for a vision of lost glory. The hopefulness of the end of the novel is contingent on the fact that the India Sonali rediscovers is one of wealth and power, not one of social injustice and subalternity.

In juxtaposing Indira Gandhi's self-fashioning as Mother India with Nayantara Sahgal's critique of Gandhi, I suggest that both excise the problem of subalternity in an attempt to ensure the nation's future. On the one hand, we have Gandhi's eugenic reproductive policies that in some senses attempt to abolish poverty by abolishing the poor. On the other hand, we have Sahgal's recursive notion of history in which the past is reborn as the future, a nostalgic move that resolves the problem of subalternity by erasing it. Though I do not mean to equate Indira Gandhi's repressive regime with Nayantara Sahgal's critique of that regime in her novel, I do suggest a similarity in the way both focus on the underprivileged, subaltern masses as a means of critiquing the nation. Thus Gandhi's "underprivileged" subject is exactly who needs to be sacrificed in her model, a sacrifice both enabled and obscured by her self-presentation as Mother India. Sahgal's admirable critique of Gandhi performs a different kind of instrumentalization. Despite the care with which she avoids ventriloquizing the subaltern (through the multiply distanced narratives of *sati* and the beggar), ultimately she eschews the problem of the subaltern and the many emergencies subalterns face by turning away from the nation to an elite postnational cosmopolitanism. Although Sahgal launches her criticism of Indian nationalism by focusing on the disenfranchisement of subaltern subjects by Indira Gandhi's state, she exchanges this point of view for a glorified version of the past and future that renders subaltern bodies invisible, a sleight of hand that resolves the problems they pose without resolving the problem of subalternity itself.

EPILOGUE

Transnational Surrogacy and
the Neoliberal Mother India

> In the '60s, the introduction of the birth control pill took the risk
> of "making babies" out of sex. Today, new technologies have taken
> sex out of the act of "making babies." And globalization is making
> it affordable. Now all one needs is a credit card. Instructions can be
> found on YouTube.
>
> —*Google Baby*

ZIPPI BRAND FRANK'S 2009 documentary *Google Baby* opens
with this meliorist account of how technology has transformed reproduction into an act determined less by chance than by the market.
In doing so it draws a series of equivalences between different historical moments and technologies, comparing the 1960s invention of
the birth control pill (with its feminist implications of taking away the
"risk" of unintended pregnancies), to new reproductive technologies for
"making babies." The inexorable logic of this movement elides the very
different implications of these technologies and moments, not least of
which is how new reproductive technologies translate the contingen-
cies of biology and circumstance (sexual orientation, age, infertility)
into a problem of the market: "All one needs is a credit card." One way
this elision works is through the quotation's address: just as the birth
control pill had the biggest impact on women from the United States,
changing their sexual mores and fertility patterns, so too is the audience for both the film and the technologies it describes largely from the
global North.[1] The very logic that "globalization is making it afford-
able" therefore references both contemporary systems of exploitation
(as suggested by the fact that elites in the global South also access this
technology) and longer histories of colonialism and imperialism.

These equivalences and elisions resonate throughout *Google Baby*, which describes how Israeli businessman Doron Mamet (inspired by his own very expensive experience with surrogacy in the United States) develops a service using donor eggs from the United States and gestational surrogates in India to lower the cost of "making babies" for couples who are otherwise unable to become biological parents. Based on the logic that "outsourcing to India is very trendy right now," his business model depends upon using relatively inexpensive Indian surrogates to drive down the cost of "baby production."[2] Mamet presents his mission in altruistic terms, explaining in an informational video to prospective clients, "I wanted to be a parent my whole life. . . . There is no reason because of what someone might think that I am not worthy of being a parent. . . . So I went and became a parent. And I would be happy to help others to become parents."[3] Referencing the fact that as a gay man some might deem him "not worthy of being a parent," Mamet leverages his sexuality to paint surrogacy as an unquestionable good (one imagines his audience bristling at the notion that Mamet is "not worthy of being a parent" based on his sexual orientation). By emphasizing his sexual identity as the site of the denial of equality and rights, and forwarding surrogacy as the way to restore those rights, he papers over the exploitative aspects of transnational surrogacy, thus obscuring his business model's dependence on the backs (or in this case wombs) of Indian women.[4] After all, Mamet was able to become a parent not only in spite of what people "might think" but also because of what he was able to pay. Relying on a model of homonormativity that, as Jasbir Puar reminds us in *Terrorist Assemblages,* "can be read as a formation complicit with and invited into the biopolitical valorization of life in its inhabitation and reproduction of heteronormative norms," Mamet reinforces an international division of labor that uses the undervaluation of Indian reproductive labor to produce and support life for national and transnational elites.[5]

Brand Frank, an Israeli documentarian, came upon the subject of *Google Baby* while studying as a Neimann Journalism Fellow at Harvard University. Struck by the number of ads on university bulletin boards calling for "young, good looking, and highly educated women" to become egg donors, Frank set out to explore how "babies had become a commodity" and how "globalization had a profound impact on the growing business of baby production."[6] This investigation of "how pregnancy could be disassembled into its elements only to be put

together again through an online mix-and-match" led Brand Frank
to the phenomenon of Indian surrogacy.[7] Initially suspecting that she
would tell a story of "exploitation" ("the outsourcing of surrogacy to
India, for a fraction of the price of western surrogates"), Brand Frank
eventually comes to read transnational surrogacy in terms of a "feminist agenda."[8] That is, although she does not uncritically celebrate the
globalization of baby production (the documentary does not flinch away
from some of its less savory sides), she comes to see surrogacy as a form
of empowerment for the Indian women who undertake it. Taking her
cue from Dr. Nayna Patel, who runs the clinic featured in the documentary, Brand Frank explains, "Dr. Patel believes that for these rural
women in India, surrogacy is almost the only way to make a life changing move. They are transforming their lives and the lives of their families and children by making education and/or housing a viable option."[9]
Rather than investigating why gestational surrogacy is "almost the only
way to make a life changing move," both Dr. Patel and Brand Frank
represent it as freeing the labor potential of otherwise unused wombs.[10]
Returning to the equivalences with which I began, just as the birth
control pill freed women from the risks of unintended pregnancies, here
freedom is understood as unlocking surrogates' economic potential and
thus "transforming their lives."[11] In this equation, surrogacy becomes a
feminist act of empowerment. The real villains in the documentary are
the surrogates' husbands, who do not seem to appreciate their wives'
labors on behalf of their families. As a review of the documentary in
the *New York Times* puts it, in the end *Google Baby* shows us that "far
worse than an extreme capitalist is a bad husband."[12]

I turn to the issue of transnational surrogacy and the outsourcing
of reproductive labor to India to think through contemporary imbrications of eugenics, feminism, and development in the era of globalization.
Looking at how "the production of immediate life through affect and
biology on one side of the world can serve to support life elsewhere,"[13]
as Kalindi Vora describes the outsourcing of biological and affective
labor to India in a recent article, I argue that eugenic feminism in its
latest guise is less about feminist nation building than it is about the
liberal feminist subjectivity of the marketplace. As characterized by
the introduction to a 2007 special issue of *New Formations,* the "new"
eugenics are new precisely because, unlike the forms of eugenics I've
examined throughout this book, they are delinked from the state and
"characterized above all by individualism and consumer choice."[14] To

some observers, this "'liberal eugenics' rehabilitates a discredited concept by sweeping away the spectre of coercion and installing instead the idea of individuals who freely choose to use technological innovation in order to improve the life-chances of themselves and their children."[15] Of course, as many essays in the special issue point out, even if eugenics is not a state-sponsored project it nonetheless involves the coercions of the market.

The new eugenics thus smooth over the inequalities structurally necessary to globalization and posit a "brave new world" in which those who have access to expensive genetic and reproductive technologies can "improve the life-chances of themselves and their children," and those who do not have such access cannot. This "privileging of the genes of the privileged," as Elizabeth Watkins calls it, is a new form of positive eugenics in which the reproduction of the economically "well-born" is not only given a distinct advantage, but also (as *Google Baby* graphically illustrates) often depends upon the economic necessity of those more fertile but less economically well-born.[16] At the same time, the co-option of transnational surrogacy to a "feminist agenda" of economic empowerment relies upon a liberal feminism that posits as its endpoint the modern, developed, reproductive subject who can freely make choices in her own best interests. What is ignored in this narrative is how, as Pheng Cheah argues in relation to the Platform for Action formulated at the Fourth World Conference on Women in Beijing in 1995, the "desires and interests" of such a subject are conveniently made to coincide with the interests of global capitalism, as the "global biopolitical field . . . fabricates the interests and needs of the individuals exploited by global capitalism, integrating them by weaving them into the very fabric of the system."[17] In this sense Dr. Patel's view of surrogacy as a form of empowerment resembles much-vaunted microcredit programs, which solve the problem of women's poverty by enabling women's entrance into largely unregulated and exploitative informal sector work.

Using the language of empowerment thereby obscures the issue of economic coercion (why, again, is gestational surrogacy "almost the only way to make a life changing move" for the rural Indian women who undertake it?) and ignores the hazards involved in this kind of work. Although the opening quotation implies by analogy that the "risks" of sexual reproduction have been removed from the act of "making babies," very real risks nonetheless accrue to the women who undertake this kind of labor, as the recent deaths of Indian surrogate, Premila Vaghela, and underage Indian egg donor, Sushma Pandey, attest.[18] In an intake interview with a potential surrogate, Dr. Patel explains, "There is also death in delivery and pregnancy. For that, neither [the clients are] responsible nor the clinic is responsible." The dissonance between the disavowal of responsibility through the language of contract and what is being disavowed (that is, death) reveals that what is being produced is not simply value, but what Vora calls "vital energy." In theorizing this labor in terms of "vital energy" instead of "value," Vora both references "the true content of value carried by the commodity and the absolute use value of labor power to capitalist production" and asserts "that what is produced by these activities exceeds what is recognizable in the commodity's exchange value." That is, she goes on to argue, tracking the production of vital energy in India for the global North lays bare "the connection between the exhaustion of biological bodies and labors in India to extend 'life' in the First World and a longer history of power relations underpinning what may seem like an emerging form of biopower in sites like commercial surrogacy."[19] The fact that vital energy exceeds its exchange value is a point to which I return shortly.

The longer histories of exploitation embedded within transnational surrogacy are covered over by the benevolent frame of "women helping women," a phrase that evokes the problematic universalism of "global sisterhood."[20] As Dr. Patel explains the transaction to a prospective surrogate: "She cannot have a child which she longs for, which you are going to give, and you cannot have a house. You cannot educate your son beyond school. For that, they are going to pay."[21] Interestingly, because the documentary chooses to focus solely on the "industry" side of "baby making," it does not present the perspective of any clients, simply giving us the abstraction of "women helping women."[22] Instead of focusing on the client–surrogate relation, the documentary draws a link between U.S. egg donor Katherine (Kat) Gaylean and Indian surrogate Vaishaili (her last name isn't given). This iteration of "sisterhood" serves as an oblique reminder that though Vaishaili's reproductive labor is indispensable, her genetic material is pointedly unwanted.[23] While Kat is the only egg donor the documentary follows, it introduces us to multiple surrogates (in one scene they are introduced by the nationality of the contracting parents), the most individuated of which is Vaishaili.[24] The documentary creates a series of equivalences between Kat and

Vaishaili: they are both married and have children; they are both doing this reproductive work to resolve housing concerns. While Kat is going to use the money to continue renovations on a large house (one scene shows her moving a large-screen TV), Vaishaili uses her money to purchase a much smaller new house. The end of the documentary juxtaposes family scenes of the women. The first shows Kat, her husband, and two daughters shooting guns in the backyard and detailing the amount of money they've spent on guns. The second shows Vaishaili's new house and features a monologue by her husband telling her friend (failed surrogate Diksha) that "women's brains are not very powerful. They are not very bright. But their brains do work on some occasions." In general the film doesn't moralize, but it is hard not to read these two scenes as critically commenting on these women's lives and underscoring how different they are from the presumed (non-gun-toting and feminist-leaning) viewer.

Thus despite the many surface differences between these two women, I suggest that the documentary is asking us to focus on the ways in which they occupy similar subject positions in their respective locations. After all, Brand Frank mentions in an interview that most of the egg donors are single—why, then, does she choose to focus on this particular married donor, and why does she underscore the connections between the two women?[25] One reason, I propose, is to flatten out the differences between them (in a sense that recalls Thomas Friedman's "The world is flat" thesis) by focusing on the intimacies that globalization creates.[26] Evoking this flatness, moreover, has the attendant purpose of interpellating Vaishaili into the kind of consumerism Kat represents. As Anne Kerr argues, "What this film shows us is that wealthy consumers and entrepreneurs are creating the conditions for poor and vulnerable women to turn their reproductive potential into tradable commodities so that they too might join the consumer classes."[27] By focusing only on the industry side, furthermore, the relationship between the client and the surrogate is obscured, thus concealing the dialectic of positive and negative eugenics that I trace throughout this book in which what appears to be a form of freedom is, when followed through to its global, postcolonial logic, revealed to be coercive. That is, the reproductive technology that grants rights (as in Doron's) and fulfills dreams (as in "women helping women") is linked to a staggeringly different toll on the surrogates' bodies and lives. In this sense, the connection between birth control practices associated with liberal feminist rights in the global North and the less emancipatory narrative of population control in the postcolonial world is repeated here, although the price of coercion is roughly inverse: the sterilized woman and the surrogate confront one another.

The language of altruism implied by "women helping women," in which the surrogate and client are equally implicated, extends to Dr. Patel, who sees herself as helping the women who serve as surrogates in her clinic. That she insists that any houses bought with payment for surrogacy be placed in the surrogate's (not the husband's) name attests to Dr. Patel's own perceived feminist agenda, as does the fact that she has established a trust fund to help her surrogates. My point is not to malign such good intentions as purely cynical or "false," but rather to underscore the impoverishment not only of what globalization has wrought but also of a feminist imagination in which gestational surrogacy is "almost the only way" to "transform lives." The fact remains, furthermore, that the transformation pictured in the film is not necessarily that of the surrogate, but of her family and most particularly her child. In the case of the Vaishaili, surrogacy does indeed allow her to buy a house, and the deed is put in her name. Nonetheless, Vaishaili's husband says he will need to "send her for surrogacy again" in order to support their son's education; the father has aspirations of training his son to become an army officer (or at least a police officer—the requirement is that he have a position that will ensure him a job at a desk, not "standing at the border with a gun in his hand").[28] Thus just like the peasant mothers I survey in chapter 4, the reproductive (here translated into productive, paid) labor Vaishaili performs is explicitly done for the masculine subject of the nation. Even though this reproductive labor is not performed directly for the nation, it aids the reproduction of the masculine national subject within a globalized economy as well as serving a global regime of positive eugenics.

Thinking of the Indian gestational surrogate as the new Mother India thereby continues one of the stories *Eugenic Feminism* has attempted to tell: that of the transformation of the symbol "Mother India" within the United States and India over the course of the twentieth century. For Charlotte Perkins Gilman, Mother India represents the sexuo-economic relationship taken to its inevitable conclusion: the overly sex-differentiated, fecund, and tradition-bound oppressed woman who serves as an object lesson for white U.S. feminist advance. Sarojini Naidu, in contrast, innovates on the male nationalist rendering of Mother India by imagining her as the progenitor, even if slumbering, of an Indian feminist modernity that precedes that of the West. In response both to Naidu's vision and to U.S. flirtations with Hindu spirituality, Katherine Mayo takes up the issue of child marriage to rewrite Mother India as a perverse symbol of stillborn Indian nationalism from which U.S. nationhood (and white womanhood) must be hysterically guarded. The post-independence Indian nationalist reclamation of Mother India departs from all of these visions by conceiving of Mother India as the heroic peasant mother, continuous with the land in her ability to bear and standing in for the authority of the postcolonial state over the revolutionary actor, an authority made timeless by its connection to her symbolically powerful figuration. This figuration shifts yet again during the Emergency, when Indira Gandhi attempts to speak both for and as the subaltern Mother India: "Indira is India, India is Indira." What this sleight of hand elides, however, is that the subaltern subjects of the nation bear the brunt of her repressive policies.

Within the context of twenty-first-century transnational surrogacy, Mother India becomes the racially evacuated womb giving life not to the nation but to the forces of transnational capital. Thus while resonant with the different iterations of eugenic feminism I trace throughout this book, the imbrications of eugenics, feminism, and development apparent in transnational surrogacy are distinctly different. Here the state is most notable for its (neoliberal) absence; the absence of any real regulation of gestational surrogacy allows it to thrive and helps to bolster India as a growing site of biomedical tourism.[29] The development of the transnational surrogacy industry in India thus depends upon the globalization of the Indian economy, a process that arguably has its roots in Indira Gandhi's regime. While the liberalization of the Indian economy officially begins in 1991, after a balance of payment crisis and bailout by the International Monetary Fund (IMF),[30] the seeds were planted by Indira Gandhi's nationalization of the banks in 1969. This popular move seemed resonant with socialist politics, but in reality, as Vijay Prashad argues, it "was designed to accomplish two things: to centralize finance capital in the interests of the big bourgeoisie and to offer credit to 'small and middle entrepreneurs' and to the agrarian bourgeoisie who were both unable to generate capital since the economic stagnation in the mid-1960s."[31] Likewise, Indira Gandhi's Twenty-Point Programme during the Emergency was, as Francine Frankel details, billed as a "'direct assault on poverty'"[32] but did not offer any real redistributive measures. Not only did the Twenty-Point Programme mirror demands issued to India by the World Bank, it also (in Point 14: "'liberalization of investment procedures'") opened up the economy to foreign investment.[33] As Prashad asserts, despite Gandhi's rhetoric of *Giribi hatao* ("Abolish poverty") in her 1971 campaign,

> the scraps to landless peasants would come to mean nothing in time as the state essentially handed over the keys to the kingdom to the industrial elite and foreign capital. When the Emergency ended in 1977 and much of its program withered, the drive to liberalize the economy, draw in foreign capital, and welcome a relationship with the IMF remained.[34]

I end *Eugenic Feminism* with a reading of *Google Baby* for what it does (and does not) tell us about the changing fate of Indian women's reproductive labor with the globalization of the Indian economy. At first glance, this rendering of transnational surrogacy would seem to be a revaluation of the pathological fecundity of the subaltern Indian woman (as traced through some of the works and moments I survey throughout *Eugenic Feminism*), turning it from a problem into a solution. One of the ways this transformation works is through the equivalences the film invites us to draw—between the 1960s invention of the birth control pill and new reproductive technologies; between the rights of childless people to have children and of impoverished women to have the basics of shelter and education for themselves and their families; and between the U.S. egg donor and the Indian surrogate. The documentary creates these equivalences by also throwing up differences, as the incommensurability of these different subject positions is both acknowledged and discounted in the name of progress. But this mapping of equivalences ignores the vital energy that exceeds exchange value, and focusing on this excess opens up a reading not of what is produced (or reproduced) but what is lost, what is foreclosed, in precisely the equivalences the documentary seeks to make.

In closing, I propose a different reading practice that draws on what Gayatri Chakravorty Spivak develops as "radical alterity": "an imaging that is the figuration of the ethical as the impossible."[35] Instead of trying to acquire knowledge of the other, or trying to make the other more like the self (with the attendant sense, as Spivak puts it, "I am necessarily better, I am necessarily indispensable, I am necessarily the one to right wrongs, I am necessarily the end-product for which history happened"), radical alterity is the recognition of incommensurability.[36] To realize the impossibility of reaching the "quite-other" is ethical in that it does not assume that the quite-other must be made over into the self. Crucially, Spivak introduces the discussion of radical alterity within the context of global feminism and gender and development, in which the supposedly ethical agenda of "righting wrongs" equals making over underdeveloped women of the global South in order for them to be appropriated by global capital (as, for instance, in the case of microcredit, which manufactures poor women's desires and then calls them interests).

Against such models that would seek to dissolve the other in the self, I suggest that the ethics of radical alterity open a possibility for modeling a non-eugenic, because nonreproductive, feminist reading practice; one that resists what the narrative itself is trying to reproduce by focusing on what it jettisons, what it labels dysgenic and thus unworthy of reproduction. In this sense a non-eugenic reading practice rejects what Lee Edelman terms "reproductive futurism": the notion that political discourse is structured around the future inhering in the figure of the (idealized) Child.[37] In resisting this reproductive drive, I use Spivak's notion of radical alterity to question the need for equivalences and the erasure of difference I see operating in eugenic narratives. A non-eugenic reading practice thus proceeds on three counts. The first is discursive, unpacking the purifying impulse contained in watchwords such as "empowerment," "progress," "utopia," and "development," to name just a few. The second is material, tracing the effects of how such rhetoric is enacted upon bodies as people and populations are sorted into the categories of fit and unfit. Finally, the last is economic, uncovering the workings of eugenics through the very logics of imperialism, development, and globalization.

Throughout *Eugenic Feminism* I've attempted to model this non-eugenic reading practice by focusing on precisely what eugenics would seek to excise even in (or perhaps, more accurately, *especially* in) its most utopian guises. In doing so I've suggested that the very demand for political purity as the way toward a brighter future is in itself wrapped up in eugenics, and that a truly transnational and postcolonial feminist reading practice must think through the positive/negative dialectic modeled by eugenics to show how important political values are potentially co-optable in the very name of progress. Nonetheless, by tracing the iterations of eugenics, feminism, imperialism, and development through the United States and India over the better part of a century, my aim has been to resist the seductions of the purifying logic of eugenics even when it is articulated in the name of a more emancipatory future, and to chart a new way forward—albeit messy and imperfect—on a different historical map.

ACKNOWLEDGMENTS

Writing this book has been a lesson in gratitude. My greatest debt is to Josie Saldaña, who not only has been an amazing advisor and friend but whose own work on development, subjectivity, and feminism continues to inspire me. Josie always knows to push me when I need it and talk me down from the ledge in moments of panic; her support and belief in this work sustained it from its earliest formulations until now. Daniel Kim has also been a formative mentor and friend; I haven't forgotten his lessons on how to build a raft. Rey Chow's rigorous engagement with this book in its earlier incarnation as a dissertation is still paying dividends. Other faculty members at Brown University who generously gave of their time and mentorship include Timothy Bewes, Madhu Dubey, Olakunle George, Nancy Armstrong, and Leonard Tennenhouse. My amazing graduate cohort—Chris Lee, Yogita Goyal, Matthew Pursell, Tess Takahashi, Zak Sitter, Monica Peleaz, Danny Voloch, Julia Davis, Alisa Hartz, Eugenia Zuroski, and Avak Hasratian—makes me nostalgic for graduate school. As a Marilyn Yarborough Teaching/Dissertation Fellow at Kenyon College, I was fortunate enough to have Kirstie Dorr, Sara Clarke Kaplan, Mrinalini Chakravarty, and Leila Neti as colleagues and friends. Sara and Kirstie have been inspiring and treasured interlocutors, and this book would not have gotten written were it not for "book writing boot camps" in Northampton and San Diego. I have learned more from them than I can say, not least about the power of friendship. Special thanks also to my mentors at Connecticut College—Julie Rivkin and Nancy Goldstein—for starting me on this path those many years ago.

Within the English Department at the University of Massachusetts Amherst I have been fortunate to find myself in vibrant and generous intellectual community. Suzanne Daly and Jane Degenhardt have been brilliant readers and friends in good times and bad. Runs with Jen Adams kept me sane. Laura Furlan, Haivan Hoang, Emily Lordi, Rachel Mordecai, Hoang Phan, Adam Zucker, Nick Bromell, Deborah Carlin, Janis Greve, Randall Knoper, Donna LeCourt, Joseph Skerrett, Jenny Spencer, and Ron Welburn have offered friendship and advice and patiently listened to me complain. Stephen Clingman has been a supportive colleague and friend and a valued interlocutor on issues of postcolonialism and transnationalism. Laura Doyle's insights on issues of gender and eugenics have been vital, as have her friendship and mentorship. During my time at UMass I've been lucky to have two excellent department chairs—Anne Herrington and Joseph Bartolomeo—who advocated for me and have been more than understanding of a variety of personal circumstances. I am grateful for the generous junior research leave that allowed me to complete a portion of this book and for opportunities to present my work at the Crossroads in the Studies of the Americas Seminar, the Interdisciplinary Seminar in the Humanities and Fine Arts, the Five College Asian/Pacific/American Studies faculty group, and the English Department Colloquium series. I also thank the many people at UMass and the four colleges who offered support and friendship: Laura Briggs, Paula Chakravarty, Floyd Cheung, Kavita Datla, David Hernandez, Laura Lovett, Srati Shah, Amina Steinels, and Banu Subramaniam. Iyko Day helped me survive the final push and patiently assisted me in thinking through many of the formulations here. Special thanks to the "Forbes crew": Nerissa Balce, Richard Chu, Jessica Delgado, Dayo Gore, and Arianne Miller.

Outside the "happy valley" there are many whose intellectual generosity and friendship have sustained me. Little did I know how lucky I was when I met Chris Lee in our first graduate seminar; he patiently talked through various iterations of these ideas with me (no matter how half-baked), read multiple versions of this book, and generously lent his brilliance to its pages (all faults, it goes without saying, are my own). This is a much better book for all of his careful attention and insight. Cathy Schlund-Vials's astute readings, endless support, and equally endless humor have been crucial in seeing this book through to completion. Friends and audiences at the American Studies Association and the Association for Asian American Studies who helped me work through these ideas, and those who read portions of this book and shared their work with me, include David Eng, Rosemary George, Aaron Lecklider, Eric Lott, Crystal Parikh, Min Song, and Chris Vials. Special thanks to

Anita Mannur for recommending *Google Baby* to me. Outside the academy, Asha Ghosh has been a friend and an excellent resource on issues of development. A portion of this book was completed at the American Academy in Rome. For their friendship and support (and babysitting), I thank Rena Diamond, Nick Wilding, Amy and Peter Campion, Anna Hepler, Jon Calame, and Lisa Bielawa. Special thanks to Anna Hepler for suggesting, and granting permission to use, an image of one of her beautiful collages for the cover. For much-needed distraction, thanks also to the "immortals": Jennifer and Scott Craver, Terry and Merele Adkins, Lars Lerup, Eva Sarraga, and the Campions. I am grateful to my extended family for support and encouragement: Sheela and Amar Amembal, Rajani Nadkarni, and especially Prakash Nadkarni.

I am so grateful to Richard Morrison for allowing me to corner him at the American Studies Association conference and talk his ear off about this book. His, and Erin Warholm-Wohlenhaus's, enthusiasm for and support of this project made its completion possible (thanks also to Erin for answering my seemingly endless questions about the process). Anonymous readers at the University of Minnesota Press and Ohio State University Press pushed me to sharpen and clarify many of the arguments here, making for a much better book, and I am thankful for their careful and generous engagement. Thanks to David Martinez for producing the index.

Closer to home, my father, Ravi Nadkarni, probably started it all in 1967 with a rant about Katherine Mayo's *Mother India* given to a surprised American Legion audience in Salt Lake City prepared to hear a lecture about "Indian culture." My mother, Sara Nadkarni, did not live to see this book to its completion, but her wicked humor, remarkably clear vision of the world, and love are with me every day and I hope found their way into these pages. My sister, Maya Nadkarni, supported me through the writing of this book in more ways than I can enumerate or ever repay. The memory of Neela Nadkarni reminds me of how precious life is. Shama Grace Yun Nadkarni calls me to all of the joys of the world outside the page, and her fierce spirit gives me hope for the future. Ray and Pong Moralee sustained me with excellent Korean food and care packages. Words cannot express my love and gratitude for Jason Moralee. He believed in and supported this book even when (especially when) I lost the faith, did everything in his power to carve out the time and mental space for me to complete it, and simply makes each day more fun than I ever hoped it could be.

NOTES

Introduction

1. Margaret Sanger, "What Birth Control Can Do for India," November 30, 1935. Typed speech. Margaret Sanger Papers, Sophia Smith Collection, Smith College, Northampton, Mass., 4, 5.

2. Sarojini Naidu, "To India," *The Golden Threshold*, 1905 (London: William Heinemann, 1916), 94.

3. Margaret Sanger, quoted in Matthew Connelly, *Fatal Misconception: The Struggle to Control World Population* (Cambridge, Mass.: Belknap Press of Harvard University Press, 2010), 99.

4. For a history of the creation and propagation of overpopulation discourse see Sarah Hodge, "Governmentality, Population and the Reproductive Family in Modern India," *Economic and Political Weekly*, March 13–19, 2004, 1157–63. http://www.jstor.org/stable/4414767.

5. Although Gandhi was not a Malthusian, he nonetheless felt that the burgeoning population was a problem due to a colonial apparatus whose very modus operandi was the exploitation of resources. Given this, India couldn't support more population as long as colonial rule continued. See Sanjam Ahluwalia, *Reproductive Restraints: Birth Control in India, 1877–1947* (Urbana and Chicago: University of Illinois Press, 2007).

6. Dhanvanthi Rama Rau, *An Inheritance: The Memoirs of Dhanvanthi Rama Rau* (London: Heinemann, 1977), 240. In Ehrlich's famous rendition, "The streets seemed alive with people. People eating, people washing, people sleeping. People visiting, arguing, and screaming. People thrusting their hands through the taxi window, begging. People defecating and urinating. People clinging to buses. People herding animals. People, people, people, people. As we moved slowly through the mob, hand horn squawking, the dust, noise, heat, and cooking fires gave the scene a hellish aspect. Would we ever get to our hotel?" Paul R. Ehrlich, *The Population Bomb* (New York: Ballantine, 1968), 1.

7. Rama Rau, *An Inheritance*, 240.

8. Ibid., 240, 243.

9. Ibid., 240.

10. Ibid., 257.

11. Sarah Hodges, "Towards a History of Reproduction in Modern India," in *Reproductive Health in India: History, Politics, Controversies*, ed. Sarah Hodges (New Delhi: Orient Longman), 16.

12. Sarah Hodges, "South Asia's Eugenic Past," in *The Oxford Handbook of the History of Eugenics*, ed. Philippa Levine and Alison Bashford (New York: Oxford University Press, 2010), 228.

13. For accounts of eugenics that similarly trace its endurance past the Second World War, see Daniel Kelves, *In the Name of Eugenics: Genetics and the Uses of Human Heredity* (Cambridge, Mass.: Harvard University Press, 1998); Wendy Kline, *Building a Better Race: Gender, Sexuality and Eugenics from the Turn of the Century to the Baby Boom* (Berkeley: University of California Press, 2005); Connelly, *Fatal Misconception;* Linda Gordon, *The Moral Property of Women: A History of Birth Control Politics in America* (Urbana: University of Illinois Press, 2007); Nancy Ordover, *American Eugenics: Race, Queer Anatomy, and the Science of Nationalism* (Minneapolis: University of Minnesota Press, 2003); and Johanna Schoen, *Choice and Coercion: Birth Control, Sterilization, and Abortion in Public Health and Welfare* (Chapel Hill: University of North Carolina Press, 2005).

14. Inderpal Grewal, *Transnational America: Feminisms, Diasporas, Neoliberalisms* (Durham, N.C.: Duke University Press, 2005), 3. Although Grewal's discussion of "transnational connectivities" in *Transnational America* is specifically concerned with the global processes of neoliberalism in the 1990s, in using this term to describe the relationship between the United States and India in the first part of the twentieth century I am following up her suggestion that "gender, race, class, and nationalism are produced by contemporary cultures in a transnational framework that is linked to earlier histories of colonization" (27). In my conceptualization of the transnational I am also borrowing upon Grewal and Caren Kaplan's important, earlier theorization of it in their "Introduction: Transnational Feminist Practices and Questions of Postmodernity," *Scattered Hegemonies: Postmodernity and Transnational Feminist Practices* (Minneapolis: University of Minnesota Press, 1994).

15. I am certainly not the first to recognize the ways in which feminism borrowed from eugenic discourse and eugenics borrowed from feminism. See Susanne Klausen and Alison Bashford, "Fertility Control: Eugenics, Neo-Malthusianism, and Feminism," in *The Oxford Handbook of the History of Eugenics;* Lucy Bland, *Banishing the Beast: English Feminism and Sexual Morality* (London: Penguin, 1995); Lesley Hall, "Women, Feminism and Eugenics," in *Essays in the History of Eugenics,* ed. Robert A. Peel (London: Galton Institute, 1998); Angelique Richardson, *Love and Eugenics in the Late Nineteenth Century: Rational Reproduction and the New Woman* (Oxford: Oxford University Press, 2003); Dana Seitler, *Atavistic Tendencies: The Culture of Science in American Modernity* (Minneapolis: University of Minnesota Press, 2008).

16. See Lothrop Stoddard, *The Rising Tide of Color against White World-Supremacy* (New York: Charles Scribner's Sons, 1922).

17. See Angela Y. Davis, *Woman, Race and Class*, 1st Vintage Books ed. (New York: Random House, 1983), chapter 12; Gordon, *The Moral Property of Women*, chapter 9; Dorothy Roberts, *Killing the Black Body: Race, Reproduction and the Meaning of Liberty*, 1st Vintage Books ed. (New York: Random House, 1990), chapter 2; Betsy Hartmann, *Reproductive Rights and Wrongs: The Global Politics of Population Control*, rev. ed. (Boston: South End Press, 1995), chapter 6; Schoen, *Choice and Coercion;* Connelly, *Fatal Misconceptions;* Ahluwalia, *Reproductive Restraints.* Some scholars view Sanger's turn to eugenics as an issue of efficiency rather than ideology. See Carole McCann, *Birth Control Politics in the United States, 1916–1945* (Ithaca, N.Y.: Cornell University Press, 1994); Ellen Chesler, *Woman of Valor: Margaret Sanger and the Birth Control Movement in America* (New York: Simon and Schuster, 1992). For a discussion of the Sanger controversy see Ordover, *American Eugenics*, 137–58.

18. Connelly, *Fatal Misconception*, 221, 322.

19. Ibid., 322.

20. Admittedly, the early years of Sanger's career were marked by her struggles *against* the U.S. government over distributing information about and attempting to increase access to birth control. Nonetheless, in her eugenic guise she is undoubtedly serving a racialized project in line with a U.S. global developmental regime.

21. See, for example, Andrea Smith, *Conquest: Sexual Violence and American Indian Genocide* (Boston: South End Press, 2005); Roberts, *Killing the Black Body;* Jael Silliman, Marlene Gerber Fried, Loretta Ross, and Elena Gutierrez, eds., *Undivided Rights: Women of Color Organizing for Reproductive Justice* (Boston: South End Press, 2004); Marlene Gerber Fried, *From Abortion to Reproductive Freedom: Transforming a Movement* (Boston: South End Press, 1999).

22. I am using Rajeswari Sunder Rajan's staging of the post-independence Indian feminist movement in her *The Scandal of the State: Women, Law, and Citizenship in Postcolonial India* (Durham, N.C.: Duke University Press, 2003).

23. See Nandita Gandhi and Nandita Shah, *The Issues at Stake: Theory and Practice in the Contemporary Women's Movement in India* (New Delhi: Kali for Women, 1992), 120–25. See Hartmann, *Reproductive Rights and Wrongs*, and Jael Silliman and Ynestra King, eds., *Dangerous Intersections: Feminist Perspectives on Population, Environment and Development* (Boston: South End Press, 1999).

24. Shah Bano was a sixty-two-year-old Muslim mother of five who sought alimony after her husband divorced her in 1978. Although she was initially awarded maintenance by the Supreme Court, this judgment was nullified amid protests from the Muslim community (who considered it a violation of Muslim personal law) by the Muslim Women (Protection of Rights on Divorce) Act of 1986. The case renewed the controversy over the issue of the Universal Civil Code.

25. This quote is commonly attributed to Sanger (see, for instance, Gordon, *Moral Property*, 196), but there is some controversy about this attribution. See

Carole McCann, *Birth Control Politics in the United States, 1916–1945* (Ithaca, N.Y.: Cornell University Press, 1994), 112, n. 42.

26. Laura Doyle, *Bordering on the Body: The Racial Matrix of Modern Fiction and Culture* (New York: Oxford University Press, 1994); Angelique Richardson, *Love and Eugenics;* Daylanne K. English, *Unnatural Selections: Eugenics in American Modernism and the Harlem Renaissance* (Chapel Hill: University of North Carolina Press, 2004); Dana Seitler, *Atavistic Tendencies.* See also Donald Childs, *Modernism and Eugenics: Woolf, Eliot, Yeats, and the Culture of Degeneration* (Cambridge: Cambridge University Press, 2001); Betsy Nies, *Eugenic Fantasies: Racial Ideology in the Literature and Popular Culture of the 1920's* (New York: Routledge, 2002); Susan Koshy, *Sexual Naturalization: Asian Americans and Miscegenation* (Stanford, Calif.: Stanford University Press, 2004); Clare Hanson, *Eugenics, Literature, and Culture in Post-war Britain* (New York: Routledge, 2012).

27. English, *Unnatural Selections,* 14.

28. Michel Foucault, *The History of Sexuality, Vol. 1: An Introduction* (New York: Vintage, 1990), 136.

29. Ibid., 139; Michel Foucault, *Society Must Be Defended* (New York: Picador, 2003), 245.

30. Thomas Robert Malthus, *An Essay on the Principle of Population,* 2nd ed. (New York: Norton, 2003), 20.

31. Francis Galton, *Memories of My Life* (London: Methuen, 1908), 323.

32. Alison Bashford and Phillippa Levine, "Introduction" to *The Oxford Handbook of the History of Eugenics,* 11.

33. Foucault, *Society Must Be Defended,* 242.

34. Foucault, *History of Sexuality,* 146.

35. Ann Laura Stoler, *Race and the Education of Desire: Foucault's History of Sexuality and the Colonial Order of Things* (Durham, N.C.: Duke University Press, 1995), 6–7.

36. Foucault, *Society Must Be Defended,* 81.

37. Ibid., 256.

38. Achille Mbembe, "Necropolitics," *Public Culture* 15, no. 1 (2003), 11–40. doi: 10.1215/08992363-15-1-11.

39. María Josefina Saldaña-Portillo, *The Revolutionary Imagination in the Americas in the Age of Development* (Durham, N.C.: Duke University Press, 2003), 23. In the Indian context, the nationalist economic critique of colonialism was premised on the idea that colonialism was an essentially impoverishing relationship that exploited Indian resources and impeded Indian development; a sovereign state would steward the nation toward greater prosperity and opportunity for all. Rather than simply a paradigm imposed from without, development becomes a key component of the decolonizing Indian nation-state. See Partha Chatterjee, "Development Planning and the Indian State," in *The State and Development Planning in India,* ed. T. J. Byres (Delhi: Oxford University Press, 1994), 51–72.

40. Saldaña-Portillo, *Revolutionary Imagination,* 6.

41. Connelly, *Fatal Misconception*, 122.

42. Ibid., 154.

43. See Stoler, *Education of Desire*, and Laura Briggs, *Reproducing Empire: Race, Sex, Science, and U.S. Imperialism in Puerto Rico* (Berkeley: University of California Press, 2002).

44. Briggs, *Reproducing Empire*, 15.

45. The landmark work that began Women in Development approaches (WID) was Esther Boserup's *Women's Role in Economic Development* (London: Earthscan, 2007), originally published in 1970 by St. Martin's Press. For an overview of feminist critiques of development see Naila Kabeer's *Reversed Realities: Gender Hierarchies in Development Thought* (London: Verso, 1994) and Nalini Visvanathan, et al., eds., *The Women, Gender and Development Reader* (London: Zed, 1997).

46. Gayatri Chakravorty Spivak, "Empowering Women," *Environment* 37, no. 1 (January/February 1995): 2. This is from an open letter she wrote in response to Gro Harlem Brundtland, then chair of the World Commission on Environment and Development.

47. Although in chapter 5 I engage with the specific definition of *subalternity* Spivak advances in her paradigm shifting essay, "Can the Subaltern Speak?," throughout *Eugenic Feminism* I use the term *subaltern* in the more general, descriptive sense coined by the Subaltern Studies Group to reference the oppressed, marginalized, and abjected others of the nation: in a word, the "unfit." "Can the Subaltern Speak?" in *Can the Subaltern Speak?: Reflections on the History of an Idea*, ed. Rosalind Morris (New York: Columbia University Press, 2010).

48. Mary Daly, *Gyn/Ecology: The Metaethics of Radical Feminism* (Boston: Beacon Press, 1978). For critiques of Daly see Audre Lorde, "An Open Letter to Mary Daly," *Sister Outsider* (Freedom, Calif: Crossing Press, 1998), 66–71; and Uma Narayan, *Dislocating Cultures: Identities, Traditions, and Third World Feminism* (New York: Routledge, 1997).

49. See, for, instance, Elisabeth Bumiller's discussion of Indira Gandhi in *May You Be the Mother of a Hundred Sons* (New York: Random House, 1990), 147–78. Although Bumiller does not claim Gandhi as a feminist, she nonetheless reads her as emblematic of Indian women in power. Population Council, "United Nations Population Award to Indira Gandhi and Qian Xinzhong," *Population and Development Review* 9, no. 4 (December 1983): 747–53. http://www.jstor.org/stable/1973563.

50. See Asha Nadkarni, "Reproducing Feminism in *Jasmine* and 'The Yellow Wallpaper,'" *Feminist Studies* 38, no. 1 (Spring 2012): 215–41.

51. For an elaboration of this in relation to late nineteenth-century Britain, see Carolyn Burdett, "The Hidden Romance of Sexual Science: Eugenics, the Nation and the Making of Modern Feminism," in *Sexology in Culture: Labelling Bodies and Desires,* ed. Lucy Bland and Laura Doan (Chicago: University of Chicago Press, 1998), 44–59.

52. As Sinha puts it, because feminists in North America (and Europe) needed

to struggle against the nation-state for full citizenship rights (most particularly the right to vote), "this particular history . . . assumes that feminism has an apparently natural antipathy for, and an ability to transcend, the nation." Mrinalini Sinha, *Gender and Nation* (Washington, D.C.: American Historical Association, 2006), 3.

53. Sinha, *Gender and Nation,* 29.

54. Partha Chatterjee, *The Nation and Its Fragments: Colonial and Postcolonial Histories.* (Princeton, N.J.: Princeton University Press, 1993); Himanji Bannerji, "Projects of Hegemony: Towards a Critique of Subaltern Studies's 'Resolution of the Women's Question,'" *Economic and Political Weekly,* March 11–17, 2000, 902–20. http://www.jstor.org/stable/4409022; Mrinalini Sinha, "Gender in the Critiques of Colonialism and Nationalism: Locating the 'Indian Woman,'" in *Feminism and History,* ed. Joan Wallach Scott (Oxford: Oxford University Press, 1996), 477–504; Sinha, "The Lineage of the 'Indian' Modern: Rhetoric, Agency and the Sarda Act in Late Colonial India," in *Gender, Sexuality and Colonial Modernities,* ed. Antoinette Burton (London: Routledge, 1999), 207–21; and Sinha "Refashioning Mother India: Feminism and Nationalism in Late-Colonial India," *Feminist Studies* 26, no. 3 (Fall 2000): 623–44.

55. Kumari Jayawardena, *Feminism and Nationalism in the Third World* (New Delhi: Kali for Women, 1986). Dhanvanthi Rama Rau is a case in point. In the years leading up to independence she brought a powerful feminist politics to nationalism and a powerful anti-imperial critique to international feminism, but after independence her energy is channeled into the state and these critiques are lost. See Mrinalini Sinha, "Suffragism and Internationalism: The Enfranchisement of British and Indian Women under an Imperial State," *Indian Economic and Social History Review* 36 (December 1999): 461–84.

56. Nira Yuval-Davis, Floya Anthias, and Jo Campling, *Woman, Nation, State* (Houndmills, Basingstoke, Hampshire: Macmillan, 1989). For more on the relation between woman and nation in general, see Caren Kaplan, Norma Alarcón, and Minoo Moallem, *Between Woman and Nation: Nationalisms, Transnational Feminisms, and the State* (Durham, N.C.: Duke University Press, 1999); Deniz Kandiyoti, "Bargaining with Patriarchy," in *The Women, Gender and Development Reader,* ed. Nalini Visvanathan et al. (London: Zed, 1997), 86–92; Kandiyoti, "Identity and Its Discontents: Women and Nation," in *Colonial Discourse and Post-Colonial Theory,* ed. Patrick Williams and Laura Chrisman (New York: Columbia University Press, 1994), 376–91; Anne McClintock, "Family Feuds: Gender, Nationalism and the Family," *Feminist Review* 44 (Summer 1993): 61–80; McClintock, *Imperial Leather: Race, Gender, and Sexuality in the Colonial Contest* (New York: Routledge, 1995); Lata Mani, *Contentious Traditions: The Debate on Sati in Colonial India* (Berkeley: University of California Press, 1998), Sangeeta Ray, *En-Gendering India: Woman and Nation in Colonial and Postcolonial Narratives* (Durham, N.C.: Duke University Press, 2000); Kumkum Sangari and Sudesh Vaid, eds., *Recasting Women: Essays in Indian Colonial History* (New Brunswick, N.J.: Rutgers University Press, 1990); Mrinalini Sinha,

Specters of Mother India (Durham, N.C.: Duke University Press, 2006); Mahua Sarkar, *Visible Histories, Disappearing Women: Producing Muslim Womanhood in Late Colonial Bengal* (Durham, N.C.: Duke University Press, 2008).

57. Mani, *Contentious Traditions*, 2.

58. Alys Eve Weinbaum, *Wayward Reproductions: Genealogies of Race and Nation in Transatlantic Modern Thought* (Durham, N.C.: Duke University Press, 2004), 39.

59. Etienne Balibar, "Racism and Nationalism," in *Race, Nation, Class: Ambiguous Identities*, ed. Etienne Balibar and Emmanuel Wallerstein (London: Verso, 1991), 54, emphases in original.

60. Weinbaum, *Wayward Reproductions*, 37.

61. Ibid., 62, emphases in original.

62. Chatterjee, *Nation and Its Fragments*, 6.

63. Charu Gupta, *Sexuality, Obscenity, Community: Women, Muslims, and the Hindu Public in Colonial India* (New York: Palgrave, 2002), first published in India in 2001 by Permanent Black; Paola Bacchetta, *Gender in the Hindu Nation* (New Delhi: Women Unlimited, 2004); Tanika Sarker, *Hindu Wife, Hindu Nation: Community, Religion, and Cultural Nationalism* (Bloomington: Indiana University Press, 2010); Sarker, *Visible Histories*.

64. Chatterjee, *Nation and Its Fragments*, 110.

65. Gupta, *Sexuality, Obscenity, Community*, 7.

66. Pradip Kumar Datta, "Women, Abductions and Religious Identities," in *Gendering Colonial India: Reforms, Print, Caste and Communalism*, ed. Charu Gupta (New Delhi: Orient Blackswan, 2012), 265–87.

67. Charu Gupta, "Archives and Sexuality: Vignettes from Colonial North India," in *Gendering Colonial India*, 329. See also Anjali Arondekar, *For the Record: On Sexuality and the Colonial Archive in India* (Durham, N.C.: Duke University Press, 2009).

68. See Alison Bashford, "Internationalism, Cosmopolitanism, and Eugenics" in *The Oxford Handbook of the History of Eugenics*, 154–72.

69. See Briggs's discussion of how the United States "simply reiterated British [prostitution] policy" in Puerto Rico. *Reproducing Empire*, 33.

70. David Arnold, "Introduction: Disease, Medicine and Empire," in *Imperial Medicine and Indigenous Societies*, ed. David Arnold (Delhi: Oxford University Press, 1988), 15.

71. See Chloe Campbell, *Race and Empire: Eugenics in Colonial Kenya* (Manchester: Manchester University Press, 2012) about imperial eugenics in Kenya. In India, however, the eugenics movement was almost entirely led by native Indians.

72. Richardson, *Love and Eugenics*, 28.

73. See Ann Tayor Allen, "Feminism and Eugenics in Germany and Britain, 1900–1940: A Comparative Perspective," *German Studies Review* 23, no. 3 (October 2000): 477–505. http://www.jstor.org/stable/1432830; Hall, "Women, Feminism and Eugenics," 36–51.

74. Mary Zeigler, "Eugenic Feminism: Mental Hygiene, the Women's Movement, and the Campaign for Eugenic Legal Reform, 1900–1935," *Harvard Journal of Law & Gender* 31 (2008): 213.

75. Quoted in ibid., 130.

76. Sinha, *Specters*, 75.

77. Stern, *Eugenic Nation*, 4. See also Bashford, "Internationalism," 164–65.

78. See Michael Latham, *The Right Kind of Revolution: Modernization, Development, and U.S. Foreign Policy from the Cold War to the Present* (Ithaca, N.Y.: Cornell University Press, 2011), chapter 4.

1. Perfecting Feminism

1. Charlotte Perkins Gilman, "The Burden of Mothers: A Clarion Call to Redeem the Race! (Lebanon Leaves)" (Mt. Lebanon, N.Y.: Shaker Press, 1895). Line numbers cited in text.

2. Elaine Hedges, afterword to *The Yellow Wallpaper* (New York: Feminist Press, 1973), 37–62; Sandra Gilbert and Susan Gubar, "Infection in the Sentence: The Woman Writer and the Anxiety of Authorship," in *The Madwoman in the Attic: The Woman Writer and the Nineteenth-Century Literary Imagination*, 2nd sub ed. (New Haven, Conn.: Yale University Press, 1979); Annette Kolodny, "A Map for Rereading: Or, Gender and the Interpretation of Literary Texts," *New Literary History* 11, no. 3 (1980): 451–60; and Jean E. Kennard, "Convention Coverage: Or, How to Read Your Own Life," *New Literary History* 13 (Autumn 1981): 69–88. For a more thorough discussion of these and other readings of "The Yellow Wallpaper" see Hedges, "'Out at Last'? The Yellow Wallpaper after Two Decades of Feminist Criticism," in *Critical Essays on Charlotte Perkins Gilman*, ed. Joanna B. Karpinski (New York: G. K. Hall, 1992), 222–33. Susan Lanser's groundbreaking 1989 article, "Feminist Criticism, 'The Yellow Wallpaper' and the Politics of Color in America," argues against these earlier readings by excavating the racial politics that inform "The Yellow Wallpaper" and Gilman's other works. *Feminist Studies* 15 (Fall 1989): 415–41.

3. Following Lanser, critics have begun to theorize the centrality of race and eugenics to Gilman's feminism. See Gail Bederman, *Manliness and Civilization: A Cultural History of Gender and Race in the United States, 1880–1917* (Chicago: University of Chicago Press, 1995); Bernice L. Hausman, "Sex before Gender: Charlotte Perkins Gilman and the Evolutionary Paradigm of Utopia," *Feminist Studies* 24 (Fall 1998): 489–510; Louise Michele Newman, *White Women's Rights: The Racial Origins of Feminism in the United States* (New York: Oxford University Press, 1999); Lisa Gaobcsi-Williams, "The Intellectualism of Charlotte Perkins Gilman: Evolutionary Perspectives on Race, Ethnicity, and Class," in *Charlotte Perkins Gilman: Optimist Reformer*, ed. Jill Rudd and Val Gough (Iowa City: University of Iowa Press, 1999), 16–44; Gary Scharnhorst, "Historicizing Gilman: A Bibliographer's View," in *The Mixed Legacy of Charlotte Perkins Gilman*, ed. Catherine J. Golden and Joanna Schneider Zangrando (Newark: University of

Delaware Press, 2000); Jennifer Hudak, "The 'Social Inventor': Charlotte Perkins Gilman and the (Re) Production of Perfection," *Women's Studies* 32 (2003): 455–77; Weinbaum, *Wayward Reproductions;* Seitler, *Atavistic Tendencies;* Dohra Ahmad, *Landscapes of Hope: Utopianism in America* (New York: Oxford University Press, 2009). Even with this new scholarship, however, there is still a tendency to view Gilman's racism as simply anachronism. The essays in Golden and Zangrando present some recent examples of this, with the exception of the essay by Scharnhorst.

4. Ahmad, *Landscapes of Hope,* 20.

5. Charlotte Perkins Gilman, *Concerning Children* (London: Watts, 1907), 8.

6. Ibid., 7.

7. Bederman, *Manliness and Civilization,* 25.

8. Kevin Gaines, *Uplifting the Race: Black Leadership, Politics, and Culture in the Twentieth Century* (Chapel Hill: University of North Carolina Press, 1996), 35.

9. See Bederman, *Manliness and Civilization,* chapter 2.

10. Gaines, *Uplifting the Race,* 81.

11. See ibid., 120–27; Stephanie Athey, "Eugenic Feminisms in Late Nineteenth-Century America: Reading Race in Victoria Woodhull, Frances Willard, Anna Julia Cooper, and Ida B. Wells," *Genders Online Journal* 31 (2000). http://www.genders.org/g31/g31_athey.html#b03; on Hopkin's complicated relationship to racial mixing see Yogita Goyal, *Romance, Diaspora and Black Atlantic Literature* (Cambridge: Cambridge University Press, 2010), chapter 1.

12. Roberts, *Killing the Black Body,* 86.

13. Ibid., 76–77. See also Athey, "Eugenic Feminisms"; Gaines, *Uplifting the Race;* English, *Unnatural Selections,* chapter 1.

14. English, *Unnatural Selections,* chapter 4.

15. Ibid., 64.

16. Charlotte Perkins Gilman and Zona Gale, *The Living of Charlotte Perkins Gilman: An Autobiography* (New York, London: D. Appleton-Century, 1935), 42.

17. Ibid., 39.

18. Lester Frank Ward, *Pure Sociology: A Treatise on the Origin and Spontaneous Development of Society* (London: Macmillan & Co., 1903), 292.

19. According to Darwin, either women or men could be sex selectors, but most of his American populizers emphasized masculine agency in choosing a mate. From this followed the idea that man, as the active agent, embodied the traits of the race, while passive woman simply embodied the traits of her sex. For more on Gilman's relationship to social evolutionary theory see Mark Pittenger, *American Socialists and Evolutionary Thought, 1870–1920* (Madison: University of Wisconsin Press, 1993).

20. Caleb Williams Saleeby, *Woman and Womanhood: A Search for Principles* (New York: J. J. Little & Ives, 1911).

21. Charlotte Perkins Gilman, "Feminism, College Education and the Birth Rate," *Forerunner* 6 (October 1915): 259.

22. Gordon, *Moral Property,* 83.

23. Ibid., 80–85.

24. Judith Allen, "The Later Gilman," in *The Feminism of Charlotte Perkins Gilman: Sexualities, Histories, Progressivism* (Chicago: University of Chicago Press, 2009), 290–326.

25. Charlotte Perkins Gilman, "The Sanctity of Human Life," *Forerunner* 8, no. 5 (1916): 128–29.

26. Mary Zeigler, "Eugenic Feminism: Mental Hygiene, the Women's Movement, and the Campaign for Eugenic Legal Reform, 1900–1935," *Harvard Journal of Law & Gender* 31 (2008): 228.

27. Charlotte Perkins Gilman, *Women and Economics: A Study of the Economic Relation between Men and Women as a Factor in Social Evolution* (Boston: Small Maynard and Company, 1898), 60.

28. Gilman was not alone in reversing this conventional view: as her contemporary Thorstein Veblen argued, the seizure of primitive woman by primitive man was crucial to the development of a leisure class defined by conspicuous consumption because "in the sequence of cultural evolution the emergence of a leisure class coincides with the beginning of ownership" and "the earliest form of ownership is an ownership of the women by the able-bodied men of the community." Thorstein Veblen, *A Veblen Treasury: From Leisure Class to War, Peace, and Capitalism.* Studies in Institutional Economics (Armonk, N.Y.; London, England: M. E. Sharpe, 1993), 16.

29. Charlotte Perkins Gilman, The *Man-Made World Or, Our Androcentric Culture,* 3rd ed. (New York: Charlton Company, 1913), 37.

30. Gilman, *Women and Economics,* 331.

31. As Robert Young clarifies, the term *hybrid* began to be applied to human populations in the nineteenth century in the context of colonial debates around race and sex. Confronted with racial otherness in the colonial project, nineteenth-century scientific controversy revolved around the possibility of fertile and infertile unions between people of different races, thus centering a debate about race on issues of sex and desire. Though positive, "amalgamation," theories of racial mixing developed, miscegenation was largely thought of as either impossible or undesirable: both linguistically and sexually "'hybrid' forms . . . were seen to embody threatening forms of perversion and degeneration." Gilman draws upon the negative connotations of the term *hybrid* to evoke the shadowy specter of racial mixing, underscoring the degradation of modern white women under the sexuo-economic relation. *Colonial Desire: Hybridity in Theory, Culture, and Race* (New York: Routledge, 1995), 5.

32. Bederman, *Manliness and Civilization,* 142.

33. Ibid., chapter 1.

34. Charlotte Perkins Gilman, "Should Women Use Violence?," in Gilman and Larry Ceplair, *Charlotte Perkins Gilman: A Nonfiction Reader* (New York: Columbia University Press, 1991), 217.

35. Bederman, *Manliness and Civilization,* 142.

36. Charlotte Perkins Gilman and Minna Doskow, *Charlotte Perkins Gilman's Utopian Novels* (Madison, N.J.: Fairleigh Dickinson University Press, 1999), 193. All further references cited in the text.

37. Ahmad, *Landscapes of Hope*, 59.

38. Gilman, *The Man-Made World*, 36.

39. Gilman, *Women and Economics*, 116.

40. Ibid., 121.

41. Ibid., 158.

42. Walter Benn Michaels, *The Gold Standard and the Logic of Naturalism: American Literature at the Turn of the Century* (Berkeley: University of California Press, 1987), 10.

43. Gilman was concerned with the problem of overpopulation as the cause of war, as she argues in "Birth Control, Religion and the Unfit," *The Nation*, January 27, 1932. http://www.thenation.com/article/154433/birth-control-religion-and-unfit#.

44. See also Zygmunt Baumann on the "gardening state" *Modernity and Ambivalence* (Cambridge, England: Polity Press, 1991).

45. Gilman's support for the war was part and parcel of her belief in social evolutionism. As Pittenger explains, "[Gilman] . . . argued in the *American Fabian* that the Cuban adventure assumed a much more cheerful aspect when viewed in its evolutionary context. . . . Like capitalism itself, war was thus an unconscious breeder of the 'banded brotherhood of tomorrow'; meanwhile, the elimination of the unfit on the battlefield disposed of undesirable elements" (*American Socialists*, 76).

46. Thomas Peyser, *Utopia and Cosmopolis: Globalization in the Era of American Literary Realism* (Durham, N.C.: Duke University Press, 1998), 86.

47. United States and William Paul Dillingham. 1911. *Reports of the Immigration Commission*. Washington, D.C.: Government Printing Office, 8.

48. Alison Bashford, "Internationalism, Cosmopolitanism, and Eugenics," in *The Oxford Handbook of the History of Eugenics*, 158.

49. Charlotte Perkins Gilman, "Immigration, Importation, and Our Fathers," *Forerunner* 5 (May 1914): 118, emphases added.

50. Ibid.

51. Ibid., emphases added.

52. Charlotte Perkins Gilman, "Solution to the Negro Problem," in Gilman and Ceplair, *Non-fiction Reader*, 178.

53. Priscilla Wald, "Naturalization," in *Keywords for American Cultural Studies*, ed. Bruce Burgett and Glen Hendler (New York: New York University Press, 2007), 173. See also Cathy Schlund-Vials, *Modeling Citizenship: Jewish and Asian American Writing* (Philadelphia: Temple University Press, 2011).

54. Bashford, "Internationalism, Cosmopolitanism and Eugenics," 160; see also Sharon Lamp and W. Carol Cleigh, "A Heritage of Ableist Rhetoric in American Feminism from the Eugenics Period," in *Feminist Disability Studies*, ed. Kim Q. Hall (Bloomington: Indiana University Press, 2011), 175–89.

55. Mariana Valverde, "'When the Mother of the Race Is Free': Race, Repro-

duction, and Sexuality in First-Wave Feminism," in *Gender Conflicts: New Essays in Women's History*, ed. Franca Iacovetta and Mariana Valverde (Toronto: University of Toronto Press, 1992), 14.

56. Gilman, *Man-Made World*, 258.

57. See, for instance, the 1960 *Time* magazine cover story on the "population explosion," January 11, 1960, and of course Ehrlich's *The Population Bomb*.

58. E. A. Ross, "The Causes of Race Superiority," *Annals of the American Academy of Political and Social Science* 18 (January 1901): 212.

59. Charlotte Perkins Gilman, "Let Sleeping Forefathers Lie," *Forerunner* 6, no. 11 (1915): 261.

2. Regenerating Feminism

1. Sarojini Naidu, *The Daily News and the Leader* (London), November 13, 1931, quoted in Hasi Banerjee, *Sarojini Naidu: The Traditional Feminist* (Calcutta: K P Bagchi, 1998), 25.

2. Ibid.

3. Naidu's first volume of poetry, *The Golden Threshold*, was published in 1905; the second, *The Bird of Time*; was published in 1912; and the third, *The Broken Wing*, was published in 1917. In 1928 her collected poems were published as *The Sceptered Flute*, and in 1961 her daughter Padmaja published some of her later poems posthumously as *The Feather of the Dawn*.

4. Makarand Paranjape, *Sarojini Naidu: Selected Poetry and Prose* (New Delhi: Indus, 1993), 3.

5. Parama Roy, *Indian Traffic: Identities in Question in Colonial and Post-colonial India* (Berkeley: University of California Press, 1998), 10.

6. As one of the harsher modern assessments of Naidu's poetry proclaims, "She is the most unfashionable poet on the Indo-Anglian poetic scene today . . . scorn[ed] for her overluxuriant imagination and mellifluous verse, her cloying sensuousness and meretricious metrics." K. Venkatachari, "The Cleft Lute: A Study in Sarojini Naidu's Poetry," *Journal of Literature and Aesthestics* 4, no. 4 (October–December 1994): 19.

7. See Roy, *Indian Traffic;* Melissa Purdue, "From Sarojini Naidu's 'Curved and Eloquent Little Mouth' to Arundhati Roy's 'Mass of Untamed Curls and Dark Eyes': Stereotypical Depictions of Female, Indian Authors in Reviews of Their Work," *Atenea* 23, no. 2 (2003): 87–102; Edward Marx, *The Idea of a Colony: Cross-Culturalism in Modern Poetry* (Toronto: University of Toronto Press, 2004); Sinha, "Gender in the Critiques of Colonialism and Nationalism," 477–504; Elleke Boehmer, "East Is East and South Is South: The Cases of Sarojini Naidu and Arundhati Roy," *Women: A Cultural Review* 11, nos. 1/2 (2000): 61–70; Malashri Lal, *The Law of the Threshold: Women Writers in Indian English* (Shimla: Indian Institute of Advanced Study, 1995); Ahmad, *Landscapes of Hope*.

8. Certainly Naidu is most often talked about through a feminist lens. Though critical examinations of her inevitably call attention to her famous disavowal of

feminism, they nonetheless retain the label "feminist" to describe Naidu. Geraldine Forbes's assertion is characteristic of this trend: "While Sarojini Naidu denied she was a feminist, I would call her ideology social feminism." *Women in Modern India* (Cambridge: Cambridge University Press, 1996), 158.

9. Sinha, *Specters of Mother India,* and "Refashioning Mother India."

10. Dipesh Chakrabarty, *Provincializing Europe: Postcolonial Thought and Historical Difference* (Princeton, N.J.: Princeton University Press, 2000).

11. Naidu, quoted in Banerjee, *Traditional Feminist,* 24.

12. Sarojini Naidu, quoted in Shirin M. Rai and Kumud Sharma, "Democratising the Indian Parliament: the 'Reservation for Women' Debate," in *International Perspectives on Gender and Democratisation,* ed. Shirin Rai (London: Palgrave Macmillan, 2000), 154, emphases added.

13. Vasant Kaiwar and Sucheta Mazumdar, "Race, Orient, Nation in the Time-Space of Modernity," in *Antimonies of Modernity: Essays on Race, Orient, Nation,* ed. Vasant Kaiwar and Sucheta Mazumdar (Durham, N.C.: Duke University Press, 2003), 274–75.

14. Naidu, quoted in Banerjee, *Traditional Feminist,* 100.

15. Ibid., 24.

16. Ibid.

17. Ibid.

18. Uma Chakravarti, "Whatever Happened to the Vedic Dasi?: Orientalism, Nationalism, and a Script for the Past," in *Recasting Women: Essays in Indian Colonial History,* ed. Kumkum Sangari and Sudesh Vaid (New Brunswick, N.J.: Rutgers University Press, 1990), 79

19. Naidu, *Selected Poetry and Prose,* 149.

20. Forbes, *Women in Modern India,* 99–100.

21. Naidu, *Speeches and Writings of Sarojini Naidu* (Madras: G. A. Natesan, 1925), 198.

22. Forbes, *Women in Modern India,* 101.

23. Naidu, *Selected Poetry and Prose,* 159.

24. Naidu, *Speeches and Writings,* 203.

25. Banu Subramaniam, "Archaic Modernities: Science, Secularism, and Religion in Modern India," *Social Text* 18, no. 3 (2000): 67–86. See also her "Imagining India: Religious Nationalism in the Age of Science and Development," in *Feminist Futures: Re-imagining Women, Culture and Development,* ed. Kum-Kum Bhavnani, John Foran, and Priya Kurian (New York: Zed, 2003), 160–77.

26. Naidu, *Selected Poetry and Prose,* 148.

27. Ibid., 149.

28. Naidu, *Speeches and Writings,* 13.

29. Bannerji, "Projects of Hegemony," 214.

30. Ketu H. Katrak, "Indian Nationalism, Gandhian 'Satyagraha,' and Representations of Female Sexuality," in *Nationalisms and Sexualities,* ed. Andrew Parker, Mary Russo, Doris Sommer, and Patricia Yaeger (New York: Routledge, 1992), 396.

31. For a further discussion of Gandhi's relationship to women and the feminine see Roy, *Indian Traffic,* and Madhu Kishwar, "Gandhi on Women," *Economic and Political Weekly,* October 5, 1985): 1691–1702.

32. Naidu, *Speeches and Writings,* 203.

33. Naidu's stance toward the English language is complicated. In the introduction to *The Golden Threshold* (1905), her first book of poetry, her mentor Arthur Symons recounts how Naidu learned English: "I . . . was stubborn and refused to speak it. So one day when I was nine years old my father punished me—the only time I was ever punished—by shutting me in a room alone for a whole day. I came out of it a full-blown linguist. I have never spoken any other language to him, or to my mother, who always speaks to me in Hindustani" (11).

34. Vasant Kaiwar, "The Aryan Model of History and the Oriental Renaissance: The Politics of Identity in an Age of Revolutions, Colonialism, and Nationalism," in *Antimonies of Modernity: Essays on Race, Orient, Nation,* ed. Vasant Kaiwar and Sucheta Mazumdar (Durham, N.C.: Duke University Press, 2003), 16.

35. Ibid., 28.

36. Sucheta Mazumdar, "The Politics of Religion and National Origin," in *Antimonies of Modernity,* 231.

37. Naidu, *Golden Threshold,* 94, line numbers cited in text; Padmini Sengupta, *Sarojini Naidu: A Biography* (New York: Asia Publishing House, 1966), 48.

38. Benedict Anderson, *Imagined Communities: Reflections on the Origin and Spread of Nationalism,* rev. and ext. ed. (New York: Verso, 1991), 24.

39. McClintock, "Family Feuds," 66.

40. Ibid.

41. Naidu, *Speeches and Writings,* 54.

42. Ibid., 36.

43. For more on the way in which Indian men, particularly Bengali men, were constructed as effeminate, see Sinha, *Colonial Masculinity.*

44. See Chakravarti, "Whatever Happened to the Vedic Dasi?"; Sinha, *Colonial Masculinity;* Ray, *En-Gendering India;* Gupta, *Sexuality, Obscenity, Community,* chapter 6.

45. See Hodges, "South Asia's Eugenic Past," 230.

46. Ibid., 229.

47. Ibid., 225.

48. Ahluwalia, *Reproductive Restraints,* 26; Sarah Hodges, *Contraception, Colonialism, and Commerce: Birth Control in South India, 1920–1940* (Burlington, Vt.: Ashgate, 2008), 9.

49. On the supposed problem of Muslim fecundity see Gupta, *Sexuality, Obscenity, Community* and Bacchetta, *Gender in the Hindu Nation,* especially chapter 3. On the council of state measure see Connelly, *Fatal Misconception,* 93.

50. Ahluwalia, *Reproductive Restraints,* 96.

51. See ibid., 127–33; Connelly, *Fatal Misconception,* 93.

52. Hodges, "South Asia's Eugenic Past," 230, and *Contraception, Colonialism, and Commerce;* Anandhi S., "Reproductive Bodies and Regulated Sexuality: Birth

Control Debates in Early 20th Century Tamilnadu," in *A Question of Silence: The Sexual Economies of Modern India,* ed. Mary E. John and Janaki Nair (New Delhi: Kali for Women, 1998), 155.

53. Narayan Sitaram Phadke, *Sex Problem in India: Being a Plea for a Eugenic Movement in India and a Study of All Theoretical and Practical Questions Pertaining to Eugenics* (Bombay: D. B. Taraporevala Sons, 1927), 19.

54. Ibid., 339.

55. See Hodges, "South Asia's Eugenic Past," and Ahluwalia, *Reproductive Restraints,* chapter 1.

56. See Chakravarti, "Whatever Happened to the Vedic Dasi?," for one of the more influential versions of this argument.

57. Hodges, "South Asia's Eugenic Past," 232.

58. Margaret Sanger, *The Autobiography of Margaret Sanger* (New York: Dover, 2004), 466–67; and "Archive: Gandhi and Mrs. Sanger Debate Birth Control," in *Reproductive Health in India,* 235–47.

59. Hodges, "South Asia's Eugenic Past," 233.

60. Naidu, *Speeches and Writings,* 98.

61. Ibid.

62. Ibid., 42.

63. Ibid., 41.

64. Gilman, "The Burden of Mothers," 22–24.

65. Naidu, *Speeches and Writings,* 12–13.

66. See Sinha, *Colonial Masculinity,* and Chakravarti, "Whatever Happened to the Vedic Dasi?," on how the Aryan ideal "was important in the nationalist construction of a sense of identity for its connotations of political and cultural achievement. These aspects are to be seen in relation to the negative qualities of an effete, unmanly, slothful and slack people as imputed by one section of European writers on India" (47).

67. Naidu, quoted in Banerjee, *Traditional Feminist,* 21.

68. Naidu, *Speeches and Writings,* 54.

69. Naidu, quoted in Banerjee, *Traditional Feminist,* 20.

70. See Chakravarti, "Whatever Happened to the Vedi Dasi?"; Sangari and Vaid, *Recasting Women;* and Sinha, "The Lineage of the 'Indian' Modern." For more on the way in which the debates around *sati* collaborated in the creation of tradition, particularly in terms of privileging scriptural evidence for the practice, see Mani, *Contentious Traditions.*

71. Spivak, "Can the Subaltern Speak?," 50.

72. Naidu, *Golden Threshold,* 46, line numbers cited in text.

73. Naidu, *Speeches and Writings,* 198.

74. As Parama Roy argues in her excellent discussion of Naidu's poetry and politics, "Within this frame of reference, woman cannot expect to be a citizen on her own account but only for something larger than herself" (*Indian Traffic,* 142). Even as Roy recognizes the paradox in this move—that it can only claim an inheritance of liberty for men through the agency of women who do not want that

agency for themselves but for their sons—I argue that Naidu's maternal feminist politics are not entirely subsumed by her nationalist ones.

75. Arguably, this blind spot (that is, Naidu's simultaneous use of the Aryan theory of history and her work on behalf of Hindu–Muslim unity), to the extent that it was generalized throughout the Congress Party, was precisely what made the Muslim League so nervous. The liberal discourse of a secular nationalism does not sit easily with a cultural discourse that is continually evoking a Hindu past as the basis of the Indian nation.

76. Kaiwar, "Aryan," 34.

77. Ibid., 50.

78. Naidu, *Speeches and Writing*, 80, 82.

79. Ibid., 87.

80. Ibid., 104.

81. Ibid., 57.

82. Ibid.

83. Sarkar, *Visible Histories, Disappearing Women*, 56.

84. Ibid., 62.

85. Chakravarti, "Whatever Happened to the Vedic Dasi?," 28.

86. Sinha, "The Lineage of the Indian 'Modern,'" 210.

87. Naidu, quoted in Banerjee, *Traditional Feminist*, 92.

88. See Laura Lovett's discussion of what she calls "nostalgic modernists" in Progressive-era United States, and how "nostalgic modernism could be extremely critical of both the past and the present even as it projected an ideal of the past in service of contemporary ends" (11). Of particular interest is her discussion of how "nostalgic idealizations of motherhood, the family, and home were used to construct and legitimate political agendas and social policies concerning reproduction" (3). *Conceiving the Future: Pronatalism, Reproduction, and the Family in the United States, 1890–1938* (Chapel Hill: University of North Caroline Press, 2007).

89. Susan Stewart, *On Longing: Narratives of the Miniature, the Gigantic, the Souvenir, the Collection* (Durham, N.C.: Duke University Press, 1993), 23.

90. Maya Nadkarni and Olga Shevchenko, "The Politics of Nostalgia: A Case for Comparative Analysis of Post-Socialist Practices," *Ab Imperio* 2 (2004): 489–90.

91. Alastair Bonnett, *Left in the Past: Radicalism and the Politics of Nostalgia* (New York: Continuum, 2010), 87.

92. Dipesh Chakrabarty, *Provincializing Europe: Postcolonial Thought and Historical Difference,* reissue (Princeton, N.J.: Princeton University Press, 2008), 247.

93. Ibid., 250.

94. Renato Rosaldo, "Imperialist Nostalgia," *Representations* 26 (Spring 1989): 108.

95. Ibid., 108.

96. Edmund Gosse, "Introduction," *The Bird of Time* by Sarojini Naidu (London: William Heinemann, 1912), 4.

97. Ibid., 5.

98. Ibid.

99. Makarand Paranjape, "Introduction," *Sarojini Naidu: Selected Poetry and Prose,* ed. Makarand Paranjape (New Delhi: Indus, 1993), 14.

100. Ibid.

101. Naidu, *Golden Threshold,* 27, line numbers cited in text.

102. Ibid., 31.

103. Ibid., 37, line numbers cited in text.

104. Naidu, "To India."

105. Meena Alexander reads it as a sign of Naidu's inability to reconcile her sexual and political passions, "Sarojini Naidu: Romanticism and Resistance," *Economic and Political Weekly,* October. 12, 1985, WS68–WS71; Makarand Paranjape contends that it reveals that even as Naidu's politics are national democratic her aesthetics are feudal, "Introduction." Parama Roy argues that the contradiction between Naidu's life and work is enabling; the archaism of Naidu's poetry allows her entrance into the male sphere of nationalist politics. Her overt femininity, as well as her celebration of "traditional" ways of life, "exonerates the poet's imperfect emulation of those gendered models" in her own life. *Indian Traffic,* 137.

3. "World Menace"

1. This is the quotation on the book jacket of the 1943 edition of *Mother India* (New York: Harcourt Brace, 1927). All references are cited in the text.

2. Kumari Jayawardena, *The White Woman's Other Burden: Western Women and South Asia during British Colonial Rule* (New York: Routledge, 1995), 95. Mrinalini Sinha, "Introduction," in *Mother India: Selections from the Controversial 1927 Text,* ed. Mrinalini Sinha (Ann Arbor: University of Michigan Press, 2000), 2. My discussion of the historical background of *Mother India* and of the controversy that *Mother India* generated is indebted to Sinha, *Specters of Mother India;* "Refashioning Mother India"; "Reading Mother India: Empire, Nation, and the Female Voice," *Journal of Women's History* 6, no. 2 (Summer 1994): 6–44; and to Manorajan Jha, *Katherine Mayo and India* (New Delhi: People's Publishing House, 1971).

3. To name just two events, on November 21, 1927, there was a conference hosted by Eleanor Rathbone in London. There was also a meeting of mass protest against *Mother India* in San Francisco on March 22, 1928 (*Katherine Mayo Papers,* Folder 206, Box 37, and Sinha, "Introduction," 2).

4. See Jha, "'Mother India' and the British" 61–65 and "'Mother India' and the Americans" 74–79 in *Katherine Mayo and India.*

5. See Sarah Hodges, "Indian Eugenics in an Age of Reform," in *Reproductive Health in India: History, Politics, and Controversies,* ed. Sarah Hodges (New Delhi: Orient Longman, 2006), particularly 125–29.

6. See the special issue of the *Journal of Colonialism and Colonial History* (2001) on "Pairing Empires: Britain and the United States, 1857–1947" for an indepth discussion of the relationship between British and U.S. empires.

7. I take this section title from the 1930 book by Wendell Thomas, *Hinduism Invades America* (Boston: Beacon Press, 1930).

8. See Andrew Rotter, "Gender Relations, Foreign Relations: The United States and South Asia, 1947–1964," *Journal of American History*, 81, no. 2 (September 1994): 518–42. http://www.jstor.org/stable/2081170; Rotter, *Comrades at Odds: The United States and India, 1947–1964* (Ithaca, N.Y.: Cornell University Press, 2000); Sinha, "Introduction"; Vijay Prashad, *The Karma of Brown Folk* (Minneapolis: University of Minnesota Press, 2000); and Joy Dixon, "Ancient Wisdom, Modern Motherhood: Theosophy and the Colonial Syncretic," in *Gender, Sexuality and Colonial Modernities*.

9. Prashad, *Karma*, 18.

10. Jha, *Katherine Mayo and India*, 2; Alan Raucher, "American Anti-Imperialists and the Pro-India Movement, 1900–1932," *Pacific Historical Review* 43, no. 1 (February 1974): 83–110.

11. See Prashad, *Karma*, especially "On Authentic Cultural Lives," and Raucher, 94.

12. See Jha, *Katherine Mayo and India*, 8.

13. The Hindu–German Conspiracy involved links between Indian revolutionaries and the German government and included (among other things) an attempt to smuggle arms into India. For more on this see Maia Ramnath, "Two Revolutions: The Ghadar Party and India's Radical Diaspora, 1913–1918," *Radical History Review* 92 (Spring 2005): 7–30.

14. As Prashad notes, of the masses of people interested in Hinduism "few cared for the living Indians in their midst or for the systematic poverty produced and maintained in India by imperialism" (*Karma*, 44).

15. See Paul Teed on how "Mayo's use of race in *Mother India* was designed in part to undermine these simple analogies between America's past and India's present." "Race against Memory: Katherine Mayo, Jabez Sunderland, and Indian Independence," *American Studies* 44, nos. 1–2 (Spring–Summer 2003): 42.

16. Despite Mayo's dubious relationship to the feminism of her time, *Mother India* has been championed as a feminist text, most notably by Mary Daly in *Gyn/Ecology*. For a similar (if somewhat more measured) feminist recuperation see Elisabeth Bumiller, *May You Be the Mother of a Hundred Sons: A Journey among the Women of India* (New York: Random House, 1990). Such recuperations have been heavily critiqued, most notably by Lorde, "An Open Letter to Mary Daly," and Narayan, *Dislocating Cultures*. There has also been a good deal of critical work done on *Mother India* and its relationship to imperialist feminist, including Kumari Jayawardena, *The White Woman's Other Burden;* Liz Wilson, "Who Is Authorized to Speak? Katherine Mayo and the Politics of Imperial Feminism in British India," *Journal of Indian Philosophy* 25 (1997): 139–51; Joanna Liddle and Shirin Rai, "Feminism, Imperialism and Orientalism: The Challenge of the 'Indian Woman,'" *Women's History Review* 7, no. 4 (1998): 495–520; Catherine Candy, "The Inscrutable Irish-Indian Feminist Management of Anglo-American Hegemony, 1917–1947," *Journal of Colonialism and Colonial History* 2, no.1 (2001).

http://muse.jhu.edu.silk.library.umass.edu:2048/journals/cch/v002/2.1candy. See also Sandhya Shetty, "Disfiguring the Nation: Mother, Metaphor, Metonymy," *Differences* 7, no. 3 (1995): 50–78, and Anupama Arora, "'Neighborhood Assets' or 'Neighborhood Nuisances'? National Anxieties in Katherine Mayo's *Mother India*," *Women's Studies* 37, no. 2 (2008): 131–55.

17. See Katherine Mayo, *Justice for All: The Story of the Pennsylvania State Police* (New York: G. P. Putnam's Sons, 1917); *The Standard-Bearers: True Stories of Heroes of Law and Order* (Boston: Houghton Mifflin Company, 1918); and *Mounted Justice: True Stories of the Pennsylvania State Police* (Boston and New York: Houghton Mifflin Company, 1922).

18. Mayo, *Justice*, 153.

19. Quoted in Jha, *Katherine Mayo and India*, 210.

20. The Government of India Act of 1919 instituted "dyarchy," a form of government in which responsibility for certain areas (such as agriculture, health, education, and local self-government) was transferred to Indian ministers.

21. Sinha, *Specters of Mother India*, 87.

22. Sinha, "Reading Mother India," 25.

23. Mayo, "India," *Liberty*, January 14, 1928, 36. *Katherine Mayo Papers*, Box 21, Folder 147a, 36.

24. Ahmad, *Landscapes of Hope*, 210, n. 59.

25. Sinha, *Specters of Mother India*, 73.

26. Jha, *Katherine Mayo and India*, 66–68; Sinha, *Specters of Mother India*, 74. Letter from the Rockefeller Foundation, signed by Major Greenwood, Esq. Ministry of Health, Whitehall, S.W. 1, London, England. *Katherine Mayo Papers*, Folder 32, Box 5. Despite this letter of introduction, Mayo claimed not to have any institutional affiliations in the United States or Britain.

27. See also E. Richard Brown, *Rockefeller Medicine Men: Medicine and Capitalism in America* (Berkeley: University of California Press, 1979), and John Ettling, *The Germ of Laziness: Rockefeller Philanthropy and Public Health in the New South* (Cambridge, Mass.: Harvard University Press, 1981).

28. See Ettling, *Germ of Laziness*, chapter 8.

29. Briggs, *Reproducing Empire*, chapter 1.

30. Alan Kraut, *Silent Travelers: Germ, Genes and the "Immigrant Menace"* (Baltimore: Johns Hopkins University Press, 1994).

31. Priscilla Wald, *Contagious: Cultures, Carriers, and the Outbreak Narrative* (Durham, N.C.: Duke University Press, 2008), 117.

32. Mayo, "India," 36.

33. See J. A. Hobson, *Imperialism: A Study* (New York: J. Pott, 1902); Rudolf Hilferding, *Finance Capital: A Study of the Latest Phase of Capitalist Development* (London: Routledge, 1981); Rosa Luxemburg, *The Accumulation of Capital* (New York: Routledge, 2003); Nikolai Bukharin, *Imperialism and World Economy* (New York: Monthly Review Press, 1973); and Vladimir Lenin, *Imperialism, the Highest Stage of Capitalism: A Popular Outline* (New York: International Publishers, 1983).

34. As Sucheta Mazumdar argues, "Instead of challenging racism, the South Asian struggle becomes an individualized and personalized mission to prove that they were of 'pureblood Aryan stock.' . . . This endows them with a sort of Mayflower status in relation to 'whiteness' or 'Aryanism' which they deny to many of their own darker-skinned countrymen." "Racist Responses to Racism: The Aryan Myth and South Asians in the United States," *South Asia Bulletin* 9, no. 1 (1989): 50.

35. Ibid. See also Sucheta Mazumdar, "The Politics of Religion and National Origin: Rediscovering Hindu Indian Identity in the United States," in *Antimonies of Modernity*, 223–60; and Ian Haney-López, *White by Law: The Legal Construction of Race* (New York: New York University Press, 1996).

36. Sinha, *Specters of Mother India*, 95.

37. Mayo, "When Asia Knocks on Our Door," *Brookline Standard Union* (June 7, 1927). 14. *Katherine Mayo Papers*, Box 21, Folder 147a.

38. For more on the relationship between metaphor and metonymy in *Mother India* see Sandhya Shetty, "(Dis)figuring the Nation: Mother, Metaphor, Metonymy." Shetty argues that the metonymic movement from suffering mother to torturing *dai* "breaks the back of the nationalist-patriarchal allegory" (53). Contrary to Shetty's argument, however, I suggest that in order for Mayo to mobilize Mother India as an allegorical figure, it is essential for her to split it into both victim and threat.

39. For more on the colonial abject see Warwick Anderson, "Excremental Colonialism: Public Health and the Poetics of Pollution," *Critical Inquiry* 21 (1995): 640–69.

40. Gupta, *Sexuality, Obscenity, Community*, 181.

41. See Anshu Malhotra, "Of Dais and Midwives; 'Middle Class' Interventions in the Management of Women's Reproductive Health in Colonial Punjab," in *Reproductive Health in India: History, Politics, Controversies*, ed. Sarah Hodges (New Delhi: Orient Longman, 2006), 200.

42. Gupta, "Introduction," *Gendering Colonial India*, 28.

43. Sinha, *Specters of Mother India*, 191.

44. See Judith Allen on how Ross recommended *Mother India* to Gilman as further proof of an androcentric culture taken to the extreme. *The Feminism of Charlotte Perkins Gilman*, 311.

45. Mayo, "India," 36.

46. Ibid.

47. Ibid., 39, emphases in original.

48. Mayo, "To the Women of Hindu India," *Slaves of the Gods* (New York: Harcourt, Brace and Company, 1929), 238.

49. Ibid.

50. Ibid.

51. Mayo, "Companionate 'Marriage'—and Marriage: A Message to Girls," *Liberty*, May 26, 1928, 1924. *Katherine Mayo Papers*, Box 21, Folder 147a, 18.

52. Ibid., 19.

53. Ibid., 20, 19.

54. Ibid., 20.

55. Ibid.

56. Ibid.

57. Ibid.

58. Ibid., 24.

59. Ibid.

60. Ibid.

61. Ibid., 20.

62. Amy Kaplan, "Manifest Domesticity," and *The Anarchy of Empire in the Making of U.S. Culture.*

63. Mayo, "Marriage," 20.

64. Ibid.

65. Mohandas Gandhi, "A Drain Inspector's Report," *Young India* (September 15, 1927).

66. Lala Lajpat Rai, *Unhappy India* (Calcutta: Banna, 1928); Dhan Gopal Mukerji, *A Son of Mother India Answers* (New York: E. P. Dutton, 1928).

67. K. L. Gauba, *Uncle Sham: The Strange Tale of a Civilization Run Amok* (Lahore, India: Time Publishing, 1929), 12.

68. Ibid., 83.

69. See Sinha, "Gender in the Critiques of Colonialism and Nationalism," 456–57; and *Specters of Mother India,* especially 136–51.

70. Quoted in Sinha, *Specters of Mother India,* 139.

71. Banerjee, *Traditional Feminist,* 44.

72. Quoted in Sengupta, *Sarojini Naidu,* 14.

73. Sarojini Naidu, C. F. Andrews, and S. K. Ratcliffe, *India's Future: 115th New York Luncheon Discussion, March 2, 1929* (New York: Foreign Policy Association), 10.

74. "Calls Rule in India 'Pure Domination,'" *New York Times,* October 28, 1928, 36.

75. Quoted in Bannerjee, *Traditional Feminist,* 54.

76. "India's Poetess to Visit America," *New York Times,* October 14, 1928, 14.

77. "Old World Woman Tells of New Independence of Sex," *Chicago Defender,* November 3, 1928, 4.

78. "India's Poetess," 14.

79. "Entertains India's Greatest Woman," *Chicago Defender,* January 19, 1929, 11.

80. Ibid.

81. Ibid.

82. Sinha, *Specters of Mother India,* 103; Harry H. Field, *After Mother India* (London: Jonathan Cape, 1929), 38–48.

83. "Sarojini Devi's Letter," *Young India* XI.1 (January 3, 1929): 1.

84. Ibid., emphases in original.

85. Quoted in Banerjee, *Traditional Feminist,* 47.

86. Ibid., 48.

87. Ibid.
88. "Sarojini Devi's Letter," 1.
89. Ibid.
90. Anupama Arora, "The Nightingale's Wanderings: Sarojini Naidu in North America," *Journal of Commonwealth Literature* 44, no. 87 (2009): 94.
91. "From and about Sarojini Devi," *Young India* XI.22 (May 30, 1929): 177.
92. Ibid.
93. Ibid.
94. Ibid.
95. Ibid.
96. Ibid., emphases in original.
97. Ibid., 178.
98. Ibid.
99. Ibid., 177.
100. Ibid., 178.
101. Ibid.
102. Ibid.

4. The Vanishing Peasant Mother

1. Mary John, "Gender, Development and the Women's Movement: Problems for a History of the Present," in *Signposts: Gender Issues in Post-Independence India*, ed. Rajeswari Sunder Rajan (New Delhi: Kali for Women, 1999), 104. See also Radha Kumar, *The History of Doing: An Illustrated Account of Movements for Women's Rights and Feminism in India, 1800–1990* (New Delhi: Zubaan, 1993); Forbes, *Women in Modern India;* and Sunder Rajan, *The Scandal of the State.* According to Sunder Rajan's narrative of the Indian feminist movement, "the post-Independence Indian women's movement is usually viewed as having three phases: the period of the 1950s and 1960s, the decades immediately following freedom, during which there was little organized activity; the period of the 1970s and the 1980s, marked by the Emergency, the International Women's Year, and the report of the CSWI on the Status of Women in India, related events which combined to produce the enormous activism of the new autonomous women's groups; and the most recent phase, following the Shahbano case in judgment in 1986, a period of withdrawal from the protest agendas of the earlier decade, into introspection, consolidation and new directions—these latter for the most part turning toward involvement in NGO work in health, literacy, welfare and development" (31).

2. For instance, prominent nationalist feminist Aruna Asaf Ali established the National Federation of Indian Women as the women's wing of the Communist Party of India in 1954, envisioning it as "a radical alternative to existing women's organization" (Kumar, *The History of Doing,* 63). Women were also involved in the Telengana People's Struggle; see Stree S. Sangathana, *We Were Making History: Women and the Telangana Uprising* (New Delhi: Kali for Women, 1989).

3. See Gandhi and Shah, *The Issues at Stake.* As they explain, "Many women

left the IWM [Indian Women's Movement] disillusioned and disgusted at the bitter debate and watering down of the Hindu Code Bill which had proposed equal inheritance rights, prohibited polygamy, liberalized divorce and custody rights. The demand for a uniform civil code for all communities was shelved" (18). The issue of the uniform civil code is a complex one, with no clear "feminist" position. See Sunder Rajan, chapter 5 of *Scandal of the State*.

4. National Planning Committee Series, *Woman's Role in Planned Economy*, Report of the Sub-Committee (New Delhi: Vora, 1948).

5. National Planning Committee Series, *Population*, Report of the Sub-Committee (New Delhi: Vora, 1948).

6. See especially chapter 13 of M. K. Gandhi, *"Hind Swaraj" and Other Writings: Cambridge Texts in Modern Politics*, ed. Anthony J. Parel (Cambridge: Cambridge University Press, 1997).

7. For a discussion of the differences between the draft outline for the plan and the plan, see Akhil Gupta, *Postcolonial Developments: Agriculture in the Making of Modern India* (Durham, N.C.: Duke University Press, 1998). See also Francine Frankel, *India's Political Economy: The Gradual Revolution (1947–2004)*, 2nd ed. (New York: Oxford University Press, 2009).

8. In 1952, the second year of the first plan, the U.S. government gave a $50,000,000 grant. Kim Berry, "'Lakshmi and the Scientific Housewife': A Transnational Account of Indian Women's Development and Production of an Indian Modernity," *Economic and Political Weekly*, March 15–21, 2003, 1056.

9. Saldaña-Portillo, *Revolutionary Imagination*, 9.

10. Boserup, *Women's Role*. Despite the importance of such critiques, WID approaches retain an essential faith in modernization, reinforcing the idea that the problem is so-called traditional culture. Similarly, by emphasizing the "efficiency" and the "instrumentality" of women in the development process they obscure the fact that women are economic actors and agents in their own right, transferring agency instead to the governmental agency doing the developing. Interpellating women as underdeveloped subjects who need to be brought from the "private" sphere of the home to the "public" sphere of the workforce, WID approaches thus reinforce the very separate spheres ideology they would seem to contest.

11. Carolyn Sachs, *The Invisible Farmers: Women in Agricultural Production* (New York: Rowman & Littlefield, 1983). See also chapter 5 of Arturo Escobar, *Encountering Development: The Making and Unmaking of the Third World* (Princeton, N.J.: Princeton University Press, 1995).

12. As Bina Agarwal shows in her magisterial 1995 study, *A Field of One's Own: Gender and Land Rights in South Asia* (Cambridge: Cambridge University Press, 1995), "the redistributive land reform programmes of the 1950s and 1960s in India . . . [were] modeled on the notion of a unitary male-headed household, with titles being granted only to men, except in households without adult men where women (typically widows) were clearly the head" (8–9).

13. Whereas in 1951, 45 percent of women worked as cultivators and 31 percent worked as agricultural laborers, by 1971 these figures had flipped, with only

29 percent of women working as cultivators and 50 percent working as agricultural laborers. Department of Social Welfare, Ministry of Education and Social Welfare, *Towards Equality: Report of the Committee on The Status of Women in India* (New Delhi: Department of Social Welfare, 1974), 163.

14. Latham, *The Right Kind of Revolution*, 108.

15. WRPE, 11.

16. See Gayatri Spivak's work on "global feminism": "A Moral Dilemma," *Theoria* 47, no. 96 (December 2000): 99–110; and "Righting Wrongs," in *Other Asias* (Malden, Mass.: Blackwell, 2008). See also Sangeeta Ray's excellent discussion of Spivak's engagement with issues of global feminism and gender and development. Gayatri Chakravorty, *Spivak: In Other Words* (Malden, Mass.: Wiley Blackwell, 2009).

17. WRPE, 16.

18. For more historical background on this document see Nirmala Banerjee, "Whatever Happened to the Dreams of Modernity? The Nehruvian Era and Woman's Position," *Economic and Political Weekly*, April 25–May 1, 1998, 4.

19. See ibid.; Maitrayee Chaudhuri, "Citizens, Workers and Emblems of Culture: An Analysis of the First Plan Document of Women," in *Social Reforms, Sexuality and the State*, ed. Patricia Uberoi (New Delhi: Sage, 1996); Rachel Simon Kumar, "Claiming the State: Women's Reproductive Identity and Indian Development," in *Feminist Futures: Re-imagining Women, Culture and Development*, ed. Kum-Kum Bhavnani, John Foran, and Priya Kurian (New York: Zed, 2003); and Sunder Rajan, *Scandal of the State*. Critical accounts of the WRPE focus on two main issues: its internal contradictions, and the fact that its recommendations were not followed.

20. Government of India (GoI), *The First Five-Year Plan* (New Delhi: Planning Commission, 1952); *The Second Five-Year Plan* (New Delhi: Planning Commission, 1956); *The Third Five-Year Plan* (New Delhi: Planning Commission, 1960). http://planningcommission.nic.in/plans/planrel/fiveyr/default.html.

21. GoI, *First Five-Year Plan*, 8:102.

22. Nirmala Buch, "State Welfare Policy and Women, 1950–1975," *Economic and Political Weekly*, April 25–May 1, 1998, WS19.

23. Maria Mies, *Patriarchy and Accumulation on a World Scale: Women in the International Division of Labour* (New York: Zed, 1986). Although Mies argues that colonization abroad contributed to housewivification of women in the metropole, the same process pertains in the colonies.

24. Leopoldina Fortunati, *Arcane of Reproduction: Housework, Prostitution, Labor and Capital* (New York: Autonomedia, 1989).

25. WRPE, 175.

26. *Population*, 93.

27. Ibid.

28. Ibid.

29. Ibid., 100.

30. This logic is reminiscent of eugenics laws in the United States (and, indeed,

Population cites U.S. precedents throughout), particularly the infamous 1924 case of *Buck v. Bell*, in which Carrie Buck, a seventeen-year-old ward of the state who gave birth to an illegitimate child, was sterilized after being deemed a "moral imbecile."

31. *Population*, 100.

32. Ibid., 102.

33. Ibid., 100.

34. Ibid., 78, 79.

35. Ibid., 80.

36. Ibid.

37. Ibid.

38. Ibid.

39. Ibid., 86–87.

40. The formula takes "the total male population" as the base and then deducts different groups—such as youth, the elderly and the infirm—to arrive at the "total adult male population of employable age." *Population*, 82.

41. WRPE, 94.

42. See also Arturo Escobar's discussion of women in agriculture. *Encountering Development*, chapter 5.

43. GoI, *First Five-Year Plan*, 1:28.

44. Ibid., 32:105.

45. Connelly, *Fatal Misconception*, 170.

46. Latham, *Right Kind of Revolution*, 100. The Indian government's decision to include population planning in the first plan emboldened the population establishment—upon learning of it John D. Rockefeller III gave $100,000 to the Population Council and promised $1.3 million more within a year (Connelly, *Fatal Misconception*, 169). For a critique of the Khanna Study see Mahmood Mamdani, *The Myth of Population Control: Family, Caste and Class in an Indian Village* (New York: Monthly Review Press, 1972).

47. GoI, *Second Five-Year Plan*, 25:55.

48. GoI, *Third Five-Year Plan*, 32:60; Connelly, *Fatal Misconception*, 182–84.

49. GoI, *Second Five-Year Plan*, 25:56.

50. Connelly, *Fatal Misconception*, 184. The shift in priorities and techniques is clearly evident if we compare the second to the third plan. See GoI, *Third Five-Year Plan*. Whereas in both the first and second plans "family planning" was a subsection in the chapter on health, in the third plan the chapter is renamed "Health and Family Planning" and states that family planning "must be at the very centre of planned development" (GoI, *Third Five-Year Plan*, 32:59). The third plan also marks a shift in that it introduces targets for population.

51. Jawaharlal Nehru, quoted in Gupta, *Postcolonial Developments*, 45.

52. Frankel, *India's Political Economy*, 131.

53. Ibid., 105.

54. Berry, "Lakshmi and the Scientific Housewife," 1057.

55. Ibid., 1061.

56. Ibid., 1059.

57. GoI quoted in Berry, "Lakshmi and the Scientific Housewife," 1059.

58. McClintock, "Family Feuds," 66.

59. The fact that Nargis, a Muslim actress, is made over into an icon of Hindu womanhood has been explored by various scholars. See, for instance, Rosie Thomas, "Sanctity and Scandal: The Mythologization of Mother India," *Quarterly Review of Film and Video* 11, no. 3 (1989): 11–30, and Parama Roy, *Indian Traffic*, 128–51.

60. Gayatri Chatterjee, *Mother India: BFI Film Classics* (London: BFI, 2002), 9.

61. Ibid., 20.

62. Sinha, *Specters of Mother India*, 249.

63. Kamala Markandaya, *Nectar in a Sieve* (New York: Signet Classic, 2002), 3. All further references cited in the text.

64. Samuel Taylor Coleridge, "Work without Hope," *The Complete Poems*, ed. William Keach (New York: Penguin, 1997), 383.

65. Quoted in Chatterjee, *Mother India*, 23.

66. Vijay Mishra, *Bollywood Cinema: Temples of Desire* (New York: Routledge, 2002). 76.

67. Marilyn Ivy, *Discourses of the Vanishing: Modernity, Phantasm, Japan* (Chicago: University of Chicago Press, 1995), 20.

68. Brigitte Schulze, "The Cinematic 'Discovery of India': Mehboob's Re-Invention of the Nation in Mother India," *Social Scientist* 30, no. 9/10 (September–October 2002): 75.

69. Connelly, *Fatal Misconception*, 173.

70. Schulze, "Cinematic 'Discovery of India,'" 80.

71. Quoted in Arundhati Roy, "The Greater Common Good," in *The Cost of Living* (New York: Modern Library, 1999), 13.

72. Ibid., 7.

73. Quoted in Andrew Robinson, *Satyajit Ray: The Inner Eye: The Biography of a Film Master* (New York: Palgrave Macmillan, 1989), 328. Salman Rushdie parodies Nargis's views in his 1995 *The Moor's Last Sigh* (New York: Pantheon, 1995).

74. Orville Prescott, "Books of the Times," *New York Times*, May 16, 1955, 21.

75. Quoted in Gilbert Rist, *The History of Development: From Western Origins to Global Faith* (New York: Zed, 1997), 71.

76. Ibid., 72.

77. Rotter, *Comrades at Arms*, 38.

78. Quoted in Latham, *Right Kind of Revolution*, 70.

79. Ibid., 67.

80. Dennis Merrill, *Bread and the Ballot: The United States and India's Economic Development, 1947–1963* (Chapel Hill: University of North Carolina Press, 1990), 3.

81. Quoted in Charles Larson, "Introduction," *Bombay Tiger* (New Delhi: Penguin India), vii.

82. Colleen Lye, *America's Asia: Racial Form and American Literature, 1893–1945* (Princeton, N.J.: Princeton University Press, 2004), 206.

83. Chris Vials, *Realism for the Masses: Aesthetics, Popular Front Pluralism, and U.S. Culture, 1935–1947* (Jackson: University of Mississippi Press, 2009), 216.

84. Prescott, "Books of the Times."

85. Ibid.

86. Shyamala Narayan, "The Language of Kamala Markandaya's Novels," 1970, rpt. in *Indian Women Novelists* (set 2, Vol. 2), ed. R. K. Dhawan (New Delhi: Prestige, 1993), 70–82; P. Shiv Kumar, "The Mask That Does Not Hide: A Perspective on *Nectar in a Sieve*," *Perspectives on Kamala Markandaya*, ed. Madhusudan Prasad (Ghaziabad, India: Vimal Prakashan, 1984), 93–97; Ramesh Srivastava, "Limitation of Markandaya in *Nectar in a Sieve*" in *Six Indian Novelists in English*, ed. Ramesh Srivastava (Amritsar: Guru Nanak Dev University, 1987), 145–54.

87. Kamala Markandaya, "Reminiscences of Rural India," in *John Kenneth Galbraith Introduces India*, ed. Francis Robert Moraes and Edward Howe (London: André Deutsch, 1974), 109.

88. Prescott, "Books of the Times."

89. Chatterjee, *Mother India*, 79.

90. Quoted in ibid., 78.

91. Christina Klein, *Cold War Orientalism: Asia in the Middlebrow Imagination, 1945–1961* (Berkeley: University of California Press, 2003), 16.

92. See Rosemary George, "Where in the World Is Kamala Markandaya?" *Novel: A Forum on Fiction* 42, no. 3 (2009): 400–409.

93. Howard Thompson, "A Handful of Grain," *New York Times*, July 4, 1959, 9.

94. Ibid.

95. Quoted in Robinson, *Satyajit Ray*, 327, my emphases.

96. Ibid.

97. Quoted in Marie Seton, *Portrait of a Director: Satyajit Ray* (New Delhi: Penguin, 2003), 70.

98. Much of what is at stake here, as Rosie Thomas argues in her important article, "Sanctity and Scandal: The Mythologization of Mother India," is the cultural text of Mother India herself. While Rukmani is the "everywoman" (to paraphrase Markandaya), Radha speaks to a specifically nationalist context (20).

5. Severed Limbs, Severed Legacies

1. Indira Gandhi, *Selected Speeches and Writings of Indira Gandhi: Vol. III, September 1972–March 1977* (New Delhi: Publications Division, Ministry of Information and Broadcasting, Government of India, 1984), 196.

2. Ibid.

3. Ibid.

4. Notably, given the ways in which Gandhi used a language of socialism but largely paved the way for liberalization to come, this is also the language of modernization theory, in which the problem is "feudalism, casteism and superstitions which were responsible for our backwardness" (ibid.). See Vijay Prashad, *The*

Darker Nations: A People's History of the Third World (New York: New Press, 2007), 207–23; and also Frankel, *India's Political Economy.*

5. Nayantara Sahgal, "Some Thoughts on the Puzzle of Identity," *Journal of Commonwealth Literature* 28, no. 1 (1993): 7.

6. Ranajit Guha, "On Some Aspects of the Historiography of Colonial India," in *Selected Subaltern Studies,* ed. Ranajit Guha and Gayatri Chakravorty Spivak (New York: Oxford University Press, 1988), 44.

7. Spivak, "Can the Subaltern Speak?," 23.

8. Ibid., 41.

9. Ibid., 30.

10. Foucault, quoted in Spivak, "Can the Subaltern Speak?," 27.

11. Ibid.

12. Rajeswari Sunder Rajan reads Rushdie's *Midnight's Children* and a short story by O. V. Vijayan called "The Foetus" to argue that their powerful critiques of Indira Gandhi nonetheless rely on misogynistic portrayals of her widowhood: "The hostility in their foregrounding of her widowhood must remain inexplicable except as culturally conditioned misogyny; and their recourse to supernatural explanations of 'feminine' power (the goddess) is a complete surrender of historical analysis." *Real and Imagined Women: Gender, Culture and Postcolonialism* (New York: Routledge, 1993), 113–14. I do not explicitly discuss how Gandhi's status as a widow complicates her self-fashioning as Mother India; for a discussion of how her culturally abject status as a widow renders her a subaltern see Sunder Rajan.

13. Indira Gandhi, *Indira Gandhi: My Truth* (New York: Grove, 1981), 78.

14. Ibid., 69.

15. My account of Indira Gandhi's political career relies upon Nayantara Sahgal, *Indira Gandhi: Her Road to Power* (New York: Frederick Ungar, 1978); Indira Gandhi, *My Truth;* Gupta, *Postcolonial Developments;* Frankel, *India's Political Economy;* and Emma Tarlo, *Unsettling Memories: Narratives of the Emergency in Delhi* (Berkeley: University of California Press, 2003).

16. Gupta, *Postcolonial Developments,* 66.

17. Latham, *Right Kind of Revolution,* 118.

18. Gupta, *Postcolonial Developments,* 67.

19. Prashad, *Darker Nations,* 207–23.

20. Tarlo, *Unsettling Memories,* 24–31.

21. Prashad, *Darker Nations,* 216.

22. Shashi Tharoor, "Experiment with Autocracy," *The Hindu,* April 14, 2000. http://tharoor.in/articles/experiment-with-autocracy/.

23. Sumathi Ramaswamy, *The Goddess and the Nation: Mapping Mother India* (Durham, N.C.: Duke University Press, 2010), 272.

24. Yasodhara Dalmia quoted in Ramaswamy, *Goddess and the Nation,* 272.

25. Ramaswamy, *Goddess and the Nation,* 173.

26. Ibid., 273.

27. Ibid., 245.

28. Thomas, "Sanctity and Scandal," 28.

29. Sunder Rajan, *Real and Imagined Women*, 110.

30. Ibid. A crore equals 10 million, or 100 lakh. Both lakh and crore are parts of a South Asian numbering system still widely used in the subcontinent.

31. Gandhi, *Selected Speeches and Writings*, 228.

32. Ibid.

33. Quoted in Tarlo, *Unsettling Memories*, 37. The "greased cartridge" references the First War of Indian Independence of 1857, which is said to have been sparked by the animal (either cow or pig) fat that was used in bullet cartridges for the Enfield Rifle. Because the cartridges needed to be bitten open by the Sepoys, the use of tallow was offensive to Hindus and Muslims alike.

34. Connelly, *Fatal Misconception*, 221.

35. Latham, *The Right Kind of Revolution*, 108.

36. Connelly, *Fatal Misconception*, 221.

37. Ibid.

38. Ibid., 225.

39. Ibid., 228.

40. Quoted in Gandhi and Shah, *The Issues at Stake*, 115.

41. Latham, The *Right Kind of Revolution*, 109.

42. See Tarlo, "Anatomising the Past: The Post Emergency Counter Narrative," *Unsettling Memories*, 31–43.

43. Ibid., 35–6.

44. See "United Nations Population Award to Indira Gandhi and Xinhong," and Betsy Hartmann's discussion of the international approbation with which Indira Gandhi's population policies were rewarded. *Reproductive Rights and Wrongs*, 252.

45. Gandhi, *Speeches and Writings*, 78.

46. Ibid.

47. Ibid.

48. Ibid., 79.

49. Ibid.

50. Gandhi, *Selected Speeches and Writings*, 605.

51. http://gos.sbc.edu/g/gandhi1.html.

52. On October 31, 1984, Gandhi was shot by two of her Sikh bodyguards in retaliation for Operation Blue Star, in which Gandhi ordered troops to remove Sikh separatists from the Golden Temple in Amritsar.

53. Tarlo, *Unsettling Memories*, 207.

54. Approaching this problem from a different angle, Gita Rajan reads Indira Gandhi through Spivak in order to posit Gandhi as the subaltern, thus suggesting that Gandhi "subvert[s] the gap in this contradiction [between *darstellen* and *vertreten*] by situating herself discursively and gesturally between these two modes of representation, and thus allowed herself to be read semiotically. In this frame, she successfully voiced the desires of the dominant ideological parties of postcolonial India, while simultaneously proclaiming her own agenda as widowed mother of India." "Subversive-Subaltern Identity: Indira Gandhi as the Speaking Subject,"

in *De/Colonizing the Subject: The Politics of Gender in Women's Autobiography,* ed. Sidonie Smith and Julia Watson (Minneapolis: University of Minnesota Press, 1992), 197. Though I appreciate Rajan's analysis, I disagree with her conceptualization of Gandhi *as* subaltern.

55. Pranav Jani, *Decentering Rushdie: Cosmopolitanism and the Indian Novel in English* (Columbus: Ohio State University Press, 2010), 7. Jani's aim in *Decentering Rushdie* is to examine the ways in which Rushdie's postnational, postmodern cosmopolitanism has come to dominate studies of the post-independence Indian novels in English. In contrast to this, Jani takes up novels that instead embody what he calls "'namak-halaal* cosmopolitanism,' a cosmopolitanism that remained 'true to its salt' in that it was oriented toward and committed to the nation as a potentially emancipatory space" (7).

56. Nayantara Sahgal, "The Myth Reincarnated," *Journal of Commonwealth Literature* 30, no. 1 (March 1995): 23–24. doi: 10.1177/002198949503000103.

57. Ibid., 26.

58. Ibid.

59. Ibid., 27.

60. Nayantara Sahgal, *Rich Like Us* (New York: New Directions, 1988), 14. All further references cited in the text.

61. Guha, "On Some Aspects," 43, emphases in original.

62. See Lata Mani's objection to Spivak's formulation, where she questions whether "noting . . . that the female subaltern *does* not speak in police records of the East India Company" means "that 'the subaltern cannot speak' at all, in any voice, however refracted" (*Contentious Traditions,* 160). Though I appreciate her critique and her careful archival retrieval of "the possibility of a female subjectivity that is shifting, contradictory, inconsistent," I believe that Sahgal's interpolation of newspaper accounts of *sati* into this multiply mediated narrative is precisely to point to the difficulty of reading the subaltern (162). In place of being able to discern her intentions, we have Sonali's grandfather's interpretations of the events which, while sympathetic, nonetheless qualify as a "speaking for."

63. Indeed, Sahgal's own grandmother was a *sati,* a fact Sahgal reports in her autobiography, *Prison and Chocolate Cake* (New York: Knopf, 1954). This is one of the many moments in the novel that suggest we should read Sonali as Sahgal's alter ego.

64. Minoli Salgado, "My Continuing Character Is India: Interview with Nayantara Sahgal," *Wasafiri* 20 (Autumn 1994): 44.

65. Chandra Talpade Mohanty, "Under Western Eyes: Feminist Scholarship and Colonial Discourse," in *Colonial Discourse and Post-Colonial Theory: A Reader,* ed. Patrick Williams and Laura Chrisman (New York: Columbia University Press, 1994), 198.

66. Jani, *Decentering Rushdie,* 185.

67. See also Inderpal Grewal's discussion of the cosmopolitan in her *Transnational America* (especially her chapter on "Becoming American: The Novel and Diaspora"). Grewal, like Jani, argues that cosmopolitanism is not necessarily an

elite formation in opposition to nationalism and predicated on mobility. Instead, she "suggest[s] that cosmopolitanism depend[s] on participation within various discourses of the global, national, and international that [move] across transnational connectivities and [enable] subjects to cross borders or claim to transcend them" (38).

Epilogue

1. Connelly, *Fatal Misconception,* 176.

2. As Kalindi Vora argues, the idea that Indian surrogates have a lower cost of living and thus do not need to be paid as much as U.S.-based surrogates is a false comparison, as the fact of the matter is that they have a lower *mode* of living: "Due to their lower incomes, surrogates often do without many necessities that commissioning parents would not do without, including basic health insurance, medical privacy, reliable electricity, clean and reliable water, a permanent home/residence, the ability to seek and find another job when one is lost, access to a variety of foods or the ability to grow them (requiring land and water), and so on." "'Limits of Labor': Accounting for Affect and the Biological in Transnational Surrogacy and Service Work," *South Atlantic Quarterly* 111, no: 4 (Fall 2012): 687.

3. See Kalindi Vora's discussion of altruism in "Medicine, Markets and the Pregnant Body: Indian Commercial Surrogacy and Reproductive Labor in a Transnational Frame," *Scholar & Feminist Online.* 2010. http://barnard.edu/sfonline/reprotech/vora_01.htm.

4. The preface of the Assisted Reproductive Technologies (Regulation) Bill–2010 similarly characterizes having a child a "right." The draft bill is available at http://icmr.nic.in/guide/ART%20REGULATION%20Draft%20Bill1.pdf.

5. Jaspir Puar, *Terrorist Assemblages: Homonationalism in Queer Times* (Durham, N.C.: Duke University Press, 2007), 9.

6. See Michelle Kung, "'Google Baby' Documentary Sheds Light on Outsourcing Surrogacy." http://blogs.wsj.com/speakeasy/2010/06/16/google-baby-documentary-sheds-light-on-outsourcing-surrogacy/. See also the director's statement on zippibrandfrank.com.

7. zippibrandfrank.com.

8. Ibid.

9. Ibid.

10. See Vora, "Medicines, Market and the Pregnant Body," on how the uterus is rendered as surplus. http://sfonline.barnard.edu/reprotech/vora_03.htm.

11. See Vora, "Limits of Labor," on how "activities of service, care, and nurture engage the biological use of [surrogate's] bodies and lives as well as labor, and the requirements of such work intrude on the laboring subject in ways that radically compromise any sense of 'autonomy' or 'separation of spheres' presumed by both liberal and Marxist discussions of workers within Western societies. Biotechnology together with globalization (and its colonial past) is the condition that makes the selling or renting of one's biological function and parts possible, a process that is

qualitatively different than the commodification of the labor that the biological body performs" (689).

12. Ginia Bellafante, "Surrogate Pregnancy Goes Global, *New York Times,* June 15, 2010. http://www.nytimes.com/2010/06/16/arts/television/16google.html ?_r=0.

13. Vora, "Limits of Labor," 688.

14. Carolyn Burdett, "Introduction: Eugenics Old and New," *New Formations* 60 (Spring 2007): 8–9.

15. Ibid.

16. Elizabeth Seigel Watkins, "Parsing the Postmenopausal Pregnancy," *New Formations* 60 (Spring 2007): 34.

17. Pheng Cheah, "Biopower and the New International Division of Reproductive Labor," in Morris, ed., *Can the Subaltern Speak?,* 200.

18. "Surrogate Mother Dies of Complications," *Times of India,* May 17, 2012. http://articles.timesofindia.indiatimes.com/2012-05-17/ahmedabad/31748277_ 1_surrogate-mother-surrogacy-couples; Mayura Janwalkar, "17-yr-old Egg Donor Dead, HC Questions Fertility Centre's Role," *Indian Express,* July 12, 2012. http://www.indianexpress.com/news/17yrold-egg-donor-dead-hc-questions-fertility-centres-role/973327/0.

19. Vora, "The Limits of Labor," 684.

20. Zippi Brand Frank, *Google Baby.* Directed by Zippi Brand Frank, 2009.

21. Brand Frank, *Google Baby.*

22. Kung, "Google Baby."

23. And, in fact, the draft legislation will prohibit a surrogate from simply being inseminated, the point being to militate against any connection between surrogate and child by making sure they share no biological material.

24. Kat is listed as a protagonist on the documentary's website; no Indian surrogate is so listed. zippibrandfrank.com.

25. Mira Jacob, "Outsourcing Pregnancy to India? This Is Just the Beginning," *Shine from Yahoo,* June 17, 2010. http://shine.yahoo.com/parenting/outsourcing-pregnancy-to-india-this-is-just-the-beginning-1753055.html.

26. Friedman lists outsourcing as the fifth "flattener." Thomas Friedman, *The World Is Flat 3.0: A Brief History of the Twenty-First Century* (New York: Picador, 2007).

27. Anne Kerr, "Google Baby: A Lesson in Global Capitalism," *Bionews,* July 4, 2011. http://www.bionews.org.uk/page_99995.asp.

28. Brand Frank, *Google Baby.*

29. An Assisted Reproductive Technology Regulation Draft Bill was drafted in 2008 and updated in 2010.

30. See Frankel, *India's Political Economy,* chapter 14.

31. Vijay Prashad, "Emergency Assessments," *Social Scientist* 24, nos. 9/10 (September–October 1996): 51.

32. Frankel, *India's Political Economy,* 548.

33. Prashad, *The Darker Nations,* 216.

34. Ibid.

35. Gayatri Chakravorty Spivak, "The Double Bind Starts to Kick in," in *An Aesthetic Education in the Era of Globalization* (Cambridge, Mass.: Harvard University Press, 2012), 104.

36. Spivak, "Righting Wrongs," 23.

37. Lee Edelman, *No Future: Queer Theory and the Death Drive* (Durham, N.C: Duke University Press, 2004), 2.

INDEX